A CAPTAIN'S WAR

THE LETTERS AND DIARIES OF
WILLIAM H.S. BURGWYN
1861-1865

William H.S. Burgwyn, Captain, Co. H, 35th N.C. Troops

Clark, *Histories*, II:591

A CAPTAIN'S WAR

THE LETTERS AND DIARIES OF WILLIAM H.S. BURGWYN 1861-1865

Edited by

HERBERT M. SCHILLER

Foreword by

RICHARD J. SOMMERS

 White Mane Publishing Company, Inc.

This White Mane Publishing Company, Inc. publication
was printed by
Beidel Printing House, Inc.
63 West Burd Street
Shippensburg, PA 17257 USA

In respect for the scholarship contained herein, the acid-free paper used in this book meets the guidelines for permanence and durability of the Committee on Production Guidelines for Book Longevity of the Council on Library Resources.

For a complete list of available publications
please write
White Mane Publishing Company, Inc.
P.O. Box 152
Shippensburg, PA 17257 USA

Library of Congress Cataloging-in-Publication Data

Burgwyn, William Hyslop Sumner, 1845-1913.
    A captain's war : the letters and diaries of William H.S. Burgwyn,
  1861-1865 / edited by Herbert M. Schiller : foreword by Richard J.
  Sommers.
        p.   cm.
    Includes bibliographical references and index.
    ISBN 0-942597-52-4 (alk. paper) : $24.95
    1. Burgwyn, William Hyslop Sumner, 1845-1913--Correspondence.
  2. Burgwyn, William Hyslop Sumner, 1845-1913--Diaries.
  3. Confederate States of America. Army. North Carolina Infantry
  Regiment, 35th. 4. North Carolina--History--Civil War, 1861-1865-
  -Personal narratives. 5. United States--History--Civil War.
  1861-1865--Personal narratives, Confederate. 6. United States-
  -History--Civil War, 1861-1865--Prisoners and prisons. 7. Soldiers-
  -North Carolina--Correspondence. 8. Soldiers--North Carolina-
  -Diaries. I. Schiller, Herbert M., 1943-   . II. Title.
  E573.5 35th.B87   1993
  973.7'092--dc20
  [B]   93-29312
                                                                CIP

For my Daughter

Anne Bothwell Schiller, M.D.

"a hard workin' little thing"

TABLE OF CONTENTS

MAPS AND ILLUSTRATIONS

ACKNOWLEDGEMENTS

I first learned of William H.S. Burgwyn's Civil War diaries and letters in 1984 when I was working on my book about the Bermuda Hundred Campaign. Several years later I was given permission by the North Carolina Department of Archives and History to edit and publish the material. My neighbor, Mary Burgwyn Newsome, kindly shared some of her genealogical material with me and introduced me to two additional family members who had much to share. First was Margaret Burgwyn Cooley, of Jackson, North Carolina, who had several wartime letters written by Will Burgwyn, as well as many of his prewar papers.[1] Second was Collinson P.E. Burgwyn, M.D., of Clarksville, Tennessee, who is a vast repository of Burgwyn family information. Coll Burgwyn must know the genealogy and inter-relationship of every family who settled in America for the first two centuries after the Pilgrims arrived. His generous sharing has enabled me to identify as many of the family members as I have. He further helped me with the identities of others and explained the complex relationships among many different North Carolina and New England families. I owe to him more than I can ever repay for the help he gave me on this project.

Chris Calkins and Bob Krick, both historians with the National Park Service, were able to help me with the identities of civilians in Petersburg and members of the Confederate States Army. The ever helpful Dennis Madison, of Richmond, Virginia, identified several individuals. Gary Gallagher, of Pennsylvania State University, was supportive in many ways. Janet Hewett provided valuable editing help. Richard Sommers' encyclopedic knowledge was, as always, invaluable in correcting many errors in identification; I am responsible for those which remain. Finally, the staff of the North Carolina Room of the Forsyth County Public Library graciously assisted me in identifying many of the regimental officers and privates mentioned in the diaries.

Herbert M. Schiller, M.D.
Winston-Salem, North Carolina

May 1, 1993

---

[1] Letters in the collection of the N.C.D.A.H. are dated August 21, September 5 and 9, 1861; July 1, August 6, 19, 22, September 3, 23, and 30, October 21, November 4, December 15, 17, 28, 1862; January 14 and 22, February 12 and 15, March 9, May 16 and 17, October 5, 1863; June 25, October 14 and 24, December 30, 1864; February 14 and 19, 1865. The remaining letters quoted are from Margaret Cooley.

Both the N.C.D.A.H. and Mrs. Cooley retain full literary rights to their respective material.

FOREWORD

The Light Division and the Pennsylvania Reserve Division, the Rock Brigade and the Iron Brigade, Terry's Texas Rangers, Rush's Lancers, the Jeb Stuart Horse Artillery, the 1st Minnesota Infantry—those were among the most outstanding out-fits of the Civil War. Famous fighting commanders were comparably conspicuous: Winfield Scott Hancock, Emory Upton, William B. Hazen, and Joseph A. Mower in Blue; "Stonewall" Jackson, Nathan Bedford Forrest, John B. Gordon, and Patrick R. Cleburne in Gray—along with many other brave battle leaders on both sides.

Such generals and such units were all the more appreciated, during the war and subsequently, because they were so rare. The Texas Brigade certainly was not the typical brigade even of the Army of Northern Virginia, and William MacRae was not the typical brigadier. More ordinary troops under more ordinary officers were less conspicuous during the Civil War and are less well known today. Their combat record was more mixed; their reverses were more frequent; their shortcomings as generals were more pronounced. Yet their endurance through such trials—unrewarded with the recognition accorded their more illustrious comrades—underscores their steady, sturdy commitment to the Cause. Thus, in these "ordinary units" and "or-dinary generals," the student may gain greater understanding of the tenor and character of a given Federal or Confederate army than can be derived from dwelling exclusively upon the more conspicuous but less characteristic components and commanders.

Two such run-of-the-mill generals of the Confederacy were Brigadier Generals Matthew W. Ransom and Thomas L. Clingman. No one will ever confuse them with Dodson Ramseur or John R. Cooke among the great fighting leaders from the Old North State. Ransom's own 35th North Carolina Infantry Regiment and the North Carolina Brigade which he subsequently commanded were comparably commonplace troops. Clingman's Tarheel Brigade was, if anything, below average with its almost unbroken series of defeats from Roanoke Island to Fort Harrison. Yet in the very ordinariness and even in the shortcomings of these troops may be found clues to the character of the Confederate army in the Eastern Theater.

These clues come from the writings of junior officers and soldiers in those units. William Hyslop Sumner Burgwyn was one such officer. The son of a wealthy planter in eastern North Carolina and the brother of the gallant Colonel Henry Burgwyn, Jr., of the 26th North Carolina Infantry Regiment, who was killed on the first day of the Battle of Gettysburg, William entered military service in March of 1861, almost half a year before his sixteenth birthday. By August of that year, he was at the front in Virginia. Early 1862 found him back in his home state on training and staff duty, but by July he had returned to the Old Dominion as a first lieutenant in the 35th North Carolina. For the next year and a half, he served with that regiment under his family friend and neighbor, Matthew Ransom. In January, 1864, Burgwyn (by then a captain) transferred to the staff of his father's long-time friend, General

Clingman. Wounded at Second Cold Harbor and captured at Fort Harrison, he endured imprisonment at Old Capitol Prison and Fort Delaware until paroled in March of 1865.

Burgwyn's diaries cover the great battles of Harpers Ferry, Antietam, Fredericksburg, Second Drewry's Bluff, Second Cold Harbor, and Fort Harrison as well as such less well known clashes as Gum Swamp, Baltimore Cross Roads, Boone's Mill, and Batchelder's Creek. Even more do they record the day-in-and-day-out activities of one officer and his troops on active campaign in central Virginia and Maryland and on guard duty in southeastern Virginia and North Carolina.

Then, too, his correspondence with and frequent visits to his family reflect their experiences on the home front at their plantation near Garysburg and as refugees in Raleigh. His well-to-do kith and kin (including such prominent Confederate officers as George Burgwyn Anderson, Junius Daniel, Duncan McRae, and Leonidas Polk) are also mentioned in his accounts. Burgwyn's own social life is extensively documented—to the point where one almost surmises that his principal duty at brigade headquarters during the first four months of 1864 was to court the young ladies of Petersburg. But after all, even by that time, three years into the war, he was not yet nineteen years old.

His extreme youth comes through clearly in his writings, as he openly records his devotion to the damsels, his absorption with his own pleasures and promotions, and his exuberance over knowing that he personally had shot a Yankee at Fredericksburg. Yet beneath such innocence and such callowness a soldier was maturing: someone who could discharge the duties of line and staff.

The Burgwyn diaries have been available for study in the North Carolina Department of Archives and History. Dr. Herbert Schiller, author of the acclaimed *The Bermuda Hundred Campaign* and editor of *The Autobiography of Major General William F. Smith*, has tracked down additional wartime letters in the hands of Burgwyn's family. In publishing these papers, Dr. Schiller is making this historically important material more readily available to the community of Civil Warriors, professional and lay. Through these papers, we may better understand how "ordinary troops" under "ordinary generals" rendered extraordinary service in the crucible of Civil War.

Richard J. Sommers
U.S. Army Military History Institute
Carlisle, Pennsylvania

INTRODUCTION

William Hyslop Sumner Burgwyn was born on July 23, 1845 at the residence of his maternal grandmother, Mrs. David Stoddard Greenough, at Jamaica Plains which is now part of Boston, Massachusetts. His twin, John Collinson Burgwyn, survived only a year. His mother, Anna (Anne) Greenough had married Henry King Burgwyn in 1838 and William was their fourth child. He was born to a heritage of affluence and wealth.

Both parents were from prestigious families, one Southern and one Northern. Henry King Burgwyn's grandfather, John Burgwin, came to America from Wales and was a descendant of the ancient Welch clan of Gwynn. He arrived in Wilmington, North Carolina, in 1750 where he established himself as a planter and merchant. He returned to Bristol to marry his second wife, Elizabeth Bush, in 1782. This couple's older son, John Fanning Burgwin, after completing his education in England, came to America and married Sarah Pierrepont Hunt, of New Bern, North Carolina. Miss Hunt was the daughter of Robert Hunt, of New Bern, and Eunice Edwards Pollok, the widow of Thomas Pollok, III, a wealthy planter in eastern North Carolina who left his family 50,000 acres and hundreds of slaves. Their second son, Henry King Burgwyn, was born in 1811 (some sources 1813).

Anna Greenough was born October 17, 1817, and was the youngest surviving child of David Stoddard Greenough, who died in 1830, and Maria Foster Doane. The Greenoughs were a prominent Boston family and David Greenough and his father were prominent attorneys. David was also a local prosperous real estate developer. Anna's mother remarried six years later to General William Hyslop Sumner, the son of the three-time post-Revolutionary Massachusetts governor Increase Sumner. The couple had no children of their own.

Prior to the marriage, Henry King Burgwyn had attended (1828-1831) the United States Military Academy at West Point, New York, but resigned. He had become involved in railroad construction in Massachusetts and Rhode Island. Anna Greenough and Henry King Burgwyn were married on November 29, 1838, and left Boston for the residence of Henry's father in New Bern, North Carolina. The following year, Henry's bachelor uncle George Pollok, the half brother of Henry's mother, died intestate and his enormous plantation was divided among several members of the Devereux and Burgwyn families. (George Pollok was related to the Burgwyns by his father's marriage to Eunice Edwards, second wife of Robert Hunt, father of Sara Pierrepont Hunt and by his sister Frances, wife of John Devereux, Jr., to the Devereux family.) Henry Burgwyn's portion was four thousand acres along the Roanoke River near Garysburg and Weldon, North Carolina, and over a hundred slaves. The couple's initial residence there ("Hillside") burned in 1849; their second dwelling, "Thornbury," was completed in 1853. It was here that the Burgwyn children grew up in an affluent plantation setting.

Henry Burgwyn, Sr., became an increasingly wealthy planter. He was among those men who were interested in scientific agriculture of the day and he published on this subject. He never sought public office although he was friends with many influential politicians throughout the Southeast. He was devoted to his family and much concerned with the education of his children, who numbered six by 1860.

Young William was very much under the influence of his other brother, Henry King Burgwyn, Jr. (born 1841), known as "Harry," his older sister Maria (born 1839), known as "Minnie," and his younger brother George Pollok, known as "Pollok." The two younger brothers, John (born 1850) and Collinson (born 1852) played little role in his development because of their youth and William's absence at school beginning at the age of nine.

Young William Burgwyn was instructed by private tutors (Reverend Frederick FitzGerald and Frederick Lightbourne) during his first few years at Thornbury. When he was nine years old he was sent away for schooling, first to Episcopal School for Boys at Burlington, New Jersey, and two years later to Reverend Frederick Gibson's school at Chestnut Hill, near Baltimore, Maryland. During 1857 and 1858 he studied at Horner's School at Oxford, North Carolina. The following year he attended Georgetown College in the District of Columbia. He departed in July, 1860, and the following month began studies at the University of North Carolina at Chapel Hill, North Carolina. He left the following year because of typhoid fever, and after recuperation studied briefly as a cadet at the Hillsboro (North Carolina) Military Academy; however, his training there was interrupted because the institution closed at the outbreak of hostilities.

In 1861, William enlisted at age 15 in the North Carolina Troops and because of his brief military training, he was appointed second lieutenant on March 1st and served that autumn as drillmaster in the Camp of Instruction located at Crabtree, three miles west of Raleigh. Attached to Colonel Johnston Pettigrew's 22nd North Carolina Troops, he worked at Brooke's Station near Aquia Creek, Virginia, (Aug. 16-26), and later Evansport, on the Potomac River, where the Tar Heel soldiers constructed batteries to prevent Federal use of the river. In the autumn of that year William was an adjutant of the Camp of Instruction at Camp Mangum, also near Raleigh. While there, on July 4, 1862, he was promoted to the rank of first lieutenant. During the reorganization of 1862, Colonel Matthew ("Matt") Ransom secured his election as First Lieutenant of Company H, 35th North Carolina Troops.

The 35th North Carolina Infantry at this time was part of General Robert Ransom's Brigade; in addition to the 35th North Carolina, commanded by Ransom's elder brother "Matt," the brigade consisted of the 24th, 25th, and 49th North Carolina Troops and Branch's (Virginia) Field Artillery. Lieutenant Burgwyn joined his regiment in early July but missed the Seven Days' Battles around Richmond in July, 1862. He began the diaries which follow shortly thereafter.

Burgwyn fought at Sharpsburg and Fredericksburg in late 1862. He then saw action in eastern North Carolina from Weldon to Wilmington in 1863 and the following year he returned to Virginia where he fought in the Battle of Drewry's Bluff in the spring of 1864 and was later wounded in the June fighting at Cold Harbor. Burgwyn was captured at Fort Harrison in September, 1864; the North imprisoned him at Fort Delaware until he was paroled in early March, 1865. An educated son of a wealthy planter family, he was accompanied throughout much of the war by a slave serving as his servant. In both letters and his diaries he recorded the monotony of camp life, the excitement of combat, the active social life of an aristocratic officer, and the tedium and hardship of confinement as a prisoner of war.

* * * *

Paroled but not exchanged in March, 1865, Captain Burgwyn was surrendered with the army of General Joseph E. Johnston late the following month. In May, 1865 he returned to the University of North Carolina and graduated three years later "with first honors." He completed his law studies the following year at Harvard. In 1869, at age 24, he moved to Baltimore where he earned the reputation of being a "discreet, able and conscientious lawyer." Burgwyn broadened his education in 1874 with the study of medicine and received his M.D. degree two years later from Washington Medical University in Baltimore. He never applied for a license to practice medicine.

Burgwyn was appointed lieutenant colonel of the Eighth Maryland Regiment during railroad labor disputes in 1877; as a result of his service he was subsequently elected colonel of the Fifth Maryland Regiment. In 1882 he left Baltimore to return to Henderson, North Carolina, to found the Banking House of W.H.S. Burgwyn and Co., which two years later became a state bank, the Bank of Henderson. At the same time he also established a large tobacco factory which he hoped would rival that of James B. Duke. He manufactured plug tobacco, pig-tail twist, and chewing tobacco, among which were such brands as "Old Dinah," "Lost Cord," "Johnny Reb," and "Prairie Bull." The tobacco enterprise ended in failure and caused financial embarrassment to himself, his brothers, and other family members. While he was overseeing the tobacco business and bank, he also began the municipal electric light and water works systems in Henderson. He was instrumental in the foundation of the educational institution which would eventually become North Carolina State University. He was disappointed to be passed over for the presidency of the institution, which went to Daniel H. Hill, Jr., son of the Confederate general. During this time he also represented North Carolina in southern interstate conventions.

In 1893 he sold his banking interests and became National Bank Examiner for the southern states. He continued in this position until 1901. During the war with Spain, he offered his services to North Carolina Governor Daniel L. Russell, and was appointed colonel of the Second Regiment of North Carolina Volunteer Troops; however, the war ended before he could see service abroad.

In 1901 he resigned his Treasury appointment to establish the First National Bank of Weldon, the first of several such ventures in North Carolina. In 1903 he founded the Bank of Rich Square and the Bank of Ayden. The following year he established the First National Bank of Rocky Mount and the Bank of Northampton in Jackson, the First National Bank of Roanoke Rapids, the Bank of Halifax, and a bank in Florida. In addition to his legal and banking interests, he was active in the Episcopal Church at the local, state and national level. Throughout his later life he was actively involved in Confederate veterans' affairs. He had a life-long interest in his own 35th North Carolina as well as the 26th North Carolina, the regiment in which his brother Henry had served as Colonel until killed on July 1, 1863, at Gettysburg. Walter Clark selected Burgwyn to write the chapters about the 35th North Carolina and about Clingman's Brigade in Clark's projected five-volume *History of the Several Regiments and Battalions from North Carolina in the Great War, 1861-1865.*

In November, 1876, in Baltimore he married Margaret Carlisle Dunlop of Richmond, Virginia. They had no children. William's father died in 1877; his mother, in 1887. William H.S. Burgwyn, renown for his courtly and dapper manner, died on January 3, 1913, and was buried beside his brother in Raleigh.[2]

* * * *

According to the records at the North Carolina Department of Archives and History, Burgwyn's widow donated six volumes of diaries; however, the first two have been misplaced. Several of his letters, however, shed light on his early wartime activities. Burgwyn was a faithful diarist and, except for times of combat, recorded his entries daily. I have tried to identify both immediate and distant family members and to explain some of the relationships not apparent in the text. I have only briefly identified general officers because such information is readily available in reference texts. Further I have only briefly summarized military action in which Burgwyn was involved since detailed narrative material is readily available.

The letters are separate from the diaries but I have brought them together where the dates overlap and have inserted the letters following the diary entry for the same day.

I have tried to leave the punctuation as Burgwyn wrote it, but he would frequently run sentence into sentence without benefit of period or semicolon. Where I felt they were necessary I have added them without indicating such additions with brackets. I have corrected obviously misspelled words without so indicating. I have changed his notation for time, e.g. 7 1/2, to a modern format. Where his use of abbreviation was obvious in context, e.g., "P" for Petersburg, I have spelled the word in the interest of readability without so indicating with brackets. Otherwise, the text is as Burgwyn wrote it.

---

[2] Samuel A. Ashe, Stephen B. Weeks, and Charles L. Van Noppen, *Biographical History of North Carolina*, 8 vols. (Greensboro: Charles L. Van Noppen, 1911), 8:73-80; Archie K. Davis, *Boy Colonel of the Confederacy: The Life and Times of Henry King Burgwyn, Jr.*, (Chapel Hill: University of North Carolina Press, 1985), pp. 7, 11, 16, 27, 30; Walter Burgwyn Jones, *John Burgwin, Carolinian [;] John Jones, Virginian*, (Privately printed, 1913), pp. 51-54; Burgwyn Genealogy, typescript in the possession of Mary Burgwyn Newsome, Winston-Salem, North Carolina; Samuel Thomas Peace, *"Zeb's Black Baby" Vance County North Carolina, A Short History*, Henderson: n.p., 1955, pp. 280, 339-401.

William H.S. Burgwyn, center, standing in Herbst's (Reynolds) Woods at Gettysburg in front of the monument of the 24th Michigan. On the right is Colonel John R. Lane, former commander of the 26th North Carolina Troops, the regiment which Henry K. Burgwyn, Jr. commanded until his death on July 1, 1863, at Gettysburg. Henry was William's older brother. On the right is Corporal Charles H. McConnell of Company B, 24th Michigan. (McConnell is frequently misidentified as Colonel and commander of the 24th Michigan at the time of the battle.)

Mary Burgwyn Newsome

CHAPTER 1

Fredericksburg [Virginia], August 27, 1861

My dearest Mother,

I got permission from Colonel [James J.] Pettigrew [22nd North Carolina Infantry] to come here today to prepare to march tomorrow; we in the soldiers don't know where. I received yours of the 23rd today about an hour ago. The lines are really beautiful. I shall commit them to memory. I hope you will get my last letter. We expect to have a fight in a few days therefore the reason of our march. God bless you dear Mother and all and trust in God.

Your most affectionate son,
W. Burgwyn

P.S. I will write again and give you my direction.

* * * *

Camp Carolina
September 5th 1861

My dear Mother,

There is a man going straight home and I seize the opportunity to write you. We left our old camp about twelve miles distant day before yesterday and came here farther up the river where the battery is to be put up to intercept the intercourse to Washington. The battery has not yet been commenced to [sic] but it will be soon and then there will be a fight but we don't know whether the enemy will land and if not we will not be engaged. Write as I say to care of Colonel Pettigrew's Regiment and write often. The gentleman who is to carry it for me is waiting. Love to all

Your affectionate son,
W. Burgwyn

* * * *

Camp Washington
September 9th 1861

My dear Mother,

I received your and Sister's[1] last night and was very glad to hear from you and also very glad to hear what it said though I heard of the result before I received

---

[1] Maria Greenough Burgwyn, also called Minnie, was W.H.S.B.'s oldest sister.

1

your letter but I was very glad to find that Father was in service. I should think the exercise would be a great benefit to him. Everything seems quieted down here though the battery has not been put up yet and when it is we will have some cannonading to undergo. I am very serious when I say I expect to come home before my two months are out unless there is something more to be done here than there is now. Tell Sister I was very glad to hear from her and will write her in a few days. Will you please find out as soon as you receive this letter if Bob [Robert Bruce] Peebles[2] has gone to Chapel Hill or not. I am very anxious to know and if you don't know please get George[3] to find out and write me *immediately*. Adjutant Havel send his best respects to you all and Colonel Pettigrew is enjoying the very best health in the world. Major [Thomas S.] Gallaway was taken down a few days ago with the measles and was removed to a house a few miles off but is getting better. Colonel Pettigrew is the only one of the field officers who has not been sick. He has now the command of a brigade equal to the command of a brigadier general.

I am enjoying very good health and have been ever since I have been here. I am very thankful I had the measles when I was a child. There is more than two thirds of the regiment sick. I must close now hoping to see you before long. Giving my best love to all

I am your most affectionate son,

W.H.S. Burgwyn

Please don't forget to see if Bob Peebles has gone to Chapel Hill or not.

* * * *

Headquarters 48th Regiment North Carolina Troops
Camp Near Goldsboro May 6th 1862

My dear Parents,

I arrived here safely Sunday morning and got permission the next day to go to Kinston and have just returned. I find Harry[4] in fine health and in good spirits. We slept together in a bed made of wheat and pine straw about three feet wide and such sleeping you never experienced. The bed was about three and a half feet high and all the night my poor corpus was in imminent peril of suffering a most terrible fall but luckily the bed was placed along side [of] one of the tent poles and the pole prevented me from falling.

I met yesterday before I left for Kinston Colonel Matt [Matthew W.] Ransom of the (35) [35th North Carolina Infantry] and asked him if he had appointed his adjutant and he said no.[5] I there applied for it and he said he would take much pleasure

---

[2] W.H.S.B.'s good friend and a resident of Jackson, North Carolina. In 1875 he would marry Margaret B. Cameron, daughter of the wealthiest man in the state. He would serve in the North Carolina House of Commons (Representatives) and later on the state Supreme Court.

[3] George Pollok Burgwyn, W.H.S.B.'s younger brother.

[4] Lieutenant Colonel Henry K. Burgwyn, Jr., older brother of W.H.S.B.

[5] Matthew W. ("Matt") Ransom was colonel of the 35th North Carolina Infantry at this time. He was a family friend and lived at "Verona," his wife's family home, four miles east of Jackson, North Carolina, approximately six miles from Thornbury, the Burgwyn family plantation and close to the Peebles' family home.

Matthew Ransom was an attorney and served in the North Carolina legislature. He was one of the three North Carolina commissioners to the Confederate government in Montgomery, Alabama. After North Carolina seceded, he became a lieutenant colonel in the 1st North Carolina Infantry. He was wounded at Malvern Hill during the Peninsula Campaign; a year later he resumed service as Colonel of the 35th North Carolina, and served in the brigade of his younger brother Brigadier General Robert Ransom.

in appointing me but would like to see a little more of his regiment before making the appointment.[6] As the Lieutenant Colonel and Major are [Oliver C.] Petway and [John G.] Jones are particular friends of mine and a great many of the officers also being my friends I think I will probably get it. Holsey arrived safely yesterday with my horse and tomorrow morning I will send Willis[7] to the plantation.

I hope this will reach you before you start to Richmond as I wish you would get me some things there. A saddle, bit, and bridle and an oil cloth suit. All, I don't think, will amount to over fifty-five dollars. The saddle, thirty; bit, five; can make out without the bridle; and oil cloth suit, twenty. I would much prefer the bit to be in this shape. [Sketch in original] I do not wish to ride with martingales. I forgot to mention a pair of saddle bags of the sort you have told me about.

I shall endeavor to obey your wishes in reading my Bible every night and to pray that God will keep us all from harm.

I will write as soon as I get any determinate position.

Your affectionate son,
W.H.S. Burgwyn

* * * *

Raleigh, May 19, 1862

Dear Father,

I reported for duty in person this morning to General [James G.] Martin and he has appointed me Assistant Adjutant General to the First Brigade at Camp Mangum. I have received the appointment and it dates back to April 1st, 1862. As you have not come up this evening I think this will reach you when you receive my former letter. I hope you will see that Holsey is not fit for a servant and let me have Willis. And as it will be necessary for me to have "Hawk Eye," had he not better ride him up.

You don't know how much bothered I am about you in regard to your Negroes that is the trouble you must necessarily have about them. I would take it seriously to mind the expediency of moving them or not and would not certainly move them before it became absolutely necessary.[8]

I can't but think that slavery has received its death blow in this war with the whole world against it. With a large community of poor white men anxious for work and who can do the work as well as the Negroes, the hot sun being no impediment as you yourself know having tried it during harvesting, now can it stand.

---

[6] On May 11, 1862, Lieutenant Colonel Henry K. Burgwyn, Jr., wrote his mother regarding his brother's quest for promotion:

> If...the adjutantcy of my regiment will be vacant Willie will want me to appoint him but I know we will not get along well together, and am really too afraid of his disposition to appoint him. I feel certain that it will be as it was at Crabtree and that under the circumstances in which we would be placed there would be difficulties and disagreements which would make us both unhappy.

Nine days later, Henry Burgwyn concluded a letter to his father with "Ransom told me he would have William elected to a lieutenancy in a few days." (Burgwyn Family Papers, S.H.C.)

[7] family slaves

[8] W.H.S.B.'s father's pro-slavery, pro-secession views may be found in his pamphlet *Considerations Relative to a Southern Confederacy with Letters to the North on the Preservation of the Union, and a Note from the Secret History of the Emancipation in the English West Indies*, Raleigh: "Standard Office" Print, 1860.

From the earliest ages slavery has existed and its most flourishing times were where it was first known and since it has gradually but surely declined. The practice of selling captives into slavery was but the barbarous practice of an unenlightened and uncivilized people and all institutions of slavery have gradually declined until now none remain but in America and in some of the Spanish colonies. After our independence the capital of the S.C. [Southern Confederacy] will be filled with natives of foreign governments hostile to the institution of slavery which will soon become the feeling of the city and the abolition of slavery in that city must necessarily be the consequence. And far and near around that city to a greater or smaller extent will the abolition of slavery be at first listened to and then agreed to and steadily but irresistibly the feeling against slavery will increase till at last every slave in the limits of the S. C. will be free to do as he like. How many years or centuries it will take to bring about the above state of things none can tell but after the example of the North in regard to the abolition of slavery since the Revolution of '76 we can but fear it will not take long.

I cannot tell how long my appointment will last as it is at the will of the governor to take it away but I think I will have one from this time till the war ends.

Hoping this will reach you and that you will send up the horse and boy if you think proper.

I remain,

Your affectionate son,
W.H.S. Burgwyn

P.S.: Have you bought a saddle for me? There has come here a horse portmanteau marked for Harry and three saddle blankets, at least I take them to be so.

* * * *

Thornbury Plantation
July 1st 1862

Dear Mother,

Father left this morning for Richmond to see about Harry and to find out how he got through the fight[9] and also to negotiate a loan.

Enclosed you will find a letter from Harry to Father which as I think you will be glad to see. We have not heard that Ransom's Brigade was actively engaged or not.

I am very sorry to see of Lieutenant Duncan Haywood's[10] death. It must come very heavily upon his family. He was a young man of very fine promise and abilities.

You directed a letter (received today) to Mr. James containing only a paper and a note by Mr. [Frederick] Lightbourne.[11] I suppose you must have forgotten the money or enclosed it in Father's letter.

---

[9] W.H.S.B.'s brother had taken in part of the Seven Days' Battles.

[10] Duncan C. Haywood, first Lieutenant of Company E, 7th North Carolina Troops, was killed on June 27th, 1862, at Gaines' Mill, Virginia. The Haywood family became related to the Burgwyns by several marriages after the war.

[11] Frederick Lightbourne was born in Bermuda and served as the second rector of The Church of The Savior in Jackson, North Carolina. He lived at the Burgwyn family plantation, Thornbury, and was a tutor to the Burgwyn children.

I shall stay here till Father returns which he says will be Saturday or Sunday. I expect then he will bring me news that will cause my immediate departure for Virginia to join Ransom's Regiment.[12]

Let me again, dear Mother, beseech you not to give heed to any flying reports for if Ransom's Brigade is engaged actively they will report almost everyone killed or wounded from the reputation of the man. From what we can hear down here no mention is made at all of any casualties in Ransom's Brigade and you can see by the papers [Major General John B.] Magruder's and [Major General Benjamin] Huger's Divisions were held as reserves and Harry is in Huger's Division.

Hoping to hear from you soon and that you are enjoying better health than when I left,

I remain, as always,

Your affectionate son,
W.H.S. Burgwyn

* * * *

BOOK ONE: AUGUST 1, 1862 - MARCH 28, 1863

Friday August 1st 1862

Started this morning at 8:00 a.m. on my brother's horse accompanying him [and] Colonel Ransom who rode in an ambulance to the camp of General [Robert] Ransom's Brigade. Camped about 4 miles from Petersburg. Passed the night with Colonel [Zebulon B.] Vance's Regiment [26th North Carolina Infantry] occupying my brother's tent fly. Weather fair but very warm.

Saturday August 2nd 1862

Left camp with the brigade riding in an ambulance of Colonel Vance's Regiment and came up with the brigade (which marched faster than the wagons) about two miles north of Petersburg. Passed the night with Vance's Regiment in my brother's tent fly as the night before. Weather warm and fair.

---

[12] The 35th Regiment North Carolina Troops was mustered in for 12 months service to the state on November 8, 1861. On January 1, 1862, the regiment was transferred to service in the Confederate States of America. In March, 1862, it took part in the fighting at New Bern, where it retreated in "utmost disorder." Following the battle it was assigned to a newly formed brigade under Brigadier General Samuel G. French. The new brigade also consisted of the 7th Regiment North Carolina State Troops, 26th Regiment North Carolina State Troops, 27th Regiment North Carolina State Troops, and several cavalry and foot artillery units. French was replaced by Brigadier General Robert Ransom in late May, 1862. The following month the 7th Regiment North Carolina Troops was transferred out of the brigade and the 25th Regiment North Carolina Troops was added. On April 21st the 35th Regiment North Carolina Troops was reorganized to serve for three years and Lieutenant Colonel Matthew W. Ransom, brother of Robert Ransom, was elected as colonel, to replace Colonel James Sinclair.

On June 19, 1862, the 35th Regiment started with Ransom's brigade for Petersburg, where they arrived on June 21st. Several new regiments were added to the brigade and it now consisted of the 24th, 25th, 26th, 35th, 48th, and 49th Regiments North Carolina Troops. (The 27th Regiment North Carolina Troops was transferred to Brigadier General John G. Walker's brigade on June 2, 1862.)

On June 24th the brigade was ordered to Major General Benjamin Huger's command on the Williamsburg Road, southeast of Richmond. The 35th North Carolina took part in the fighting at King's School House on the 25th and at Malvern Hill on July 1st. Ransom's brigade returned to Drewry's Bluff, south of Richmond on July 7th and moved to Petersburg on July 29th. (*N.C. Troops*, 9:354-355).

Brigadier General Robert Ransom

Sunday August 3rd 1862

Marched back again with the brigade from where we came from the day before, it being rumored the Yankees were landing in great numbers at City Point. Rained very hard for about half an hour at 10:00 o'clock a.m. Marched back on the same road for two miles and bivouacked there for the night. The night fair and [illegible] rain. I used my brother's flies.

Monday August 4th 1862

Remained at our last night's camp all day. About 10:00 a.m. I was elected First Lieutenant of Company H [35th North Carolina Infantry] (Captain [David G.] Maxwell [and] Colonel Ransom superintending the election.) There was but one dissenting vote in my election. Weather excessively hot but fair.

Tuesday August 5th 1862

About 3:00 p.m. started from our camp and marched toward Petersburg to within two miles of it and encamped pitching our tents which had arrived the day before from Drewry's Bluff. The weather warmer than it ever seemed to me to be and our march consequently very fatiguing.

Wednesday August 6th 1862

Obtained permission to go to the city to get my trunk left there when I came on. Took a bath (which was very much needed) and dinner at Jarratts Hotel; also put on clean clothes through out which had a very salutary effect after keeping my clothes for a week. Weather very warm and fair.

* * * *

Petersburg, August 6, 1862

Dear Mother,

Harry has before this told you why I have not written you but today I having obtained leave to come to Petersburg I sit down to tell you everything that has occurred.

The night Harry left us the brigade received marching orders to go to Drewry's Bluff as it was supposed. It marched as far as two miles the other side of Petersburg on the road to Drewry's Bluff when we arrived there orders came for us to march back again from where we came from, the real object being to attack the Yankees who it was reported had landed in large numbers from their gunboats. The brigade proceeded about seven miles down the City Point Road and there halted about twelve o'clock p.m. It rained very hard for some little time and consequently everybody got perfectly wet. The brigade, except Colonel [William J.] Clark's Regiment (which was left behind to do picket duty) was then marched back about two miles and halted for the night. We stayed there the next day and the next until about three o'clock p.m. when we were marched three or four miles nearer Petersburg and there halted and we expect to stay there some time our tents having arrived on August the 4th. Colonel Ransom having ordered an election to be held I was elected 1st Lieutenant of Company H (Captain Maxwell) with but one dissenting voice and am now here for the purpose of getting my baggage out to my company.

Colonel Ransom has acted perfectly upright and [illegible] about my election and did what he could do to get me elected. I did not leave the plantation till Wednesday the 30th. Colonel Ransom had disappointed me the two previous days and I went to Garysburg both the days that he disappointed me not knowing but that he was going each day. Tell Harry I have not heard the result of his petitions to be sent to North Carolina and that I do not think Major [James S.] Kendall[13] has withdrawn his resignation. I have not seen him for two days.

I cannot tell you where to direct exactly only to Petersburg, 35th Regiment, North Carolina Troops, Ransom's Brigade. I hope you are taking advantage of this warm weather and regain your accustomed strength and that Father is better than when I left him. Tell Harry I have not received my belt or bugle and if he has not given it to anyone to give [it] to me to keep it till I see him again. Give my love to all and tell Father I will write him from camp.

Your affectionate son,
W.H.S. Burgwyn

* * * *

Thursday August 7th 1862

Remained in camp all day. About 12:00 noon orders came to hold ourselves in readiness to march at a moment's notice and to prepare a day's rations but we were not ordered away which was very satisfactory. Weather fair and very warm.

Friday August 8th 1862

Remained all day in camp. Was detailed as officer of the guard. The regiment was detailed as a working party to work on the field works around Petersburg about half mile from camp. Weather warm and fair.

Saturday August 9th 1862

Remained all day in camp. Nothing of importance occurring. Colonel Ransom came to Captain [Nicholas McK.] Long's[14] tent and remained nearly all day but did not take command of his regiment. Lieutenant Colonel Jones came to camp after dress parade but left again. Weather 96° and very warm.

Sunday August 10th 1862

Remained again all day in camp and nothing occurred to distract the daily routine of the camp. Lieutenant [Thomas W.] Richardson of Company D with a detail of ten men started for Raleigh to bring back 510 conscripts to fill up the regiment. Weather at 97° but rained at night fall.

---

[13] Kendall had been elected major on April 21, 1862, and he was transferred to the staff of the 26th North Carolina Regiment. He resigned on July 21, 1862, because "the relations...between myself and others of our field & staff are such that to remain longer in connection with the regiment would be incompatible with my honor as a gentleman and soldier." *N.C. Troops*, VII, p. 463.

[14] Captain Long was Quartermaster of the 35th North Carolina Regiment. He was grandson of Colonel Nicholas Long (1728-1797), a large landowner in Halifax County, N.C. Colonel Long owned "Mush Island," a 2,700 acre plantation east of Weldon, N.C., along the Roanoke River; much of this property was acquired after the war by Matt Ransom. Col. Long's son, Thomas W. Mason Long, M.D., would marry W.H.S.B.'s younger brother's (George) daughter (Maria Greenough Burgwyn) after the war. Captain Long was first cousin of Ellen Williams Long, wife of Confederate General Junius Daniel.

Monday August 11th 1862

Received permission to visit Petersburg today. Went there with my captain, Captain Maxwell, and remained there until 5:45 p.m. Took dinner at the Bollingbrook Hotel. Fare but poor; charged me one dollar moderate. Weather very warm and fair.

Tuesday August 12th 1862

Met Mr. James who had just arrived the day before from home with fifteen Negroes pressed into service from my father's plantation. Went over to see them and found them at Colonel [Junius] Daniel's Brigade. They seemed satisfied with their situation. About 5:00 o'clock p.m. the wind rose and blew very much. It rained slightly. Weather before the storm very warm and fair.

Wednesday August 13th 1862

Nothing extraordinary or unusual occurred today. The regiment went out to work in the morning and evening as usual. Weather much colder than day before and the night unusually cold. It is rumored that we are going to join Stonewall Jackson.

Thursday August 14th 1862

Did not go out this morning with the regiment to work, having been appointed adjutant *pro tem*. The regiment is throwing up rifle pits and in a day and a half 500 men of the regiment threw up 619 feet of rifle pits. Weather cool and fair.

Friday August 15th 1862

Went out with the regiment this morning for the purpose of seeing the way to construct rifle pits. Made application to Colonel Ransom to relieve me from acting adjutant but he refused, my captain and one of the lieutenants not being on duty with the company. Weather cool again but fair.

Saturday August 16th 1862

Was ordered by Colonel Ransom to lay off a new encampment for the regiment in rear of the present camp. Was assisted by Lieutenant Richardson. The regiment moved to the new camp immediately after dinner. Colonel Ransom relieved me after dinner. Weather cool the night very cold for this time of year.

Sunday August 17th 1862

Was ordered out at 6:00 a.m. as usual in the week with the regiment to work on the fortifications and remained working till we finished our part which was 10:00 a.m. After dinner the regiment went out to work again. Weather cool but fair; night very cold for the time of year.

Monday August 18th 1862

Finished the breastworks around Petersburg today about 11:00 a.m. Spent the evening lolling about camp. Weather moderately warm and fair. Four of us officers spent $6.50 for watermelons to celebrate the finishing of the breastwork and made preparations to go to the city next day.

THIRTY-FIFTH REGIMENT.

1. M. W. Ransom, Colonel.
2. John G. Jones, Colonel.
3. J. T. Johnson, Colonel.
4. Simon B. Taylor, Lieut.-Colonel.
5. Wm. H. S. Burgwyn, Captain, Co. H.
6. Robert B. Peebles, Adjutant.
7. David G. Maxwell, Captain, Co. H.
8. P. J. Johnson, Captain, Co. K.
9. Walter Clark, 1st Lieut. and Adjutant.

Staff of the 35th Regiment North Carolina Troops

Clark, *Histories*, II:591

Tuesday August 19th 1862

Received orders about 2:00 o'clock this morning to be ready to march at 10:00 o'clock a.m. and to prepare three day's of cooked rations. The men were ordered to set about preparing their things immediately. We started about ten and by the most determined exertions the troops succeeded in marching fifteen miles by nightfall and encamped opposite to Drewry's Bluff. The dust was almost intolerable; so thick you could not see sometimes the men of your own company but the heat was not very great. The men were very much exhausted. We bivouacked in the woods.

* * * *

Thirty-Fifth Regiment, North Carolina Troops
August 19th 1862

Dear Mother,

I write in haste to tell you that this morning at 2:00 a.m. we received orders to hold ourselves in readiness to march at ten o'clock with three day's cooked provisions. Our major says we are going to Richmond and I don't think there can be any doubt but that we will join Stonewall. I do not know whether Harry's regiment is ordered off or not but I supposed it is if it has not been taken out of Ransom's Brigade of which I have heard nothing.

I will write if I can from Richmond or at the first stopping place though I do not know whether we will be allowed to take our baggage with us or not but if we go to Stonewall I imagine we will not be allowed to carry anything with us. I sent over Pompey[15] yesterday to see if Harry had come but found he had not. I hoped he could last night or that he will come before the regiment leaves for it will be in a very disorganized condition with no field officers present. We finished working on the works around Petersburg yesterday by noon and this immediate order accounts for compelling us to work on Sunday showing that as soon as we could possibly finish them we would be ordered off.

Give my love to all and hoping I will hear from you good accounts from Harry, I remain,

Your affectionate son,
W.H.S. Burgwyn

* * * *

Wednesday August 20th 1862

Commenced our march at 7:00 a.m. toward Richmond. Left the Turnpike road opposite to the pontoon bridge that crosses the James about six miles below Richmond. After a little halt commenced the crossing of the pontoon bridge and did not stop to rest till we arrived in the suburbs of Richmond at 2:00 p.m. The heat was greater than the day before and the dust was horrible, worse than the day before but we only marched about nine miles.

---

[15] W.H.S.B.'s slave and body servant.

Thursday August 21st 1862

Remained all day in yesterday's encampment expecting every hour to be ordered to march. The weather warm and later only fair but it clouded up in the afternoon and it rained very heavily in the night and the lightening was very vivid and the thunder loud.

Friday August 22nd 1862

This morning drizzly and remained so until about 12 noon. Weather moderately warm. Remained all day in camp. Visited some fortifications nearby camps also the grave of Powhatan and the rock where [Captain John] Smith was bound to await the fatal stroke when Pocahontas saved him.

* * * *

Thirty-Fifth Regiment North Carolina Troops
Camp near Richmond August 22nd [1862]

Dear Mother,

We left our camp near Petersburg (as I wrote you on our departure) on Tuesday the 19th and arrived here day before yesterday after two days very severe marching. The first march was about fifteen or seventeen miles and we started about 10:00 a.m. The roads were almost intolerable it had been some time since we had had any rain and the dust was so great at times that I could hardly see the men of my company and you can imagine what we suffered. The next day they commenced the march at 7:00 a.m. and marched nine miles by 2:00 p.m. the dust of everything was more intolerable than the day before but I did not feel the march half so much as the one of the day before and am now I believe better than I was even before I started. This is only a temporary stop here for we leave today they say for Stonewall. The troops are in fine spirits and do not seem to dislike going to him as much as one would expect. I heard yesterday Harry had forwarded a surgeon's certificate that he was unable to return to camp; his men are very anxious that he should return for they don't relish the idea of going to Stonewall without any field officer in command. The officers have determined to elect their field officers except the colonel for they expect him to go up and I have no doubt but that they will elect some competent men. I think it would be better if you sent me some three or four dollars of stamps by Harry for I would not be able to get any about Gordonsville. Don't forget the drawers. Better send cotton flannel to him. Please also send me another blue flannel shirt like the one I have. We are not allowed to take much baggage and those things are the best to take that will not show dirt and will keep you warm at night. I don't think I can afford to let Harry have his blankets again. The weather has been unusually cold and I will need them all in winter. Can't he bring me some? Kinchen[16] has preserved all his things and though we are allowed to take with us but the smallest measure of [illegible] possible he has brought all his tools and things with him. I will write from our next encampment. With much love to all, I am,

Your affectionate son,
W.H.S. Burgwyn

---

[16] Harry's slave and body servant.

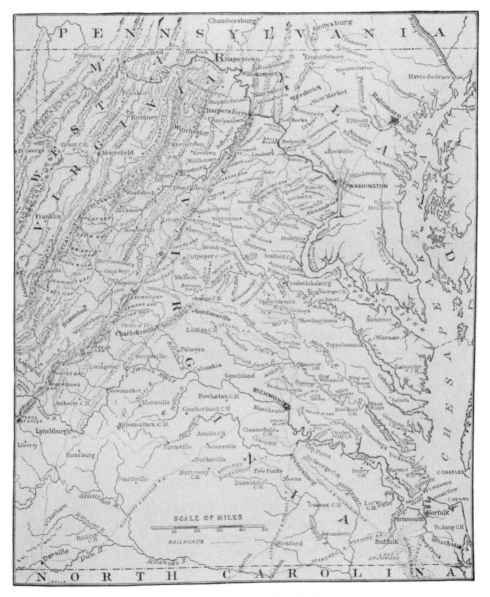

Map of Virginia and Maryland

Battles and Leaders, II:1

CHAPTER 2

Saturday August 23rd 1862

Received orders early this morning to be ready to march at 7:00 a.m. Was told by Colonel Ransom that my father and Colonel Burgwyn my brother were both in Richmond. Received permission to go there and remained there all day. Return with Harry about 6:00 p.m. The regiment had encamped. Weather a little cloudy but no rain, moderately fair. Rained about duskfall but did not last all night.

Sunday August 24th 1862

Remained in camp all day. Had a tedious work in ruling off a regimental morning report I not having any. Weather little drizzly early in the morning but cleared up during the day. The wind pretty high about 10:00 a.m.

Monday August 25th 1862

Received permission to visit Richmond to see my father. Went in an ambulance with my brother and remained there all day. Met some schoolmates of Georgetown College, D.C., who had just succeeded in running the blockade and coming to Richmond to join the army. Weather tolerably fair and moderately warm.

Tuesday August 26th 1862

Received orders to march this morning at 10:00 a.m. Started but was turned back for want of transportation. Went in bathing about 4:00 p.m. in the James River and saw men across it. Weather moderately warm in the morning; warmer in the middle of the day and also rain.

Wednesday August 27th 1862

Awoke at 3:00 a.m. this morning, the drum beating so soon to prepare to march at 7:30 a.m. Was allowed to take no baggage with us on the trains but what we could carry on our backs. The wagons carrying only tent flies and the regulation's amount of baggage. Taking the army roads for Jeffersonville, Culpeper County, Virginia, where we were going as far as we could on the railroad. Arrived in Richmond at 9:30 a.m. and left on the cars at ten minutes of 6:00 p.m. Weather cloudy and sprinkly when we left but no rain at night. My brother received the order transferring his regiment to that not to start with us. [1]

---

[1] Henry K. Burgwyn, Jr. was transferred to Pettigrew's Brigade. Before the brothers separated, Henry gave William a parting meal, supplies, and food. Further, Henry gave him whiskey and saw that William was "instructed in its use." (Davis, *The Boy Colonel*, pp. 189, fn. 36.)

Thursday August 28th 1862

The cars arrived at their destination about 4:00 a.m. and as soon as the men could be got off they returned to Richmond. Our camp was on either side of the railroad where the cars stopped about twelve miles from Culpeper Court House; the bridge across the Rapidan having been burned by the Yankees prevented the cars from going any farther. We are encamped about a mile from where Jackson defeated the Yankees under Pope.

Friday August 29th 1862

Moved our camp about half a mile from the railroad in a dense wood where we had a most delightful campground and went in bathing by day in the river near the burned bridge. In the evening Brigadier Generals Jordan or [George B.] Anderson's[2] Brigade [2nd, 4th, 14th, and 30th North Carolina Infantry] arrived. Weather moderately fair and warm.

Saturday August 30th 1862

Remained in camp all day. Weather cloudy and towards night clouded up for rain. Received orders to prepare to march next morning for the purpose of giving the troops an airing.

Sunday August 31st 1862

About 7:00 a.m. it commenced raining and continued with some slight interruptions til 12:00 noon. All the men got wet having nothing to cover themselves with. The wagons not yet having arrived from Richmond. Did not march as was intended.

Monday September 1st 1862

Was ordered to march at 7:30 a.m. and consequently commenced our march for Culpeper Court House at that time. Marched on the railroad and forded the Rapidan and another river, the bridge over them being burned by the Yankees in their retreat. Reached Culpeper Court House about 4:00 p.m. having stopped sometime on the way. Immediately after stopping for the night, commenced to rain and rained very hard for about ten minutes getting all the men [wet] and the wagons did not come up in time to use the tent flies.

Tuesday September 2nd 1862

Left Culpeper Court House for Jeffersonville a distance of fifteen miles about 5:00 a.m. and after a tedious march reached Jeffersonville about 4:00 p.m. Weather fair and moderately warm. Our brigade marched in front, General [John G.] Walker having marched in front the day before. Forded the Hazel River at 11:00 a.m.[3]

---

[2] George Burgwyn Anderson was a second cousin of W.H.S.B.; their grandfathers were brothers.

[3] Burgwyn's regiment, the 35th North Carolina, along with the 24th, 25th, and 49th North Carolina and Colonel James R. Branch's Field Artillery, composed Brigadier General Robert Ransom's Brigade. Along with Walker's Brigade (3rd Arkansas; 27th, 46th, and 48th North Carolina, 30th Virginia, and French's [Virginia] Battery) commanded by Colonel Vannoy H. Manning, comprised Walker's Brigade.

Wednesday September 3rd 1862

Recommenced our march from Jeffersonville about 5:00 a.m. and marched about three miles north of Warrenton Court House a distance of about fifteen miles. Weather cool in the morning fair all day. Our brigade marching in rear and our regiment in rear of all. Half as an advanced guard and half for a rear guard for the wagons.

Thursday September 4th 1862

Left our camp near Warrenton about 7:00 a.m. and marched as far as Gainesville about seven miles by 11:00 a.m. Weather fair and warm but night very cold. Met wagons trains, ambulances, and carts continually passing with wounded men from the last battle.

Friday September 5th 1862

Recommenced our march from Gainesville about 7:00 a.m. and proceeded to within six miles of Leesburg a distance of ten miles. Weather warm and fair. The dew very great for in the morning. My bed clothes were almost as wet as if it had rained.

Saturday September 6th 1862

Marched at 6:00 a.m. this morning and pushed on to cross the Potomac as near as possible to join the main army under Jackson. Marched to within four miles of the river a distance of about twelve miles. Weather very excessively warm and the dust almost insufferable and having to march almost entirely in the sun the men suffered more than on any previous march about two-thirds having fallen out.

Sunday September 7th 1862

Commenced our march at 6:00 a.m. and reached the Potomac River about 10:00 a.m. Walker's Brigade being ahead we were detained some time. Had to ford the river, it taking us up to the seat of our pants and about three-quarters of a mile wide. First put my foot on the Maryland shore precisely five minutes of 11:00 a.m. The men as they would step on shore would raise a shout. The weather very warm. Dust very great but there was some wind stirring which prevented us from feeling the march as much as the day before. The name of the ford where we crossed the Potomac was called Cheek's or Cheak's Ford.[4] We halted at a little town called Buckeystown about nine miles from where we cross the Potomac.

Monday September 8th 1862

Left our last night's bivouac at 7:00 a.m. and marched about a mile and a half to the north side of the Monocacy River which runs in front of the little town of Buckey's. Remained there all day. Weather very warm and fair. The dust almost insufferable.

---

[4]Cheeks Ford crosses the Potomac River and joins the road between Berlin, Maryland, and Lovettsville, Virginia, four miles east of Harper's Ferry.

Tuesday September 9th 1862

Left the north side of the Monocacy at 7:00 a.m. and marched about three miles passing [Major General Lafayette] McLaws Division. Received orders about 12:00 noon to march back and rush to the place we left about 2:00 p.m. Halted for three hours drawing rations but did not have time to cook them. Left at 5:30 p.m. for the Potomac for the purpose of blowing up a bridge and aquaduct about two miles below Cheek's Ford. Reached the place about 11:00 p.m. a distance of about nine miles and as we were crossing the bridge were halted by a Yankee picket. A bitter skirmish took place and we lost a captain from his imprudence in rashly exposing himself. Did not succeed in blowing up the bridge or aquaduct it being too substantial a structure and we were afraid to stay till it could be drilled for fear of being cut off by the Yankees under [Major General Nathaniel P.] Banks who were in large force about five miles and at Poolesville [Maryland].

Wednesday September 10th 1862

Left the aquaduct about 4:00 a.m. and marched toward Buckeystown to within two miles of it and halted. Left the place about 7:30 p.m. to recross the Potomac to prevent being cut off. Marched all the remainder of the night. Marched about fourteen miles today and the two nights marching almost exhausted the men. Weather was warm and fair. Four Yankee pickets rode up in front of our brigade to within twenty yards but it was so dark we did not perceive them till too late.

Thursday September 11th 1862

Continued our march to cross the Potomac and reached Point of Rocks about daybreak. Crossed the river just below as soon as possible and encamped on the opposite side all day. Rained at night. Weather cloudy all day but warm. Wrote Mother a few lines too and sent it by Dr. Lassiter (who was going there in an ambulance to carry Dr. O'Hagen's [regimental surgeon] Negro boy who shot himself this morning. I borrowed the doctor's horse which came very opportunely for the constant marching had very early broke me down.

Friday September 12th 1862

Left the south side of the Potomac River at 7:00 a.m. and marched as far as Hillsborough on the Harpers Ferry road, a distance of about fifteen miles. Passed through some of the most magnificent country in Virginia and as fine I ever expect to see. Weather cloudy but very warm.

Saturday September 13th 1862

Left Hillsborough about 8:00 a.m. We marched in rear of the trains and all marched about four miles and halted sometime waiting for orders as our troops on the Maryland side were shelling the enemy at Harpers Ferry and we were only about five miles from Harpers Ferry. Marched about two miles nearer Harpers Ferry and halted for the night. After dark about 8:30 p.m. the whole went on picket about a mile from Harpers Ferry and everyone expected to be in a fight as it was supposed the Yankees would endeavor to cut their way through our brigade and not surrender. Weather moderately warm and cold at night.

Sunday September 14th 1862

Returned from picket to camp at daybreak and cooked provisions. Remained all night in camp. Our troops on the opposite side of the river and on this side also kept up an uninterrupted firing and shelling and it was supposed that Longstreet whipped Banks very severely today. We heard the firing off very distinctly and it was very great. Weather cold at night and cool in the day. The first lieutenant of Captain [Thomas B.] French's [Virginia] Battery, Walker's Brigade, was killed.

Monday September 15th 1862

Returned from picket at daybreak. Rations of beef were issued but no flour. About 7:00 a.m. the Yankees at Harpers Ferry surrendered. We marched about twelve miles within three miles of Harpers Ferry the bridge over the Shenandoah [River] being destroyed and the river unfordable. Took 14,000 prisoners. Two generals, 50 pieces of cannon from 18,000 to 20,000 stand of new arms, etc., etc. Weather warm in the day and at night also for the time of the year.

Tuesday September 16th 1862

Was wakened up at 1:00 a.m. and ordered to march to Shepherdstown [Virginia] about twelve miles. Reached it about 9:00 a.m. and crossed the Potomac at 1:00 p.m.. Marched about a mile and a half and bivouacked for the night. Weather warm and fair. Men very much exhausted from the want of sleep.

Wednesday September 17th 1862

Was wakened up at 3:15 a.m. and marched to take our position in line of battle. Great battle being about to come off. [5] After getting our position and then another we were marched about 8:00 a.m. where the fight was most severe and our men were about to be repulsed. We formed in line of battle our whole brigade and charged through a storm of shells and grape; once in jumping over a fence the regiment was about to waver. I caught the colors from the flag bearer and assisted in rallying the men but my colonel took the flag from me almost immediately after I took it but I still remained in front of the regiment cheering them on; about [a] quarter of a mile farther as we came in sight of the Yankees they poured in a murderous fire into the 49th [North Carolina Infantry], the regiment immediately on our right, but we charged up to the brow of the hill and gave it to them with all our might. They ran like sheep and then their artillery commenced on us. We were just on the falling side of a hill and that was the only thing that saved us. They poured grape shell and canister at us till we were ordered to another part of the same woods about 400 yards off to drive the Yankees from it. We charged them and fired upon them at about a 100 yards and they ran like sheep. Then their artillery commenced on us in truth and all say the shelling of Malvern Hill was not equal to it. We were in almost the same sort of position as before we moved but not so good and the grape and canister would come over us about three or four feet. They fired at us all day as hard as they could and after dark they threw some shell. We moved our position about a mile about sundown to go on picket leaving part of Walker's Brigade in the wood. We held the woods with our brigade all day where three [regiments] of our brigade had been driven from before we came up. The Yankees had their camp the night before the battle in the woods we held today. Their batteries were about 300 yards off from us.

---

[5] During the battle of Sharpsburg, Ransom's Brigade took part in the counterattack on General John Sedgwick in the West Woods.

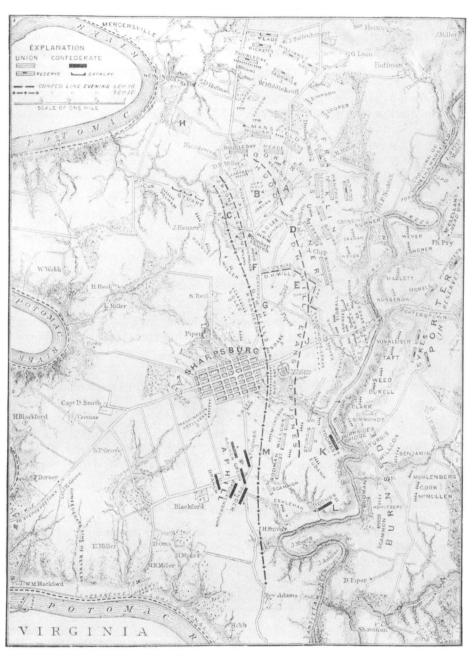

Battlefield of Antietam, Maryland

Battles and Leaders, II:636

Thursday September 18th 1862

Marched back about 7:00 a.m. to take position in the same woods we held yesterday. Expecting to have a very decisive and bloody battle but the two commanding generals agreed to a truce to bring the dead and consequently there was no firing of any consequence all day. Just after getting fixed to sleep for the night we were silently and hastily got under arms and took up our line of march to recross the Potomac. Weather cloudy and about 4:00 p.m. it rained a little while. General T.J. Jackson rode through the woods where we were with his staff. He had on an old coat and India rubber overcoat and was mounted on a mighty sorry looking claybank horse.

Friday September 19th 1862

Arrived at the Potomac River about 1:30 a.m. and crossed immediately. Bivouacked about a mile and a half on the opposite side. Marched by night to Martinsburg [West Virginia] a distance of about fifteen miles by the way we came. Weather cloudy in the morning but a most beautiful sunset.

Saturday September 20th 1862

Left Martinsburg at 9:00 a.m. for Shepherdstown precisely where we came from the day before. Reached there about 4:00 p.m. Was ordered to return from where we came at 6:00 p.m. and after being on the road eight hours reached Martinsburg about 2:00 a.m. next day. The men were completely exhausted and gave out but about half being able to reach Martinsburg. Weather cloudy. We marched today counting the night about eighteen miles.

Sunday September 21st 1862

Remained all day in bivouac near Martinsburg to rest the men and to cook two days' rations. The men very much exhausted and need the rest imperatively. Weather fair and the men suffering very much in the night from want of bed clothes, baggage and clothing being lost.

Monday September 22nd 1862

Remained all day in bivouac near Martinsburg. Felt very badly. Was told by my surgeon that I was taking jaundice. I had been unwell for some days. My boy [Pompey] returned to me about 2:00 p.m. having been directed to Winchester wrongly. Received a letter from my Mother dated August 27th which raised my spirits considerably. Wrote home by a resigned officer. Weather fair.

Tuesday September 23rd 1862

Feel no better today but worse. Wrote two letters, one to my Mother, the other to my brother Harry by Captain Long our quartermaster who was sent home to get clothing and *cetera* for the regiment. Wrote for a complete outfit as I was extremely destitute, having lost everything. Weather fair.

* * * *

Thirty-Fifth Regiment North Carolina Troops
Camp near Martinsburg, Virginia, September 23rd 1862

Dear Harry,

I suppose ere this you have heard of the capture of Harpers Ferry with 14,000 Yankees, etc., etc., and of a great battle near Sharpsburg on the 17th instant. I was present at both but at Harpers Ferry there was no fighting but what the artillery did.

On the 16th we waded the Potomac and bivouacked about a mile and a half on the other side opposite Shepherdstown. Next day about 3:00 a.m. we were moved to our positions in line of battle but had it changed constantly. About 9:00 a.m. we were ordered into the thickest of it where our troops had been repulsed. The brigade was formed in line of battle and marched splendidly through a severe shower of grape, cannister, and shell but not a man wavered till we came to a fence right in front of us which we had to climb and consequently threw us into more or less confusion and just then the shells and things came thick and fast and at this very time my second lieutenant was shot and it threw us into more confusion. I jumped in front of the regiment and tried all I could do to form the regiment. Colonel Ransom and myself think I rallied them quickly and then General Ransom gave the command "Forward." The men hesitated a little and I seized the colors from the color bearer and called on the men to follow. Then Colonel Ransom made me give them up to him and I turned round and called on the men to follow waving my sword and encouraging them. The whole brigade then marched forward in line of battle and kept dressed better than a dress parade. We had not gone far before we came to a line of woods and somebody commenced shouting as some hundred Yankee prisoners came through our lines. We were then ordered to charge through the woods which were about a hundred yards in width widening in direction of our right to about 400 yards. The Yankees had possession of the skirts of the woods opposite us and we were ordered to clear the woods of them. They sent the regiment on our right, the 49th [North Carolina Infantry], with a severe fire wounding and killing a great many but the fire not being far enough to the left to hurt us. We charged up to the skirts driving the Yankees in front of us and then fired upon them lying down. They fled like geese and then their artillery opened upon us about 300 yards distant. Just at the skirts of the woods where we were lying down was sloping and their artillery passed over us. We stayed there some time and were then marched round to the right by the right flank halted, fronted, and ordered to charge the enemy that were in the skirts of the woods. General J.E.B. Stuart ordering us to do so we charged beyond the front of the woods and there found two batteries, one not over two hundred yards from us. They immediately opened upon us but pointed their guns too low and we immediately fell back in the woods to a place something like the other place and lay down. And then commenced such a storm of grape, cannister, and shells that they say was far worse and more severe than Malvern Hill but we were in a little hollow and the grape and cannister passed about three or four feet above us, the Yankees making it graze the tops of the hill. We were shelled there all day till about 5:00 with some slight interruption when the Yankees endeavored to retake the place.

Colonel Ransom praised me very much about my action there and Major General Ransom says they told him I acted most gallantly. We marched from Rapidan Station to a little town in Maryland without one day's rest and we have twice entered Maryland and been twice driven back making four times we have waded the Potomac. We retreated or fell back after the battle of Sharpsburg across the river and in our haste lost all our baggage and bed clothing but no regiment but ours lost the officers' baggage or bed clothing. I have no more time to write more as I have written Mother and have got to write her some more as our quartermaster goes to Raleigh today to get clothing, guns, etc., etc., for the men.

> Your affectionate brother,
> W.H.S. Burgwyn

* * * *

Wednesday September 24th 1862

Remained contrary to our expectations in our bivouac. Felt much better than yesterday but had no appetite. Weather little rainy but a fair night some wind about nightfall.

Thursday September 25th 1862

Felt worse than expected to feel with no appetite and constant feeling of nausea. No orders to leave for which I was very thankful, as I was unable to march. Weather fair.

Friday September 26th 1862

Had frost this morning. For the first time felt almost the same as the day before but got a little better late in the day. Ate a good deal for supper which I took with Lieutenant Colonel [Samuel H.] Walkup of the 48th [North Carolina]. Received intimation we would leave early next morning. Weather fair.

Saturday September 27th 1862

Left early this morning in the direction of Winchester [Virginia]. After all day's marching we arrived about night fall to within about four miles of Winchester, having marched eighteen miles. I marched all the way but with great fatigue. Weather fair.

Sunday September 28th 1862

Remained all day in bivouac where we halted the night before. Feel only tolerable having passed only a poor night. The night inordinately warm and my only blanket kept me sufficiently warm. Weather fair.

Monday September 29th 1862

Remained in the same place as yesterday all day. Received permission to visit the surrounding country to get provisions. Was enabled to get a very good dinner and also to buy a chicken. Lieutenant [William F.] Beasly of the 48th [North Carolina] accompanied me. Weather rained a little about 1:00 p.m. but afterwards was fair.

Tuesday September 30th 1862

Sent my boy Pompey out foraging this morning and also to get some bread baked in the form of a loaf. He succeeded in getting me the bread baked and I was presented with some coffee and sugar. Weather tolerably fair. Wrote home by [Mr. David] Clark [6] our adjutant's [Lieutenant Walter M. Clark] father who had come to see him.

---

[6] David Clark was a prominent, wealthy planter in eastern North Carolina and served briefly in early 1862 as brigadier general of the state militia. David Clark's appointment as a militia officer was a source of some resentment on the part of Henry King Burgwyn, Sr., who had hoped for a similar appointment. His son, Walter McKenzie Clark, later became a noted North Carolina Supreme Court justice and historian, and editor of *Histories of the Several Regiments and Battalions from North Carolina, in the Great War 1861-1865.*

Map of Northern Virginia

* * * *

Thirty-Fifth Regiment North Carolina Troops
Bivouac in the woods 4 miles north of Winchester
September 30th 1862

Dear Father,

Before this I hope you have received those letters written since the Sharpsburg battle and consequently are informed of my safety, and that Captain Long has handed you one written to be carried by him. I did not tell you in the letter given to Captain Long that I was pretty bad off with jaundice for I knew it would distress you all and be of no good but now since I am almost entirely recovered, thank God, I let you know it. I felt very badly while it was on me but we happened to remain in bivouac near Martinsburg for about a week and it was on me the worst those days but three days ago we marched from Martinsburg to this place a distance of eighteen miles and as the surgeons told me it would do me good to travel I managed to march it and think it cured me.

I am very anxious to hear from you all and hope Captain Long will bring me letters and good news. I think all the army is falling back and day before yesterday we were all in fine spirits at the news that General [James] Longstreet's Corps was ordered to Richmond but I am afraid it is not so. We are in Brigadier General Walker's Division and Major General Longstreet's Corps. With the exception of this jaundice I have been well enough to keep up on all the marches and pray God I always will be able. We are making out here as well as can be expected with no blankets or baggage and hope soon to get supplies from our Quartermaster Captain Long. I never before was really anxious for the war to close but now nothing could please me better than for it to close though I am perfectly willing to undergo everything that is ordered though I wish they would send us somewhere near home to winter quarters. But as I firmly believe everything that is done is done for the best I try to await patiently for easier times.

Colonel Ransom has been unwell lately and now has a sty on his eye that pains him very much so he says. I wish Harry's regiment had never been transferred from the brigade. I would have had a much easier time of it. We are constantly hearing cheering news of our troops in the west and it has been reported but not confirmed. I don't think that General [Don Carlos] Buell with 20,000 men has been captured by General [Braxton] Bragg and General [Sterling] Price. I hope it is so. We have been having unusually good weather since we left Rapidan Station for troops in bivouac but I am afraid the weather will turn cold and rainy. I am obliged to close now hoping to hear good news from all and with much love, I am,

Your affectionate son,
W.H.S. Burgwyn

* * * *

Wednesday October 1st 1862

Moved about half a mile nearer Winchester in a woods for the purpose of getting a better bivouacking ground. Feel much better today. My appetite commencing to return. Weather sprinkly all night but fair in the day.

Thursday October 2nd 1862

Early this morning weather rainy but cleared up about 12:00 noon. The brigade was reviewed at 5:00 p.m. Thought the review was but a poor one. Weather fair and warm. Felt as well as I could feel as just recovering from the jaundice.

Friday October 3rd 1862

Remained stationary all day in yesterday's bivouac. Weather fair and warm. Felt in very fine spirits this morning and heard in the afternoon that Warrenton, Virginia, had not been captured by the Yankees and consequently our baggage was safe.

Saturday October 4th 1862

Nothing occurred today to disturb the usual monotonous routine of camp life in the form of a bivouac. Weather very warm and fair but commenced blowing about 5:00 p.m. and night cool. Little rain early in the night.

Sunday October 5th 1862

Early this morning the weather was uncomfortably cold but the sun coming out bright the middle of the day was pretty warm. Went to bed with a very hard chill on me and suffered very much all night. Was detailed as brigade officer of the guard but too unwell.

Monday October 6th 1862

Nothing occurred to vary camp life. Time passed very slowly and books are as avariciously pounced upon whenever or wherever seen as gold would be. Weather uncomfortably warm but fair.

Tuesday October 7th 1862

I am feeling very badly today from the effects of a violent attack of dysentery which also makes me feel very weak. Escaped another chill which as it being my chill day I expected. Weather fair and very warm.

Wednesday October 8th 1862

General Ransom ordered elections to be held in all the regiments of his brigade to fill vacancies of company officers. I, at Colonel Ransom's recommendation, recommended three young men Robert B. Peebles and Virginius Copland of Northampton and [Fabius] J[ulius] Haywood[7] of Wake counties but they were not elected. Weather fair and warm.

Thursday October 9th 1862

We moved our camp about half a mile farther off from the turnpike road in a close piece of woods. Weather warm and fair. Colonel Ransom was taken worse today but later in the day was improving.

Friday October 10th 1862

Was detailed as brigade officer of the guard and was sent with six men to where we get water to guard a Mr. Eastan's premises. Slept in his drawing room and had a nice dinner and supper with him. Weather rainy all day.

---

[7] Son of Dr. Fabius Julius Haywood and Martha Helen Whitaker; he had been wounded and captured at Malvern Hill.

Saturday October 11th 1862

After breakfast at Mr. Eastan's I was relieved by another officer of a new guard. The regiment was detailed on fatigue to destroy the Winchester and Potomac Railroad and they had to destroy it about eight miles from Winchester. Weather cold and cloudy.

Sunday October 12th 1862

Went out in command of the fatigue party of my company to destroy the railroad left the day before. I had with me twenty of my men to destroy 100 yards of railroad which we accomplished in an hour. Weather cloudy and rainy in the afternoon and night.

Monday October 13th 1862

Remained in camp and had nothing to do today. Wrote home by a Mr. Pearson of General Ransom's staff. Weather cloudy all day and towards night rainy.

Tuesday October 14th 1862

Yesterday was the first drill we had since we left Richmond and General Ransom drilled his brigade in the afternoon for two hours. Company drill from 10:00 to 11:30 a.m. Weather cloudy and clear by turns. Colonel Ransom having obtained a furlough of thirty days.

Wednesday October 15th 1862

Had company drill at 10:00 a.m. till 11:30 a.m. and instead of brigade drill in the afternoon we were ordered to police the camp. Wrote home to father and had the letter mailed in Winchester, Virginia. Weather fair in the morning but cloudy towards night.

Thursday October 16th 1862

A fatigue party of fifteen men from each company and every regiment was detailed to tear up some more of the railroad they tore up some time ago. I remained in camp in command of the remainder of the company. Weather cloudy and at dusk thunder and rain all night.

Friday October 17th 1862

Received orders about 1:00 a.m. to cook three days rations of flour and be ready to march at daybreak. Were kept prepared expecting to move every movement all day but at nightfall they issued rations of beef and it was thought we would not leave till next day. Weather fair and warm; the sun coming out in full force.

Saturday October 18th 1862

After reveille this morning orders came around revoking the orders of yesterday to move and we have settled down. Quiet again though expecting the cold weather will render it necessary to fall back. Weather fair and night cold.

Sunday October 19th 1862

Went to a Mr. Eastan's about a mile off and got quite a good dinner for fifty cents. Read the lessons for the evening and morning of the Episcopal Church having bought me a Prayer Book and borrowed a Bible. Weather fair and night cold.

Monday October 20th 1862

Orders were sent round today that General Walker's division would be reviewed at 2:30 p.m. by General Longstreet. But he not coming, General Walker reviewed them himself. The presentation of a horse to General Ransom by the officers of his brigade took place today. Weather fair.

Tuesday October 21st 1862

Had regimental review today at 4:00 p.m. Our major commanding [John M.] (Kelly) reviewed the regiment. About dark it clouded up and in the early part of the night it rained a little and then it turned colder. The wind blowing very hard. Weather fair all at night raining and windy. Wrote home.

* * * *

Thirty-Fifth Regiment North Carolina Troops
Camp 4 miles north of Winchester
October 21st 1862

Dear Mother,

This will be carried to Raleigh by a Mr. Barclift who has been detailed to go there and see about bringing on the clothing which Captain Long went for but he (Captain Long) having resigned[8] it was necessary for somebody to be detailed to go after them and they detailed this Mr. Barclift. I know if you received my letter written when Captain Long left the regiment and which was carried by him you have got all those things I wrote for prepared but in case you did not receive it I will give you a new list hoping you have been taught how to follow and carry out a list of things to be had by Mr. Lightbourne's constant and never failing promptitude.

A jacket and pants made of the thickest and warmest and most lasting cloth. I would prefer a gray ink kind but the color is of no importance. The jacket made double breasted and the pants long and full wide in the legs. Keith the tailor has my measure and he can cut them out and if necessary make them. Two flannel undershirts. Three thick colored flannel shirts. Three cotton flannel drawers. The [sic] pair of cotton socks. Half dozen handkerchiefs. Comb and brush; fine tooth comb. Tooth brush. Two cravats. A Beauregard sentinel cap made of worsted like Katie makes them to keep my head and ears warm. A good pair of warm gloves with long cuffs. Three towels. Three cakes of soap. Pen and ink (I will supply the paper and envelopes) and about five thickness of blankets about as wide and long as those you fixed for me before and fixed in the same manner. Sewing materials. You see I ask for a complete outfit for I lost everything I had with me at Sharpsburg and my trunk and things I sent back to Warrenton are of no more use to me than if I did not have them but as soon as I can find any way or get up with them I will send them to you at Raleigh.

---

[8] His wife Sallie Williams was terminally ill and she died on November 20, 1862.

You can send the clothes by this Mr. Barclift if he will take them which you can find out by getting Father to ask him or if he will not or cannot take them a man from my company, Corporal William G. Morris, who I have this day detailed to go to Mecklenburg County, N.C., to get clothes for the company, will on his return take charge of them. I have instructed him three or four days before he starts to return to drop a line to Father telling him the precise day he is coming through Raleigh and you can have the things at depot and give them to him there. His furlough is for twenty days from this time and you can judge somewhat when he will be coming through. When you send the clothes please put me up a box of eatables, some butter and as much good browned corn bread you can stuff in if you think it will not mold, and anything else you may think good to send. And now for the news. On the 17th instant about 7:00 a.m. orders came around to prepare three days rations of flour and to be ready to march at daybreak. Daybreak came. Everything was ready and packed up to leave and we were all expecting to hear the drums beat to fall in but no orders came. Twelve o'clock came and still no orders. Night came and orders came round for the butchers to go and kill beeves and the men went to cooking their rations of beef and still we were under apprehension we would be obliged to march in the night for no contrary orders had come but early next morning orders came revoking the orders of yesterday and we settled down quiet again. The cause of the orders it is said the enemy were advancing and that the whole army were under the same orders and it was expected a large battle would come off that day but Jackson's old division and one other was sent down and I believe drove the Yankees back. Yesterday the ceremony of presenting General Ransom a horse by the officers of his brigade took place. The orator on the occasion Captain [William C.] Clark, 24th Regiment North Carolina Troops, made a very good speech and the general astonished us all by the fine effort he made; both of the speeches were worthy of the occasion. I believe the horse cost five hundred dollars.

Yesterday General Walker had his division out to be reviewed by General Longstreet but he did not come and General Walker reviewed it.

The glorious news about Bragg and his gallant army has filled us all with great exultation and we all hope most important things will result from so decisive a battle.

The weather is turning very cold and it is a wonder now the men are able to stand it in their naked condition.

I am thankful to say since I have recovered from my attack of jaundice I never have enjoyed better health and though I must suffer more or less I have not even a cold.

Excuse my bad writing but my hands will not move freely on account of the cold and I am in such a hurry I cannot read over the letter.

Love to all.

Your affectionate son,
W.H.S. Burgwyn

* * * *

Wednesday October 22nd 1862

Very windy all day and consequently very disagreeable. About 4:00 p.m. orders came around to prepare one day's rations and be ready to leave at sunrise next day. Weather very windy but fair. Sent home Corporal Morris to get blankets for the company.

Thursday October 23rd 1862

Commenced our march in the direction of Winchester at sunrise and at Winchester took the Front Royal Turnpike and marched as far as Millwood Town by 2:30 p.m. a distance of fifteen miles only halting once. Weather not as windy as the day before also fair.

Friday October 24th 1862

Recommenced our march in the direction of Paris, Virginia, and waded the Shenandoah at 10:30 a.m. Water so cold I thought I could not get across. From Paris went to Upperville Town ten miles from Millwood Town. Weather fair.

Saturday October 25th 1862

Remained near Upperville, Virginia, all day and went through the town but could not succeed in buying anything for a protection against the weather such as blankets, etc. Weather fair all day. Received a letter from Father dated 5th and 19th instant.

Sunday October 26th 1862

A cold rain all day and very disagreeable and very hard on the men. My tent fly, though a tolerable good one, leaked some and I got a little wet in the night from the fly blowing down and the ropes coming off the pegs. Was detailed as brigade officer of the day.

Monday October 27th 1862

A cold high wind rose about 1:00 a.m. and continued all day making a large fire very necessary for comfort. Sent one wagon today to bring our tent flies from Warrenton, Virginia. Weather fair and windy.

Tuesday October 28th 1862

Had regimental inspection at 12:00 noon. Immediately after inspection orders came around to be prepared to march at a moment's warning and we expected to march as soon as we could be got ready. Weather fair. Received a letter from Mother dated 5th instant.

Wednesday October 29th 1862

Received orders about 2:30 a.m. to be ready to march immediately and about 3:00 a.m. the wagons started off in the direction of Paris, Virginia, and we were expecting to march every minute but did not start till 11:00 a.m. and marched to Paris and encamped a mile south of it. Went immediately on halting on picket two and a half miles from Upperville, Virginia. But we were relieved about 10:00 p.m. by another regiment. Weather rain.

Thursday October 30th 1862

Received orders about 12:00 noon to hold ourselves in readiness to march and it was expected we would have a brush with the enemy at Upperville, Virginia, but we did not start. Orders came around about 8:00 p.m. the regiment would be inspected and mustered at 7:00 a.m. and leave at 8:00 a.m. Weather fair and tolerably warm.

Friday October 31st 1862

Our regiment in the march today was detailed as guard to the wagons and consequently did not commence our march till 11:30 a.m. and marched till 8:15 p.m. but having to wait on the wagons we did not march but twelve miles. Weather fair and warm.

Saturday November 1st 1862

Recommenced our march for Culpeper Court House about 8:00 a.m. Crossed the Hedgeman River about 1:30 p.m. and encamped for the night one and a half miles south-east from Amissville at 3:00 p.m. having marched fifteen miles. Weather fair and warm.

Sunday November 2nd 1862

Recommenced our march at sunrise for Culpeper Court House and encamped [a] mile and a half south-west of Culpeper at 4:00 p.m. having marched eighteen miles. Waded the Hazel River at 11:00 a.m. Weather fair.

Monday November 3rd 1862

Remained all day in camp near Culpeper Court House. Received permission to visit Culpeper to get one of my boots mended. Received orders about dusk that reveille would be at 4:30 a.m. and we would march at 8:30 a.m. Weather fair.

Tuesday November 4th 1862

Commenced our march in the direction of Rapidan Station and marched about half way when we came to a halt and encamped a mile and a half from the railroad half way between Culpeper Court House and Rapidan Station. Clear, fair. Wrote Father today.

* * * *

Thirty-Fifth Regiment North Carolina Troops
Camp half way between Culpeper Court House and Rapidan Station
November 4th [1862]

Dear Father,

You will see by the heading of the letter we have made a pretty considerable move since I last wrote you or Mother.

We left our camp north of Winchester on Thursday the 23rd day of last month and at Winchester took the turnpike road in the direction of Front Royal and marched as far as Millwood Town a distance of about fifteen miles and only halted once during the whole march. Next morning half an hour by sun [sic] we took the road to Upperville ten miles off waded the Shenandoah at 10:30 a.m. The water so cold I thought I never would be able to get across; it seemed as if my legs were cut off just where the water struck them. We crossed the Blue Ridge at Ashby's Gap and passing through Paris reached Upperville about 4:00 p.m. Remained in Upperville till Wednesday the 29th when we took the road back to Paris and encamped within half mile of the town. Remained near Paris till Friday the 31st when we took the direct road to Salem; about two miles from Salem turned off to the west and marched about four miles on the turnpike towards Springfield marching that day about twelve miles. Next morning about 8:30 a.m. turning off to the right we kept on in the direction of Culpeper Court House and waded the Hedgeman River about 1:30 p.m. and kept on in the direction of Amissville and encamped [a] mile and a half south east of it.

About sunrise next morning we recommenced our march and crossing the Hazel River in the usual manner, viz., wading and feeling the same difficulty in crossing, viz., the extreme coldness of the water. We reached Culpeper Court House about 3:30 p.m. Marching a mile and a half west from the town we encamped making eighteen miles we marched that day. We remained all day near Culpeper and early this morning marched to our present position and expect in a few days to leave on the cars for Richmond or Petersburg and think it probably before this will reach you. I may have an opportunity of telegraphing you from Richmond or Petersburg.

I received on the 25th of last month your letter of the 5th and 19th instant and on the 28th Mother's of the 5th being the only letters I have received from home since the one received September 22nd dated August 27th and I assure you they were very acceptable. ·

During all the marchings and exposures I have stood it as well as could be and am now in as good health as I ever was with the exception of a slight cold which I think I am recovering from.

I must now close hoping I will hear from you now more regularly as we are not so far off and will probably be nearer. With much love to all and hoping you have recovered from your attack of the liver which I had hoped you were entirely over, I am,

Your affectionate son,
W.H.S. Burgwyn

* * * *

Wednesday November 5th 1862

Remained all day in camp and was busily occupied in making my muster and pay rolls and got them about half done. Weather fair in the morning but it clouded up and rained a little at night.

Thursday November 6th 1862

Was busily occupied all day with my muster and pay rolls and finished them as well as I could by night. Weather cold and looking very much like snow. My boy Pompey taken down by chills and fever.

Friday November 7th 1862

About 10:00 a.m. it commenced snowing and continued all day till night but it did not snow hard consequently the ground was not covered for more than an inch. Was busily employed today in making out a muster roll for General Ransom. Weather cold and snowy.

Saturday November 8th 1862

Received orders about 9:00 a.m. to be ready to march and at 2:30 p.m. orders came to march and we all were in hopes of going to Richmond or Petersburg but we marched in the direction of Madison Court House and crossed the Robertson River about 5:00 p.m. and encamped a mile south having marched eight miles. Weather sometimes snowing and very cold.

Sunday November 9th 1862

Recommenced our march for Madison Court House about 8:30 a.m. and reached Madison Court House about 11:00 a.m. having marched about eight miles. The Blue Ridge in many places presented a magnificent sight being partly covered with snow and the sun shining on it. Received a letter from Mother dated 25th instant [sic]. Weather fair.

Monday November 10th 1862

Obtained permission to visit Madison Court House to get my boots mended. Got them mended. Returned to camp in time to move our camp at 2:00 p.m. to a mile south of Madison Court House on the Gordonville Turnpike road. Weather fair and tolerably warm.

Tuesday November 11th 1862

Remained all day in camp near Madison Court House, Virginia. Had company drill from 2:00 to 4:00 p.m. Weather fair and warm. I was much surprised today to hear Colonel [Stephen D.] Ramseur of the 49th [North Carolina Infantry] had been appointed Brigadier General.

Wednesday November 12th 1862

The Quartermaster sent two wagons to Gordonville today to get the clothing for the regiment just arrived there from Raleigh, North Carolina. Had two drills today from 9:00 to 11:30 a.m. and from 2:00 to 4:00 p.m. Weather fair in the morning but cloudy towards night and also very warm. Wrote my mother and brother Harry.

* * * *

Thirty-fifth Regiment North Carolina Troops
Camp near Madison C.H. November 12th 1862

My dear Mother,

In my last letter to Father dated November 4th we all were in great hopes we would be in Richmond or Petersburg in a day or two and when the orders came to march we were expecting to get on the train for Richmond but all our anticipations were blighted when after marching seven or eight miles and halted for the night we found out we were going to this place and now nobody can form any opinion about where we are going to or when we are to leave this place. Since my last to Father it has been unusually cold; on Friday the 7th it commenced snowing about two in the morning and snowed all day till night but not very heavily only covering the ground about an inch deep. The men have managed to keep alive by building large fires and making rude shelters of pine with one axe to a company. The next day it snowed at different times but at no time for any length or much. About two o'clock p.m. the same day, that is the 8th, we commenced our march for this place and waded the Robertson River about 5:00 p.m. and encamped half way to this place about 5:30 p.m. During the night I was awakened by snow falling in my face but fortunately it did not snow much. Next morning at 8:30 a.m. we recommenced our march for this place and reached here about 11:00 a.m. and have been here since.

On the morning of the 9th just before we started for this place I received your letters from Thornbury dated October 25th and 26th ultimo which revived me considerably and your writing from Thornbury reminded me of those times gone to come no more when every letter was headed *Thornbury*. I hope you have enjoyed yourself very much and I feel certain you have from your letter and it must have been a great treat to you to have Harry to spend a day or two with you there so like old times. I have lately heard of Harry's fight at Williamston (I think it is) and how well with four companies he stopped and defeated the intentions of the Yankees. I have also heard with considerable surprise that Colonel Ramseur has been appointed brigadier general. I can't see what thing he has done worthy of a brigadier general's commission. Colonel [John R.] Cooke of the 27th Regiment North Carolina Troops has been appointed brigadier general over our acting major general's brigade (Walker's) who has been made full major general and Ransom now commands his brigade and the division. I still "Thank God," keep in the best of health, and am only in great need of clothing which I expect to get every day.

With much love to all and hoping Father has got entirely well, I remain,

Your affectionate son,
W.H.S. Burgwyn

* * * *

Thursday November 13th 1862

Was detailed with my company to go on picket about three miles north of Madison Court House. Obtained dinner at a house nearby where I was stationed but got a very inferior dinner. Weather fair and warm.

Friday November 14th 1862

Was relieved this morning about 10:00 a.m. by a detachment from the 25th [North Carolina]. On arriving in camp found a large bundle of carpet blankets sent me by my Uncle Tom [Thomas Pollok Burgwyn] for me and my men's use and a keg of edibles. Weather fair and warm.

Saturday November 15th 1862

Remained in camp all [day] and with the exception that the regiment was inspected by General Ransom nothing occurred too different from the daily routine of camp life and duty. Weather fair. Was inspected at 9:00 a.m.

Sunday November 16th 1862

Weather all day cloudy and rainy at night. Sent for my trunk to Gordonsville by a wagon of the regiment going there. Received a letter from Mother dated November 2nd and a little note from Father concerning the blankets sent me by my uncle.

Monday November 17th 1862

Weather cloudy and drizzly and rained at night. Wrote Mother today and Captain Maxwell. Discharged four men from the company; two for being over forty years old and two for being only sixteen years of age when enlisted.

* * * *

Thirty-Fifth Regiment North Carolina Troops
Camp near Madison Court House
November 17th 1862

Dear Mother,

On returning day before yesterday from picket with my company I found at the quartermaster's office the bundle of carpet blankets presented by Uncle Tom and the keg of eatables presented by you and last night I received yours of the 2nd sent from Thornbury.

You can imagine how gratified I was to receive the blankets as a present from Uncle Tom to be distributed amongst my men. It shows he has a great feeling for me well knowing how highly the men would appreciate such generosity and as soon as I receive the blankets you are going to send me I intend to give them out but till then I will need them myself and they are the very sort of blankets my men are now thoroughly supplied with blanket and clothing the man who I detailed to go home and get them has returned and they have as much as they can carry. Nothing could have come more acceptable, dear Mother, than your box of eatables with the full supply of butter which is as fresh as if it were just made and the honey also was very acceptable.

I sent yesterday by a wagon to Gordonsville for my trunk and if the wagon returns tonight I will write you. I will then have a pretty good supply of underclothing but if you were to see my pants and coat you would laugh. My pants at the bottom are so ragged I have to hem them up and all the lining [in] most of my coat is torn out.

Mr. Barclift who brought me the blankets and keg told me there was a box at Weldon for me and that he asked the express agent at Weldon and Richmond to forward it on to Gordonsville who promised him they would and I hope to receive it tonight by the wagon that is to bring my trunks. I have written to the express agent at Weldon and Richmond both about it. I suppose the box contains the cloth and blankets and I hope I will receive it soon and I know you all are making the utmost endeavors to get me the things. My man who went home for the blankets forgot to write Father telling him he would pass through Raleigh. I wrote you on the 12th about Harry's fight which your letter of the 2nd speaks about and was very glad to hear he did so well and lost so few men.

Tell Uncle Tom at the first opportunity I will write him a long letter and thank him for his donation to me and my men. I continue to enjoy good health and don't fear the cold as I have such good blankets to keep me warm at night. Pompey is really puffed out so fat. I must haste with love to all.

Your affectionate son,
W.H.S. Burgwyn

* * * *

Tuesday November 18th 1862

Received orders about 4:00 a.m. to march at 8:00 a.m. and at that time commenced our march in the direction of Madison Court House where we all we[re] disappointed expecting we would have to go to Culpeper Court House but in town we took the Orange Court House Road and reached it about 2:30 p.m. having marched fifteen miles. We crossed the Rapidan on planks about 1:00 p.m. Weather rainy and misty all day and the roads very disagreeable. Received orders about 7:00 p.m. to march next morning at 9:30 a.m.

Wednesday November 19th 1862

Commenced our march at 7:30 a.m. and with great fatigue owing to the state of the roads which were very wet and of a clay soil. Marched twenty miles by 4:00 p.m. Weather rainy and misty all day and rained hard about 2:00 a.m. in the night. Was detailed about 5:00 p.m. as brigade officer of the guard.

Thursday November 20th 1862

Commenced our march at 7:30 a.m. for Guiney's Station and marched to within two miles of Spotsylvania Court House a distance of twenty miles by 3:30 p.m. Weather rained hard during part of the day also at night. Was relieved at 4:00 p.m. as officer [of the] guard.

Friday November 21st 1862

Started again at 7:30 a.m. marching in rear of the wagon train and about 10:00 p.m. reached camp six and a half miles below Fredericksburg, Virginia, marching a very circuitous route, owing to the orders being changed. About twenty-two miles. Weather cloudy and little rain in the day but none at night.

Saturday November 22nd 1862

Left camp at 10:00 a.m. for Fredericksburg and marching by a country road halted three miles south of it at 4:00 p.m. marching five miles. Weather cloudy but sun coming out sometimes no rain. General [Robert E.] Lee passed us while halted on the road and General Longstreet also has headquarters about mile off.

Sunday November 23rd 1862

Remained in camp near Fredericksburg, Virginia, all day. Lost my knapsack containing all my clothes and my Colt's pistol which troubles me greatly. Weather fair and cold. Wrote mother and a letter to [remainder blank]

Monday November 24th 1862

Remained stationary all day. Offered $5.00 reward for my knapsack but could not find it. Weather fair and moderately warm.

Tuesday November 25th 1862

Remained in camp all day. Received permission to detail a man to go to Hanover Junction to bring my trunk and others of officers of the regiment. Found my knapsack that I had lost. Weather fair all day but rained hard all night.

Wednesday November 26th 1862

Our brigade was inspected today at 11:00 a.m. by Major [Henry E.] Peyton (General Lee's staff). My company [Company H] was praised highly by General Ransom and Major Peyton. My detached man returned but could not find my trunk. Weather fair and cold.

Thursday November 27th 1862

Received orders at 7:30 a.m. to be ready to march at 11:00 a.m. and at 12:00 noon moved about a mile south or our last camp for the purpose of getting wood. Weather fair; night cold.

Friday November 28th 1862

Obtained permission from General Ransom to detail a man to go to Culpeper Court House to look for my trunk. Received a letter from my brother Harry dated November 20, '62. Weather fair and warm.

Saturday November 29th 1862

Got the detail written and signed today and sent him off but he was not permitted to get on the train. Wrote my Uncle Tom today thanking him for his gift of carpet blankets. Weather cloudy and looked like snow.

Sunday November 30th 1862

Wrote my brother Harry and Father today. Had regimental inspection at 10:00 a.m. General Jackson's Corps arrived in the vicinity today. Weather cloudy and very much like snow.

* * * *

[Only the last page of this letter survives and a corner of the page is missing. From the content it must have been written on November 30th or a few days later. Burgwyn seems to have addressed it to his father.]

There must be some [missing in original] obstacle that prevents my [missing in original] not heard from there since [missing in original] from Mother dated 2nd November [missing in original] 16th. All the letters to my company come directly through and they never or very seldom ever miss receiving their letters. I am certain Mother writes once a week and as you see it has been twenty-eight days since her last letter was written.

I received a letter from Harry dated 20th in which he says "[illegible] and father I hear is in Petersburg tonight I shall go in town tomorrow to see him" and he has doubtless told you he is endeavouring at my request to get me transferred which I hope he will effect as soon as possible.

General Ransom has behaved very officer-like to me since joining his brigade and on an inspection of the regiment he gave me the praise over the other companies and on an inspection of his brigade by the Inspector General (Major Peyton) he complimented my company over all the companies in his brigade and recently he has granted me liberties which he said he would not do but in a that [sic] and this. So Surgeon [missing in original] and through I have been [missing in original]-mand since Sharpsburg [missing in original] (Maxwell) intends as I am [missing in original] when he is able to return.

I have under[stood] Governor Vance intends raising some State Troops; if it is so I would like to get a position in them which I think considering all the hardships I have experienced in this campaign I may be entitled to, being constantly exposed to the weather. My beard has grown astonishingly, being now more than an inch in length and I imagine a person would take me to be much older than I am and I am presumptive enough to think I am competent to fill the majority of a regiment which I would like to get.

I think we may leave this place shortly to go farther south but I would not be at all surprised if we were to stay here all winter and I hope before long I will be transferred.

I am looking every day for a letter from you only having received one since the battle of Sharpsburg.

With much love to all and I hope you have entirely recovered, I remain

Your affectionate Son,
W.H.S. Burgwyn

* * * *

Monday December 1st 1862

Received a letter from Mother dated November 13th directed to Culpeper Court House. Had company drill at 2:00 p.m. Weather cloudy and cold with little sun about mid-day.

Tuesday December 2nd 1862

Received a letter from Mother dated November 29th. Captain Long, quartermaster, returned to camp to settle up his account. Weather sunny in the early part of the day but cloudy in the evening and night.

Wednesday December 3rd 1862

Our brigade was reviewed by General Ransom at 10:00 a.m. preparatory to a review tomorrow by General Lee. Weather cloudy and misty. Wrote Mother and the express agent at Gordonsville, Virginia, about a box there for me.

* * * *

35th Regiment North Carolina Troops
Camp 4 miles south of Fredericksburg, Virginia
December 3rd, 1862

Dear Mother,

On the 1st instant I received yours of the 13th misdirected to Culpeper Court House, Virginia, which [I] did not receive sooner because directed there yesterday I received yours of the 29th instant from Raleigh with great pleasure. I did not mention anything about the box of clothes because I had received no notice that any such box had been sent; in mine of the 17th November from Madison Court House in which I sent Sergeant Barclift who brought the blankets to me informed me there was a box at Weldon for me and that he advised me to write to the express agent at Weldon and Richmond, which I did, and have not heard anything further from it before yesterday when Captain Long, who arrived yesterday to settle up his accounts, told me it had been forwarded from Weldon to Gordonsville and advised me to write the express agent at Gordonsville and ask him to send it to Richmond to await my call or order which I have done hoping and expecting to receive my transfer from this to Harry's Regiment in a short time and that then I will get it and bye the bye please ask Harry how he succeeds and write me as soon as you can for I have not much reliance upon Harry's promptitude in writing and I know you will and besides I am duly anxious to get away from the regiment since I have no confidence in any of my field officers except Colonel Ransom, though I am very well liked in my company and know they would dislike my leaving them very much.

I was very much surprised to hear Grandpa [John Fanning Burgwyn][9] had been struck with paralysis; it must be very slight indeed to effect him so slightly. I am also very much pained to hear how badly Uncle Tom is getting on in the use of his limbs. I can't imagine what has made him grow worse.

I am truly [missing in original] you have had such a pleasant time on the plantation. If it should please God for you never to visit it again you at least will with pleasure and with pleasing associations remember you[r] last visit to the old place where all of us have passed many a sunny hour and [illegible] with but few about and they having only long enough to make the reappearance of the sun more striking. Should the Yankee hoards conquer our fair and once happy land no place will ever be remembered by me with such fondness and love as Thornbury and always will be as glad to go back to it again as when in years past I returned from my five months sojourn at some school which I thought the happiest time of my life and wondered how people could voluntarily stay away from their homes but few persons have had such a home as I have had but should we successfully finish this war I hope we once more may have another such one surrounded by all that is dear and old time.

I am very sorry you had to lose Mrs. Cotton's house but as it is I am firmly convinced it must be for the best for probably this winter the Yankees may by a successful hit or raid penetrate as far as Raleigh and probably burn the town.

I hope Emmy may succeed in getting a house in Raleigh for I think in these times relations ought to stay as close to each other as convenience will allow so that any assistance needed may at once be obtained and I should dislike very much in case I obtain a furlough, which I think very probable if I am transferred, that Emmy and her household should live in some place where I would have to make a trip to see them.

When I get home again I will be so much accustomed to living in a small place and without even entering a house that your present place will seem like a palace in appearance and a pyramid in size. I would have been very glad to have seen Father but I know he would have suffered so much inconvenience in coming that I am glad he did not undertake to come. I am very glad to see he is so much better he can

---

[9] J.F. Burgwyn was born in Thornbury, England, in 1783 and died on June 18, 1864. He was the oldest son of John Burgwyn and Elizabeth Bush of Bristol, England.

travel about. His and Ally's [10] escape was truly great and but as you say for his presence of mind he would most probably been killed as for poor Ally I hope his "insenseless" did not last long.

I have written a good long letter for a camp letter. I hope Father and Uncle Tom have received my letters of the 29th and 30th ultimo. With much love to all and hoping you will write soon and let me know how Harry succeeds in my being transferred, I remain always,

Your affectionate Son,
W.H.S. Burgwyn

P.S. Pompey says "give my best respect to Mother and Mistress and all my young masters and tell them that I am as hearty as a buck." I have acknowledged the receipt of all your letters. How does Father like his new overseer?

* * * *

Thursday December 4th 1862

General Lee did not review us today and after going through a movement in brigade drill we came to camp. Had battalion drill in the evening. Received a letter from Mr. Maxwell dated December 2nd. Weather fair.

Friday December 5th 1862

Commenced raining about 10:00 a.m. and about 12:00 noon turned to sleet and at 1:00 p.m. commenced snowing and continued till about 10:00 p.m. Snowed about three inches deep. The moon was eclipsed tonight.

Saturday December 6th 1862

Very cold all day though the sun came out in full brightness. The snow melted very little. Received letter from my father from Thornbury dated December 1st who informed me he has appointed a new overseer.

Sunday December 7th 1862

Wrote Captain Maxwell today. Weather fair and very cold; colder than the day before. Wagons were detailed to haul wood for the officers today.

Monday December 8th 1862

Very cold today. Last night colder than any night we ever had. Weather fair. Put water on my head this morning in washing and it froze before I had finished wiping my face.

Tuesday December 9th 1862

Weather a little more moderate than the last two days. The snow not yet all melted. Weather fair. The sun coming out in its unrivaled splendor but very cold at night.

Wednesday December 10th 1862

Remained in camp all day. Weather warmer than it had been for the last week. The snow melting very much. Was much disappointed in the mail's not coming this evening for I expected to hear from my brother Harry relative to my transfer.

---

[10] W.H.S.B.'s next to youngest brother, John Alveston Burgwyn.

Thursday December 11th 1862

About 4:00 a.m. heard the two signal guns agreed upon for the signal to prepare for immediate action and about 7:00 a.m. commenced our march for the line of battle. First took position on the Plank Road to from [sic] Fredericksburg to Orange Court House then on the Telegraph Road to Richmond and finally returned to our first position in the Plank Road where we remained all night being allowed fires. We passed the night as comfortably as we could effect. Weather fair and moderately warm but heavy front at night. Saw Generals Lee, Longstreet, Stuart, McLaws all together on a commanding position viewing the field of battle. The enemy succeeded in putting across their pontoon bridge and crossed in small numbers on the right but I don't think succeeded in getting their artillery across.

Friday December 12th 1862

Remained where we passed the night all day but on the other side of the Plank Road. Nothing but artillery was made use of to any effect today. None of our regiment being hurt. Weather fair and comfortably warm.

Saturday December 13th 1862

At 5:00 a.m. we were formed into line ready to take our position in the line of battle. At 1:30 p.m. moved to our first position through a storm of shell in a ravine on the right of the Plank Road.[11] Remained there about an hour and [a] half (Lieutenant [John H.] Connelly Company B and two men from Company A was killed there) and moved by the right flank to a position one hundred and fifty yards in front not by any means as good a position losing while there our major (Kelly) and thirty-five officers and men killed and wounded. Remained there till some time after dark and then moved to where we stayed the night before. From 11:00 a.m. until dark there was an incessant roar of small arms and artillery and the enemy's loss is dreadful. Weather fair and comfortably warm.

Sunday December 14th 1862

About 5:00 a.m. moved from last night's bivouac and took our position on the left of the Plank Road quarter of a mile from our advanced line of pickets on a level piece of ground which I thought exposing us unnecessarily. Only one man wounded today in Company K. At dark moved to our night's bivouac on the 12th and remained there till about 12:00 noon. Weather fair and warm. Not much fighting today only with the pickets and a little shelling which only occurred at intervals.

Monday December 15th 1862

At 12:00 noon moved to our position on the left of the place we stayed the day before on a line with it. At 2:00 a.m. moved to take position as pickets on the right of the railroad to Gordonville and immediately in front of the enemy. My company and Company D and K were sent as an advance picket to the right front. I am pretty certain I shot a Yankee myself and my men were firing constantly at the Yankee pickets. Weather fair and windy.

* * * *

---

[11] At the Battle of Fredericksburg Ransom's Brigade supported McLaws' brigades, which were behind the stone wall below Marye's heights. Ransom's Brigade extended from the Plank Road to the Telegraph Road and reinforced McLaws throughout December 13th.

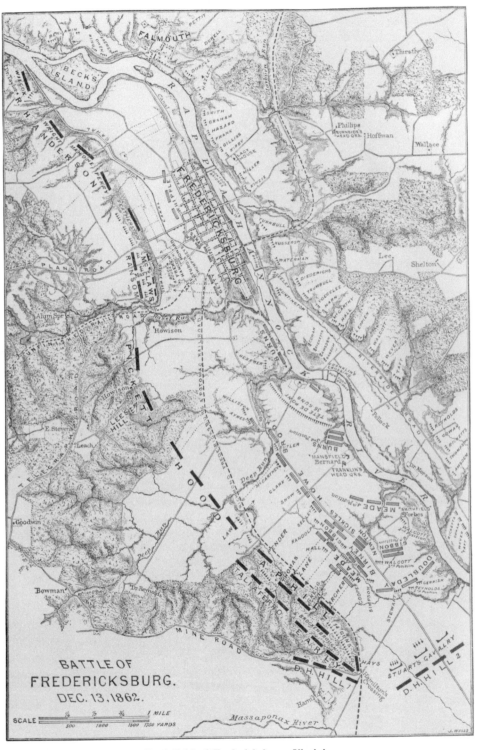

Battlefield of Fredericksburg, Virginia

On Picket immediately in front of the enemy
December 15th 1862. 12:00 o'clock

Dear Mother,

I ordered Pompey to ask Captain [Charles J.] Gee (Commissary) after the battle of the 13th to write home and tell you I had passed through the dreadful day unhurt, but as I have not seen Pompey since and won't know whether he has done it or not. Yesterday there was comparatively no fighting of any consequence except shelling which did bring to our positions very little damage, but day before yesterday I don't suppose this continent ever has, or will soon witness such a day's fighting. Early on the 11th at 4:00 a.m. we heard the two signal guns signal to prepare for a fight, and that morning we marched to take our position in line of battle. That day and the day after musketry was very little heard nothing but shelling. On the first day (the 11th) the enemy were engaged in constructing their pontoon bridges which they did in defiance of us, and commenced crossing the same day, and the day after also, but the next day they commenced on our right where Jackson was and attacked A.P. Hill, and being defeated there came round to the left and attacked Longstreet. Though our regiment did not fire a gun on the 13th we lost our major and 38 killed and wounded though we were in as good a position as we could get under the circumstances. Musketry came over us so fast that it made a complete tune, and the air seemed as full of minie balls as it ever was of flakes of snow or drops of rain. As the grape and shell were coming from everywhere we were so close to them, and our ground so much higher than theirs that most of their fire passed over our heads, consequently so few killed and wounded. This morning about 4:00 a.m. four companies of the regiment including mine were ordered on picket in front of our lines and just in front of the enemy with nothing to cover us, but the high ground we are on. Every moment or two our pickets are firing at some unlucky Yankee who chanced to show his skin any where about and I myself have done more firing than any other person in the picket detail, being so fortunate as to send one to his last resting place which is more than the rest can be certain of, and am now waiting while writing this for some Yankee picket to make his appearance in range. Every now and then a ball from a Yankee comes whizzing round my head and the shells burst frequently right over us though today has been a perfect calm in comparison with the last four days. Our batteries are just now opening on the enemy. I think because they are evacuating the town as some of my men have just informed me they appear to be leaving in large quantities. From the commanding position we hold, I see the dead Yankees strewn around where they were in deadly conflict, and the Yankees have not endeavored to bury them. I never expected to see such a sight as I saw on the 13th. The innumerable batteries of the enemy throwing thousands of shells into the burning city of Fredericksburg and it was just about dark enough to make the effect more striking and grand [end of manuscript]

* * * *

Tuesday December 16th 1862

Sent some of my men on the battlefield to get themselves overcoats, blankets, and after finding the enemy had evacuated the town and they got themselves more than a supply. I obtained an overcoat which I very much needed. Was sent back to our old camp about 12:00 noon with the remainder of the regiment. Weather is the same; morning raining but cleared up about 9:00 a.m.

Wednesday December 17th 1862

Remained all day in camp. Weather cold; towards night it snowed a little but of no consequence. Wrote Father today. Received letter from Father dated December 10th. One from Mother dated December 9th. One from my brother Harry dated December 13th.

* * * *

Thirty-Fifth Regiment North Carolina Troops
About old camp four miles south of Fredericksburg
December 17th, 1862

Dear Father,
The battle is over. No more the enemy's cannon thunders forth its terrible missiles of death and the roar of musketry is for the time silenced and nothing now remains but the dreadful spectacle of the terrible combat and God in His merciful providence has preserved me unhurt and untouched through the five days and nights and a half of the dreadful carnage.

On the 15th instant I wrote Mother by pencil and sent it to camp by Pompey to give it to Captain Gee (our commissary) who sent it off and on the 13th the day of the principal fighting sent word by Pompey to Captain Gee to write you and let you know I had passed through safely which he did and I think you must ere this have received the first and probably the second and consequently are relieved of anxiety on my account.

The day I wrote Mother last, the 15th, I was on picket in front of the enemy and remained there for thirty-six hours till I was relieved and sent to camp. Just before being relieved finding the enemy's pickets not firing at me or showing themselves I conjectured they had retreated (which they had) and gave permission to some of my men to visit the field of battle and supply themselves with overcoats and things which they needed and consequently they obtained from dead Yankees as many overcoats, shoes, and boots, and haversacks, and enough provisions to restore three or four regiments. I have now an overcoat an [sic] taken from a dead Yankee also a fine pair of boots and a cap. Some of my men also found watches on the Yankees.

Without doubt the enemy has suffered more than they ever have before and our loss is small in comparison to that of the Yankees than it ever was in any previous battle but I think but for our position we would undoubtedly have been beaten.

On the north and south side of the Rappahanock there is for about three quarters of a mile a level plain comparatively and there high and steep hills rise which extend all along the river in that relative position. On the hill on the Yankee side was posted their artillery and immediately at the bottom our men in trenches consequently the enemy advancing would be exposed to the fire of the artillery and our musketry. Fortunately just in front of our line the trenches there was a small undulation in the ground and the enemy advancing can not be seen till they had marched over that undulation consequently there was no danger of the men firing too soon. The Yankees would march in a perfect line till our first fire when owing to the nearness our fire would be so dreadful that they could not stand it. Fifteen times did the Yankees charge in face of the dreadful fire where part of our brigade was posted and every time they would be forced back with terrible slaughter. As soon as the Yankees made their appearance our men would give the van rank and when they about faced to fly gave them the front and at only sixty yards you must know the fire must have been dreadful and brutally thunderous and then after being repulsed by the musketry the artillery would rake them with grape and canister.

I am waiting anxiously for a letter,
W.H.S. Burgwyn

* * * *

Thursday December 18th 1862

General Ransom called the officers of his brigade to his tent this morning to collect their charity for the people of Fredericksburg. He (General Ransom) subscribed one hundred dollars. One third of his month's pay. I also one third of month's pay. Weather fair but very cold at night.

Friday December 19th 1862

Colonel Ransom arrived this [afternoon] about 3:00 p.m. Had division review at 3:00 p.m. but owing to my being on guard I did not go out. Colonel Ransom brought me a letter from my brother George from Thornbury. Was relieved as officer of the guard about 5:00 p.m. Weather fair but cold.

Saturday December 20th 1862

Remained all day in camp. Weather fair and not so cold as yesterday in the daytime but very cold at night.

Sunday December 21st 1862

Asked Colonel Ransom if there was any chance for a furlough. He said he did not know but would see the general and find out what he could do for me. Weather cold and towards night cloudy; very much like snow.

Monday December 22nd 1862

Sent my detailed man after my trunk, the detail having been approved by General Lee. Weather very warm for season of the year and also fair.

Tuesday December 23rd 1862

Was excused by the doctor on account of my bowels. Wrote Mother and George. Weather very warm for the season and also very fair.

Wednesday December 24th 1862

Was again excused by the doctor on account of my bowels. The regiment was inspected today at 2:00 p.m. by the division inspector, Captain [Thomas] Rowland. Weather warm at during night it rained slightly. Early in the day weather fair.

Thursday December 25th 1862

Dull gloomy Christmas. Weather early misty, cloudy and cloudy almost all day. Weather warmer than I ever knew it to be at a Christmas.

Friday December 26th 1862

Was again excused and felt worse than before. Lay in bed almost all day. Received orders this evening to police the camp and that there would be division review and inspection by General Longstreet at 3:00 p.m. tomorrow. Weather cloudy and warm.

Saturday December 27th 1862

In accordance with orders received yesterday the division was reviewed at 3:00 p.m. by Generals Lee and Longstreet. Weather cloudy and very much like rain. My detailed man returned but could not find my trunk. The disappointment is great. I was again excused by the doctor.

Sunday December 28th 1862

Weather today fair and warm. Captain [John] Farrell, 24th [North Carolina] Regiment returned today but did not bring a box for me at Richmond. Wrote Mother today from whom I had not heard since the 12th which letter was dated the 7th. Much disappointed in not getting a letter today.

* * * *

Thirty-Fifth Regiment North Carolina Troops
Camp near Fredericksburg December 28th 1862

Dear Mother,

I take my pen in hand to write you again dear Mother though I do not think my last has hardly had time to reach you but I have nothing to do and I have borrowed pen, ink, and paper which enables me to do it but the materials are not of the most desirable description.

It is with sorrow I have again to complain of the negligence of the mails for I have not received a letter since the 17th (acknowledged) which was dated the 9th. I was in hopes I would get a letter on the 25th to enliven the day for a duller Christmas I never wish it to be my lot to pass. Nothing but a suspension of drill commemorated the day and no whiskey or eggs could be procured to make eggnog and consequently there was no disturbance or gaiety in the camp at all.

I am beginning to think some of you must be sick since I cannot hear from you though I do not allow myself to entertain such a suspicion. Yesterday the division was reviewed by Generals Longstreet and Lee but owing to my being unwell on account of diarrhea which I have been troubled with for the last five or six days I did not go out but I am in hopes I am improving.

I think the Yankees have been so thoroughly whipped here and at Kinston [North Carolina] they will not make any more land movements this winter though I apprehend much from Bank's fleet which I think will most probably attack Wilmington. I don't think they would venture up the Roanoke unless the country they ventured up was already in their possession since it affords such fine opportunities for men to line the banks and pick them off without being in danger and also on account of the depth of the river.

George wrote me a short letter by Colonel Ransom which said Father had gone to Raleigh but it did not say what for.

I am afraid the rumor I told you of in my last about our going to North Carolina was without much foundation though I believe Colonel Ransom yet entertains hopes of our either going there or [to] Richmond.

I hope before this reaches you I will receive a letter from you or Father bearing good news. General Lee at present refuses all applications for furloughs but I think he will withdraw his order soon as he sees the Yankees intend no aggressive movements this winter.

Hoping to hear from you soon and that you are all well and with much love I remain

Your affectionate son
W.H.S. Burgwyn

P.S.: Please send me in your next a dollar's worth of postage stamps.

* * * *

Monday December 29th 1862

Had an election for Second Lieutenant and Captain [Hugh M.] Dixon was unanimously elected Second Lieutenant but the election only to be considered valid in case Lieutenant [Silas C.] Hunter's resignation be accepted which has not yet been heard from.[12] Wrote Captain Dixon and Lieutenant Hunter. Weather fair and warm.

Tuesday December 30th 1862

The regiment was to be inspected by the brigade inspector but the rain prevented him from accomplishing it. Received orders to send in to General Longstreet's head-quarters a complete list of the men of the company and the time of any absence from the company. Weather cloudy rained a little about 3:00 p.m. but appeared to clear off in the night.

Wednesday December 31st 1862

Weather cloudy and much cooler; about dusk it commenced snowing but did not snow much. The regiment was inspected at 11:00 a.m. by brigade inspector. Was busily occupied today by making out the report ordered by General Longstreet mentioned in yesterday's remarks. Received a new set of muster and pay-rolls.

Thursday January 1st 1863

Finished my muster and pay rolls and the report for General Longstreet. Reported for duty but was excused from drill by Colonel Ransom to make out my muster and pay rolls. Weather fair and moderately warm; a most beautiful day.

Friday January 2nd 1863

Was detailed to take command of a working party today and at 5:00 a.m. started for Fredericksburg to work on the fortifications around it; finished about 2:00 p.m. and arriving at camp found orders to move to a new camp at daybreak tomorrow. Read a letter from Captain Maxwell dated December 26th. Weather fair and warm.

---

[12] Silas C. Hunter had been appointed first lieutenant of Company H on May 27, 1862. He resigned because of "rheumatism to which he is liable on exposure to wet or cold." His resignation would be accepted on February 9, 1863. Hugh M. Dixon had been promoted to captain of Company H, 35th N.C., on October 10, 1861, and resigned for unknown reasons on May 27, 1862. He would be elected second lieutenant on February 9, 1862. (*N.C. Troops*, IX, pp. 427, 428.)

Saturday January 3rd 1863

At daybreak we started and marched opposite our new camp and halted for about fifteen minutes. There commenced our march and instead of going to a new camp kept on the Telegraph Road for fifteen miles and halted for the night. There never was a more complete surprise. Weather fair and warm; rode in the ambulance half the way.

Sunday January 4th 1863

Commenced our march in the direction of Richmond on the Telegraph Road at daybreak and reached Hanover Junction about 4:00 p.m.; ten miles. Rode all day in an ambulance. Weather cloudy but moderately warm a little rain at dusk but more at night.

Monday January 5th 1863

Recommenced our march for Richmond on the Telegraph Road and marching sixteen miles to within eight [miles] of Richmond. Rode four miles of the way in ambulance. Weather fair and warm. Crossed Middle River on our march.

Tuesday January 6th 1863

Recommenced our march at 7:00 a.m. At 11:00 a.m. reached Richmond marching through it without halting and halted two miles from Drewry's Bluff. Marching fifteen miles. Weather fair in the morning but rained from 1:00 p.m. to 3:00 p.m. Fair at night.

Wednesday January 7th 1863

Marched again at 7:00 a.m. and halted at 12:00 noon. Two and one-half miles north of Petersburg. Having marched twelve and one-half miles. Weather fair. The place we halted today is the same as the place we slept the first day I came to the brigade on August 2, 1862.

Thursday January 8th 1863

Remained all day in the camp. Weather fair but cold and cloudy at night. Received permission at 6:30 p.m. to visit Petersburg and returned by 12:00 midnight. Telegraphed mother to [in] Raleigh I was here.

Friday January 9th 1863

Received permission again to visit Petersburg and having borrowed Adjutant [Walter M.] Clark's horse started about 9:00 a.m. Returned to camp at 3:30 p.m. Weather fair and moderately warm but snowed a little at 1:00 a.m. but snow all melted the same day.

Saturday January 10th 1863

Wrote Mother today. Weather rainy all day. My brother George came to see me today from the plantation and brought me some provisions. Finished the rolls for the men's state bounty today.

Sunday January 11th 1863

Received a letter from Mother dated January 3, 1863. Went in town this evening with my brother George. Weather cloudy and warm but faired off in the evening. Felt very badly from a severe cold I caught.

Monday January 12th 1863

Returned from Petersburg to camp at 9:00 a.m. Made me a chimney to my tent fly. Feel better today than yesterday but still far from well. Weather fair and warm. General Ransom went to Richmond today.

Tuesday January 13th 1863

Remained in camp all day. Wrote my brother Harry. Weather fair and very warm for the time of year. Some more cooking utensils were issued out to the companies which had become absolutely necessary.

Wednesday January 14th 1863

Remained all day in camp. Commenced a letter to my Aunt Emmy [Sarah Emily Pierrepont Burgwyn][13] but did not finish it. Weather fair and unusually warm. Looked like rain towards night.

* * * *

Thirty-Fifth Regiment North Carolina Troops
Camp near Petersburg January 14th 1863

Dear Emmy,

I have delayed writing you so long that I confess dear Emmy you would have a right to think I never did intend to write you but you know by my letters to Mother and Father that we have not been permanently situated for any time since we first left this place on the 27th of last September and in fact ever since the battle of Sharpsburg September 17th writing materials have been so scarce and so almost impossible to get that you must and will I am confident receive that as part of my excuse and even now I am waiting orders to move and am liable at any time to be interrupted in what I am doing and be ordered off on some extra duty. I cannot, I don't think, write what will be more interesting to you than give you a summary of the campaign and relate more particularly those things that have occurred that I know will be of interest to you.

On the 1st of September, 1862, we commenced our grand march for Maryland and marching without intermission reached the Potomac River on the 7th about 10:00 a.m. It was here about half a mile wide and about waist deep. The men when they would arrive on the Maryland shore gave a shout and all seemed anxious to meet the enemy. On the 9th we marched as far as the Monocacy River three miles south of Frederick City and having halted there about two hours we marched back from where we came and having halted about two hours we started on a midnight march in the direction of Virginia for the purpose of blowing up a bridge across the canal which ran parallel with the Potomac River on its north side.

Just before we started orders were given for the men to fire off the old loads in their guns and carefully reload them as it was expected we would have to fight

---

[13] Henry K. Burgwyn, Sr.'s, sister. During the war she was a refugee in Raleigh with her brother Thomas Pollok Burgwyn.

to accomplish our object. It was with a heavy heart I received orders for us to go on this expedition since we were looking for a decisive battle soon and I was afraid this expedition would separate us from Jackson's or Longstreet's Corps and I thought we would not have an opportunity to get in the fight that was to occur. Arrived at the bridge about midnight and just after halting the deathlike stillness was broken by the Yankee pickets firing with their whole force upon our men after they had discovered and halted us. They immediately fled and we captured a horse and two or three swords. Soon after Captain [George T.] Duffy of the 24th [North Carolina Infantry] was brought along as it was said mortally wounded (but who has since recovered) and soon our officers finding the bridge too solid to blow up without drilling it and being afraid the Yankees would be upon us in an overwhelming force we fell back to the place we were the day before. That night at dusk we commenced our march for Virginia to make our debut at Harpers Ferry and to assist in its reduction. That night we marched all night and the tremendous fatigue we endured will make me never forget it. About daybreak we waded the Potomac at the Point of Rocks and the men utterly exhausted were given a day's rest on its south side. You will see for the last ten days ever since we left Rapidan River we had been marching fifteen and eighteen miles and the last two days and nights without intermission and it was wonderful how I managed to stand it but I never enjoyed better health. The next day, the 12th, we commenced our march for Harpers Ferry and about 12:00 noon on the 13th came in hearing of the firing at Harpers Ferry. That night and the night of the 15th we were on picket and holding the approaches from the south to the place. About 8:00 a.m. on the 15th Harpers Ferry surrendered and we obtain by the surrender 14,000 prisoners, 50 pieces of cannon, two generals, and from 18,000 to 20,000 stand of new arms. We only lost one officer in the battle. At 10:00 a.m. that day we marched across the mountains and wading the Shenandoah bivouacked for five or six hours. About midnight we were ordered to march in the direction of Shepherdstown which we reached about 8:00 a.m. Crossing the Potomac by our invariable method, viz., wading, we bivouacked on its north side. At 3:00 a.m. on the memorable 17th of September we marched to take our position in the line of battle. About the fight and the way our troops acted and the hard fighting we did needs no encomiums that it was let it judge for itself; sufficient to say we were engaged from morning to night and held all the time with our brigade alone and half the time with two regiments to assist us a piece of woods where brigade after brigade had been driven from and the enemy with all the batteries they could bring to bear on us raking us without intermission with grape, canister, and shell. Next night about dusk we commenced our falling back on the south side of the river and at midnight in the darkest night I ever saw waded across the Potomac which was so wide it seemed to me I never would get on the other side.

We then lay on the south side near Martinsburg and Winchester till October 23rd when we left marching southward. On the next day we waded the Shenandoah opposite Ashby Gap, the water almost so cold we could hardly cross it. By the 1st of November we camped near Culpeper Court House where we camped three months before when on our march to Maryland. On the 23rd of November camped about three miles south of Fredericksburg and remained in camp till 11th of December when about 4:00 a.m. the stillness of the morning was broken by the firing off of two large guns which was the signal that we were attacked.

As soon as we could be got under arms and having issued to the men eighty rounds of cartridges, twice as much as commonly given, we started for the scene of action. All that day and the day after no small arms were engaged of any consequence and the enemy having completed the pontoon bridges in the evening of the 12th commenced crossing their forces. That day, the 13th, they shelled the town we being placed on a high hill overlooking the town had an uninterrupted view of the magnificent grand sight of the shelling a town. At dark the sight was sublime beyond description. The flashes of light from a hundred guns, the bursting of the innumerable shells, the city on fire in many places, and the enemy's artillery placed in a semicircle on the north bank of the Rappahannock and on the commanding positions of the Stafford heights which when they would fire presented the spectacle of a semicircular line of about [a] mile and a half long from which large flashes of fire were constantly coming. They did not continue to fire long after dark and all was silent and still but there was a terrible meaning in that deathlike stillness. The whispered commands, the suppression of a cough, the silent tread of the men taking their place in line of battle for the coming battle was awfully foreboding but also equally exciting and you could see that the men were fully alive to the danger and tremendous results at stake and if the Yankee generals could have seen the willingness that men took dangerous and exposed positions and the determination written on their faces to conquer or die he would have trembled to think of the consequences that would occur in placing his hired mercenaries against them.

On the morning of the 13th there was a heavy fog which cleared off about 10:00 a.m. and I thought though this was not such a sun as that of Austrilitz I hope it will prove as fortunate to us as that was to Napoleon. About 1:30 p.m. we moved through a storm of shell to a position in a ravine about sixty yards closer to our batteries to support them. While in that position though it seemed impossible for us to be hurt we lost one officer and two privates killed. We stayed there about an hour and then moved our position about a 100 yards closer to the batteries still through a storm of shell and musketry which killed and wounded five or six men; and just as I had formed my company in line and was dressing and making them step up to the line and preventing them from lying down for the shell and minie balls were coming over our heads powerful, I saw a shell coming about three feet from the ground right towards us which was spent sufficiently to let me see it as it went. I only had time to say "You fellow" when it struck a man in the company on my left sending him to his final resting place. We were then ordered to lie down and while lying down two spent minie balls struck a color corporal lying on my right side and a spent shell about a foot long came tumbling over the ground right in front of me and if it had not struck an oak post that had been pulled up the night before for fire wood in all probability I would not now be here to write you.

We lay down there exposed all the time under the most severe storm of shell, grape, canister, and musketry that I imagine was ever seen on this continent but the Yankees being below us it mostly passed over our heads. About sundown the firing slackened and we were hoping it was over for the day and the men had mostly all got up to stretch themselves, having been all day lying on the damp ground when of a sudden there was such a tremendous roar of all the instruments of death that the Yankees could bring to bear on us that it fairly shook the earth. One of my men fell dead without a struggle or moan; our Major [John M.] (Kelly) was killed so dead he did not move a muscle and we lost heavily in killed and wounded. The Yankees were making their last and most desperate and most deadly charge that they had yet made but were repulsed with tremendous loss in about ten minutes and then the battle was over. The next day and night when they retreated there was no firing of any consequence and the next day we went into our old camp. We are now here expecting every day to go to North Carolina and I hope soon to be able to see you all.

January 15th: I have just received a letter from Mother dated Christmas enclosing one from Grandpa. Also another from Mother dated January 13th enclosing one from Sister which I was very much gratified to receive.

Tell Grandpa there is no one from whom I receive letters with more pleasure than from him and because I know they are such a task for him to write I prize them more highly. George paid me a visit last Saturday and I am much surprised and pleased to find him so much improved. Tell Mother I never shall receive or look for her letters but with the greatest pleasure and impatience for they always contain the very thing I want to know and as yet always bring good news about her health and the 'family's.

I have written you now dear Emmy the longest letter I ever wrote or expect to write in camp and shall look for an answer from you with impatience. Give my best love to Katie [Katherine M. (Maggie) MacRae][14] and tell her I attribute the sentinel cap in the box to her generosity and love for me with a great deal of fatigue and trouble on her part. Hoping you have had a pleasant visit at Mrs. Devereaux's,[15] I am always,

Your affectionate nephew,
W.H.S. Burgwyn

---

[14] Daughter of Julia Theodosia Burgwyn (Henry K. Burgwyn, Sr.'s sister) and the Reverend Cameron F. MacRae. Katie was a niece of Emily Matilda Barclay, wife of W.H.S.B.'s uncle, Thomas Pollok Burgwyn. Reverend MacRae was chaplain of 15th North Carolina Infantry for a short period of time. His only son, John Burgwyn McRae served in the 13th Battalion, North Carolina Troops.
     Katherine's first cousin was Colonel Duncan K. MacRae, 5th North Carolina Infantry.
[15] Mrs. John Devereux (Margaret Mordecai). She was the daughter of Moses Mordecai and Anne Lane. Her home was "Will's Forest," which she had inherited from the Lane family.
     John Devereux was Henry K. Burgwyn, Sr.'s and Emmy's second cousin. John Devereux was a major and served as Chief Quartermaster of North Carolina Troops during the Civil War. He also managed the details of the state's blockade-running efforts.

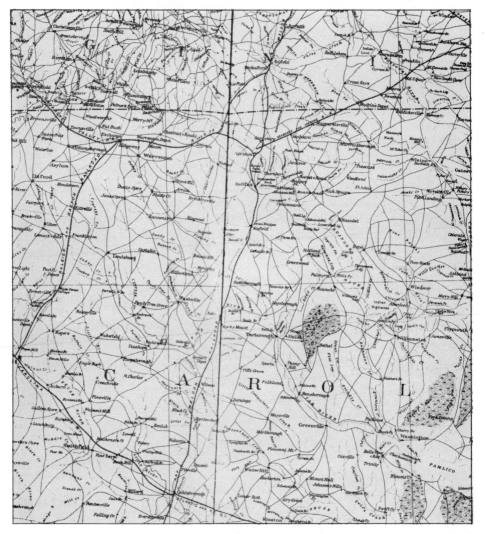

Map of North Carolina from Virginia to Goldsboro, including Thornbury, Burgwyn's home, on the Roanoke River below Halifax

O.R.A.: Plate CXXXVIII

CHAPTER 3

Thursday January 15th 1863

Finished my letter to Emmy. Received a letter from Mother dated December 25th enclosing one from Grandpa [John Fanning Burgwyn] dated December 23rd another from Mother dated January 13 enclosing one from Sister dated January 13th. On brigade guard today. Received permission to go to Garysburg and see my brother Harry. The regiment being under orders to leave tomorrow for Goldsboro [North Carolina]. Weather fair in the day and warm but rained hard and long at night.

Friday January 16th 1863

Got the conductor to put me on the train and started for Garysburg at 6:00 a.m. Reached there at 10:00 a.m. Saw my brother Harry and determined to go to the plantation and go up tomorrow to Raleigh as I thought the regiment would not pass till tomorrow. Weather rainy but cleared up about 9:30 p.m. and turned cold; wind blowing hard.

Saturday January 17th 1863

Started from plantation at 7:45 a.m. for Raleigh which I reached about 5:00 p.m. Surprised all the family very much. Met Father when the trains passed each other between Gaston and Weldon. Weather fair but very cold.

Sunday January 18th 1863

Remained in Raleigh and enjoyed myself immeasurably. Went to church twice in the morning and evening. Weather fair and cold. Had a very pleasant evening at home with my aunt Esther and Cousin Kate [MacRae] and all our family and Miss [Malvina] Henry[1] who was invited to open the evening.

Monday January 19th 1863

Started to join my regiment at 5:00 a.m. Reached Goldsboro at 8:00 a.m. Was detained there all day from no cars crossing. Met Major [A.H.] Galloway and Major [George P.] Collins and being irritated spent the night with the latter. Found the brigade gone to Warsaw on the Wilmington and Weldon Railroad. Weather cold and fair.

---

[1] Daughter of Louis DeBonaire Henry and Margaret Haywood. Henry was a prominent North Carolina Democrat who had died in 1846.

Tuesday January 20th 1863

Started to join my regiment at Warsaw in the box cars that transported Colonel [James K.] Marshall's regiment [52nd North Carolina Infantry] to Magnolia. Was taken sick soon after coming to the regiment and after going to the hotel. Was taken very sick with the cholera morbus [acute gastroenteritis] which lasted all night. Weather rainy and cool.

Wednesday January 21st 1863

Felt no better this morning and Dr. [Francis N.] Luckey of the 25th [North Carolina Infantry] gave me a pass to go to the hospital at Goldsboro. Taking Pompey with me I went there and tried to get transferred to Raleigh but could not succeed. Stayed at the Griswald Hotel in the same room with Lieutenant Colonel [John A.] Flemming and Captain [Peter Z.] Baxter both of the 49th North Carolina Infantry. Weather drizzling and cold and rained at night.

Thursday January 22nd 1863

Felt some better this morning. Obtained with Colonel Flemming and Captain Baxter quarters in a very light and comfortable private house owned by Mr. Slocumb and his wife who in conversation I found knew our family. Wrote Mother today. Weather cold but cloudy fair.

* * * *

Goldsboro, January 22nd 1863

Dear Mother,

I arrived here safely on Monday morning and I was detained all day in this place on account of the train having run against another one and mashing up the engine. When I came here I found the brigade had gone to Warsaw on the Wilmington and Weldon Railroad and next day went down on the train that transported Colonel Marshall's regiment, the 52nd [North Carolina]. I found out Pettigrew's Brigade had been ordered to Magnolia on the same railroad about seven miles from Warsaw. On the same night I arrived at Warsaw, the 20th, I had a severe attack of cholera morbus and having no place to stay came next day to this place. I am now almost well. I am staying at a private house and report every day at a hospital here. I shall return to camp either tomorrow or next day.

General Cooke's Brigade has been taken from General Ransom and he now only commands his own brigade. He is now under General [Samuel G.] French. Harry and myself will be now very close together and I hope we will continue so.

Don't be uneasy about me for I am almost well and will go to the regiment either as I say tomorrow or next day.

They are concentrating the troops about Kenansville and Magnolia ready to meet the enemy on their advance on Wilmington but I don't think they will fight there. With much love to all,

Your affectionate son,
W.H.S. Burgwyn

* * * *

Friday January 23rd 1863

The pain in my bowels almost well. Did not report to the hospital today. Weather cloudy and cold but no rain. Occupied myself in reading some books borrowed from the proprietor (Mr. Slocumb).

Saturday January 24th 1863

Felt almost well today. Wrote Father to Raleigh and desired Mother to forward it. Weather drizzly in the morning but no rain in the after part of the day. Two young ladies staying at the house entertained us acceptably with vocal music.

Sunday January 25th 1863

Sent word to the hospital I would join my regiment today. Started for Magnolia at 3:30 p.m. and reached it about 5:00 p.m. Walked out to my brother's regiment about two miles from depot. Rode into town with my brother to see General Pettigrew whom he wished to see on business. Weather fair and sun came out.

Monday January 26th 1863

Remained all day in camp of the 26th Regiment North Carolina Infantry. Saw the brigade (Pettigrew's) march out to witness the execution of a deserter ([Sergeant Andrew] Wyatt) 26th North Carolina Infantry but he was reprieved by the solicitation of the colonels of the brigade. Weather fair but clouded up at night but no rain.

Tuesday January 27th 1863

Started for camp this morning at 10:00 a.m. riding one of my brother's horses his orderly riding the other. My boy Pompey walking. Found the regiment about half mile south of Kenansville. Weather commenced raining about 1:30 p.m. and rained all day and night.

Wednesday January 28th 1863

Pass a restless night a little feverish. Lieutenant Hunter returned to camp on the 21st. Weather rainy before 12:00 noon and about 4:00 p.m. hailed a little and turned much cooler. Put me up a chimney to my tent. Sent out in the country to get me a box made to put my clothes in instead of a trunk.

Thursday January 29th 1863

Had brigade drill at 2:00 p.m. The drill ground being at the unusual distance of a mile from camp. Weather warm and tolerably fair. The ball was put off from today till tomorrow. Frank Johnson's band was hired.

Friday January 30th 1863

Had two drills today at 9:00 a.m. and 2:00 p.m. Company and battalion drill. Harry on his way to reconnoiter a place called C--- [*sic*]. [Illegible] called to see me. Went to the ball about 8:00 p.m. Frank's band did not arrive until 1:30 a.m. next day. Weather fair.

Saturday January 31st 1863

Owing to Frank Johnson's not coming till late we recommenced the dance at 11:00 a.m. today and danced till 3:00 p.m. I did not go today. Wrote Mother today. Was detailed as officer of the regimental guard today. Received orders at 7:30 p.m. to hold ourselves in readiness to march at a moment's notice. Weather fair.

Sunday February 1st 1863

Was relieved as officer of the regimental guard at 4:30 p.m. Received a letter from Harry directed to Richmond dated January 1st. One from a Dr. P.C. Neal dated December 29th. Weather cloudy very much like rain. Determined to send my boy Pompey home for a week.

Monday February 2nd 1863

Sent boy Pompey to 26th Regiment [North Carolina Infantry] to let Harry know I send him tomorrow to plantation. Weather rained a little in the latter part of the night but no rain in the day. Commenced a letter to Father. Received a letter from Captain Maxwell dated January 26th; one from private D. M. Morrison [Company H] dated January 22nd.

Tuesday February 3rd 1863

Sent Pompey to the plantation. Commenced snowing about 4:00 a.m. and continued till 7:00 a.m. Snowed about three inches deep; the remainder of the day much brighter. The snow melting much. Finished my letter to Father. Received a letter from Mother dated January 7th. Officer [of the] guard again today but did not post sentinels owing to [illegible].

Wednesday February 4th 1863

Was busily occupied in making out muster and pay rolls and a correct set of bounty rolls. Weather very cold and did not post sentinels owing to it.

Thursday February 5th 1863

Wrote Mother today and just after finishing my letter and the rains still pouring down. Was ordered on picket about a mile. Stayed all night on the soaked ground with my oil cloth only to cover with and it raining all the time. Passed a hateful night.

* * * *

Camp Thirty-Fifth North Carolina Troops
Near Kenansville January[2] 5th, 1863

Dear Mother,

I received your very welcome letter day before yesterday and as I was extremely busy all day yesterday I had to put off answering it till today.

I almost envied you your nice little room all by itself and perfectly warm for here the snow is on the ground two or three inches deep tho you may have a chimney, camp life is none the warmest or most pleasant and for the last day or two it has

---

[2] Internal evidence indicates this letter was written February 5, 1863.

been very cold indeed. It commenced snowing day before yesterday morning about 4:00 a.m. and snowed very hard for about three hours and now it is raining like all the world and consequently not so very cold as it was.

Last Tuesday I sent Pompey to [the] plantation for a little leave of absence for he has been very faithful to me and though he did not seem very anxious to go I thought I could spare him now as well as any time.

He is to start for Raleigh Monday and remain there Tuesday and return to me Wednesday. I sent by him both coats you let me have because when I get the other one I would not be able easily to carry them and I would not have any use for them.

If you can easily do it please put two more pockets in it on each side at right angles to the two you have put in so that when my arms are at full length they will be in there; make them pretty deep.

Harry has given me his blue Lexington [V.M.I. cadet] coat. Please put two horizontal bars of gold cord on each side of the collar as you did on the jacket to designate my rank.

I am very glad Mrs. [J.W.] Newsom has finished my [illegible]. I will when I receive them write her a note thanking her. I will give you a description of myself; as I now write I am sitting on a log that forms part of my bed and which prevents the straw I lie on from spreading out which bye the bye is a very hard and uncomfortable seat since it is not more than three inches from the ground and consequently I am in rather a double sort of position my chin on my right knee which portion is constantly reminding me my whiskers have grown considerably since August lst and that my pants are none of the finest or most free from wool or cotton. My left leg extended to its full length to make my position as comfortable as it can which nevertheless I have to change by getting up every now and then. My paper and ink and piece of paper I use to keep from soiling the writing paper and a piece of a Muster Roll under all and all resting on the lid of Lieutenant [John R.] Baker's[3] box trunk which answers the purpose of trunk and table at meal times and consequently renders it necessary for me to cover it with something to prevent too much of the grease that profusely adorns it from coming in contact with my writing paper and thereby ruining it and last of all I cast fearful glances up at the tent to see if the rain in its fury and heedlessness has not penetrated through the pale covering that covers me from the inclemency of the weather and thereby abruptly putting an end to my correspondence. But as the rain has not as yet penetrated the tent cloth and I have just rested myself by getting up and stretching I recommence my epistolitory conversation.

I have given strict injunctions to my valet de chambres and man of all work and deeds (Pompey) that he must not dare to show himself here unless he brings me a trunk for since my wardrobe is reduced to three white shirts I must have something to shield them from the smoke of pine and he, like a faithful servant, has promised if a trunk or anything that bears the slightest resemblance to one can be found or seen and money paid by it I shall have it. If you, dear Mother, can aid him in getting me one please do so for I cannot get along without one.

I am truly sorry Mr. [Frederick] FitzGerald's[4] little boy is dead for I really felt a great love for it and if phrenology is a true thing he must have been a great man if he had lived.

---

[3] Co. H, 35th N.C.

[4] First Rector of The Church of the Savior, Jackson, North Carolina. He lived with the Burgwyns at Thornbury before the war, moved to Raleigh in 1860, and was serving as major with the 12th North Carolina Infantry and in hospitals in and around Raleigh.

This is a long and the most gay letter I have ever written you and I suppose it is owing to the good news about Charleston and Galveston. Tell Grandpa I am looking for a long letter from him every day and have got some nice foolscap paper to reply to it.

With much love and hoping you are either napping or reading pleasantly in your pleasant little room, I am,

Always your most affectionate son,
W.H.S. Burgwyn

* * * *

Friday February 6th 1863

Stopped raining about 12:00 noon. Took breakfast and dinner at a citizen's house nearby. Weather turned much colder after it stopped raining. Was relieved by a company from the 49th Regiment [North Carolina Infantry] about 4:00 p.m. Found everything on my return to camp safe and dry.

Saturday February 7th 1863

Met today my particular friend Bob Peebles who came to see me and who was staying at Magnolia awaiting his trial to come off on Monday night. Weather fine and warm. Heard from Peebles Harry intended trying for a furlough. Intend to try myself when Captain Maxwell comes back.

Sunday February 8th 1863

Got permission to visit town today to go to church but did not go as the church was too crowded. Took dinner at the hotel in the town. Wrote Captain Maxwell. Weather cloudy in the first of the morning but fair and warm afterwards.

Monday February 9th 1863

Instead of a drill today had the regiment fixing up the fence that had been torn down preparatory to our leaving here for a new camp tomorrow. Received orders about 3:00 p.m. to leave for the new camp at 7:30 a.m. tomorrow. Weather fair and very warm but clouded up at night.

Tuesday February 10th 1863

Started for our new camp one and a half miles north of Kenansville at 7:30 a.m. At 12:00 noon obtained permission to go to Magnolia to attend a ball given there by the 11th North Carolina Regiment. Having gone to the Middleton's to see my friend Bob Peebles; was introduced to a Miss Martin and escorted her to the ball. Left about 3:00 p.m. and stayed all night at her M [sic] with Bob Peebles. Weather fair and very warm but cloudy at night. Received a letter from Mother dated February 6th and 14th.

Wednesday February 11th 1863

Took breakfast at Mr. Middleton's and returned to my brother's regiment at 9:00 a.m. and at 10:00 a.m. started for camp. Had company drill at 2:00 p.m. Weather fair and warm all day but cloudy at night with a few drops of rain. Paid my men that were present their state bounty equal to $24.30.

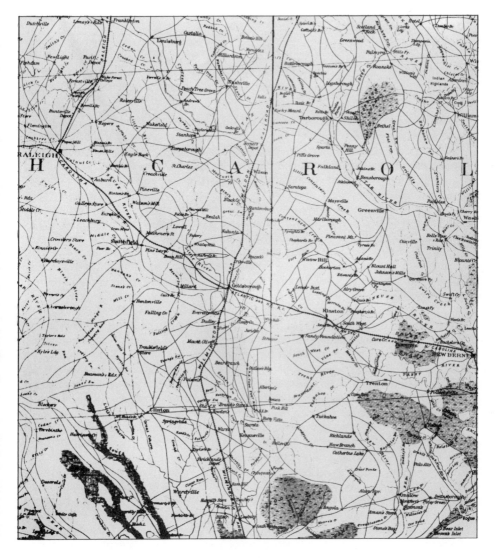

Map of North Carolina from Goldsboro south along the Wilmington & Weldon Railroad toward Wilmington

O.R.A.: Plate CXXXVIII

Thursday February 12th 1863

Had brigade review at 2:30 p.m. Adjutant Clark received the acceptance of his resignation today. Wrote Mother a short letter. Was surprised that my boy Pompey did not return to me today since when he left I ordered him to return by the 12th. Weather fair and very warm.

* * * *

Camp Thirty-Fifth Regiment North Carolina Troops
Near Kenansville, North Carolina, February 12th 1863

Dear Mother,

I received yours of the 6th just day before yesterday and you see I did not have time to answer it in time for you to get the answer before Pompey should come to Raleigh and be obliged to leave; as it is though he should have come down evening; he has not arrived here yet and I am afraid he may have been taken sick.

Just after I had finished and sealed my letter to you of the 5th ultimo which I hope you have before this received I was ordered on picket duty about [a] mile and a half from camp and you can imagine what a time I had. It was raining as you know at 4:00 p.m. when I started out and it rained without intermission all night and till 12:00 noon next day and in this country the rain does not it seems to me to soak in the ground as much as it does at Raleigh and when I got to the picket ground the whole place was covered with water about an inch deep. There was no covering of any sort whatever at the place and we had just to stand up and take it; you may judge the night we passed.

Day before yesterday I had another opportunity to "trip it on the light fantastic." There was a ball given by the 11th [North Carolina] Regiment, Pettigrew's Brigade, and I having obtained permission attended it and enjoyed myself. I enjoyed myself much more than I otherwise would for before going to the ball I went to see Bob Peebles staying at a Mr. Middleton's at Magnolia and it so happened that there was a bridal party staying at his house with all the bridesmaids and Peebles having introduced me I escorted one of them to the ball Miss Martin sister of the groom, Lieutenant Colonel [William J.] Martin of the 11th [North Carolina] Regiment. I also met there a Miss Everett who informed me she had been to school at Saint Marys with Sister and who I found a most agreeable lady indeed and very intelligent. She said she was a particular friend of Sister's and I was glad to hear it since I was very much pleased with her indeed though she was not very pretty. The trunk you speak of would be the very thing as not very new but I am afraid it would be entirely too large and that would be a most serious fault. I hope you have succeeded in getting me one for I need one very much. I also find myself very unpleasantly situated in going to these parties since the first I went to I went in my jacket and the [illegible]. I had to borrow a suit. I think I shall write father and ask him to give me his uniform suit and have it made to fit me.[5]

I will write again immediately but there is a friend come to see me and I must close. Harry tried to get a furlough but it was disapproved.

Ever your most affectionate son,
W.H.S. Burgwyn

* * * *

---

[5] Henry King Burgwyn, Sr., had attended the United States Military Academy at West Point, New York, from 1828-1831 but he did not complete the course of study.

Friday February 13th 1863

My boy Pompey arrived today at 12:00 noon being delayed in Raleigh by the cars till Thursday night. My brother Harry came to see me; his regiment and the brigade being ordered to Goldsboro. Received the acceptance [of] Lieutenant Hunter's resignation today and forwarded it to him. Weather fair and warm.

Saturday February 14th 1863

Sent Pompey to Magnolia in a wagon for my trunk and he returned about 4:00 p.m. Found in the trunk a long letter from Father and a short one from Mother. No drill today. Was detailed as officer of the regimental guard at 4:00 p.m. Weather fair and warm.

Sunday February 15th 1863

Wrote Mother today. I wrote out furloughs agreeable with General Orders Number 5 Department Headquarters for two of my men and forwarded them. Weather rained a little about 12:00 noon and looked very much like rain the remainder of the day. Was relieved as officer of the guard at 4:00 p.m.

* * * *

Camp Thirty-Fifth Regiment North Carolina Troops
Near Kenansville, North Carolina, February 15th 1863

Dear Mother

Day before yesterday Pompey came to me about 12:00 noon and brought all the things to the depot (Magnolia) and I sent for them yesterday. The overcoat is done to perfection and the pockets are precisely in the right place. The uniform coat fits me better than if it was made by any tailor in Raleigh and it seems as new as ever. The trunk is the very thing that I wanted since it is perfectly good to hold my clothes and if I lose it I shall not lose anything of much value.

Day before yesterday Harry called by to see me on his way to Goldsboro, his brigade being ordered there as I conjecture to take the place of [General Junius] Daniel's which has gone to Kinston viz., [General Nathan G.] Evans having gone to Charleston, South Carolina. I am very sorry the brigade has gone for I could now and then visit it for a short time. I read with pleasure Father's letter and your note attached to it and am very glad he has made so advantageous a disposal of his bonds of $20,000. I only wish he had the remainder to dispose of likewise. You may depend upon it I shall get a furlough as soon as Captain Maxwell comes which I look for daily and I anticipate a very pleasant time as Harry says now General Pettigrew has approved his application for a furlough.

I hope you were pleased with Pompey's behavior and consider me a more proficient hand in training a servant than Harry. Pompey tells me that William amongst his other marvelous stories, says while at New Berne he marched two months day and night without sleeping a wink while you know he never [illegible] any at all.

I am glad George has gone to Chapel Hill for I imagine his manners and behavior are now better for his stay at the plantation.

Harry has just bought him a buggy and having asked me to lend him my horse "Sultan" I readily consented though I expect to hear of his running away with him and breaking his buggy all to pieces. Tell Sister though I do not write to her as often as she does me it should be no reason why she should not write me and I will write her hereafter regularly if I am permitted to stay regularly in camp or not be kept busy every week moving our camp. We have now a very pretty camp and the men have fixed themselves very nicely and it seems a pity they should be forced to move again soon unless military movements require it. You need not hereafter complain of Dinah's or the other Negro women for forgetting on cold or wet days to put on the warm or thick clothing for the other wet night on picket will you believe I totally forgot I had that nice oil cloth cape you sent me and never did think of it till two or three days afterward.

Since I commenced this letter it has begun to rain and rained hard for a short time and now it has slacked and seems going to clear up. Many thanks to you for sending me my watch and when I get home I will have to make you a handsome present for your many charities to me in a money line.

You know I cannot be so extravagant in camp as to use more than one sheet of foolscap paper so I must close.

With much love to all, I am ever,

Your most affectionate son,
W.H.S. Burgwyn

* * * *

Monday February 16th 1863

Received the furloughs for the men who left at sundown. Received orders about 7:00 p.m. for the men to cook two days rations and report to Lieutenant Colonel Flemming at 8:00 a.m. tomorrow. Wrote Mrs. J.W. Newsom thanking her for knitting my [illegible]. Weather drizzly all day and night.

Tuesday February 17th 1863

Started under Lieutenant Colonel Flemming at 9:00 a.m. for a Mr. Higgins for meat and corn who lives in Onslow City about forty-two miles off. Arrived 6:00 p.m. Reached Haw Branch Church about twenty-two miles. Spent the night at a Mr. Frank Thompson's about two and a half miles farther on. Crossed Northeast River from Kenansville eight and a half miles. Weather rained all day and night.

Wednesday February 18th 1863

Recommenced our march at 7:00 a.m. and at 3:00 p.m. reached Mr. Higgins' a distance of nineteen and a half miles. Weather rained hard during the day but cleared off about 4:00 p.m. Crossed the Northeast or branch of New River about eight miles from Mr. Higgins'. Quartered the men in the Negro houses of the place. I stayed in Mr. Higgins' house.

Thursday February 19th 1863

Was sent to a Mr. White's about five miles toward Kenansville for the purpose of getting some meal or corn ground. Stayed all night at Mr. White's. Never saw so fine a lot of Negro women before in my life and he said it was owing to his never permitting his Negro women to work in the winter. He only started with four hands and is now worth one hundred thirty Negroes and 3,500 acres of land.

Friday February 20th 1863

Got in the wagon that carried the meal and rode till we came to a halt about fifteen miles from Mr. Higgins'. Took dinner in the country about one mile from camp. Weather fair and moderately warm.

Saturday February 21st 1863

Commenced our march at 7:00 a.m. and at 3:00 p.m. reached Hawesville a distance of fifteen miles. Weather cloudy all day and rained very hard all night accompanied with thunder and lightening.

Sunday February 22nd 1863

Started at 7:00 a.m. about half way to Kenansville. Heard the brigade was ordered to Wilmington, consequently we marched directly to Magnolia and did not pass Kenansville. Found Lieutenant Dixon at camp. Received a letter from Dr. Neal. Weather rained in fore part of the day but cleared up cold in the after part. Paid tonight my men and their eight month's wages are $5,078.14. Passed the night in the deserted camp of the 44th North Carolina Regiment about one mile from Magnolia. Drew pay of my own for six months and Sundays = $571.00.

Monday February 23rd 1863

Started from our last night's bivouac for Magnolia to get on the train about 10:00 a.m.; halted at the camp of the 11th [North Carolina] Regiment (Colonel [Collett] Leventhorpe) owing to the train's not coming and remained there all day and night. Weather fair and cold. Passed the night in the house Colonel Leventhorpe had for his headquarters.

Tuesday February 24th 1863

Started on the train for Wilmington at 7:45 a.m. and at 12:30 p.m. reached it. Marched to the camp of my brigade about two miles from the city. Weather cold and windy. The wagons started about 12:00 noon the day before to go to Wilmington by land and they employed many other wagons to haul the things to camp.

Wednesday February 25th 1863

Obtained permission to visit Wilmington. Left a note at a Mr. Myers,[6] druggist of the city, for my cousin Hazel Burgwyn[7] letting him know I was here and to come and see me. Wrote Mother. Weather cloudy and fair and moderately warm.

Thursday February 26th 1863

Had a pleasant time today in playing "Town Ball." Weather misty and rainy all day but no rain at night. Heard from Lieutenant Horne of our regiment; he saw my brother Harry get off the Raleigh and Goldsboro train at Goldsboro therefore I think he had received a furlough.

---

[6] Possibly Charles D. Myers, who lived near H. W. Burgwyn and who sold groceries, liquors, cigars, and willow ware.

[7] Hasell Witherspoon Burgwyn, M.D. was the son of George William Rush Burgwin. (Also, see Hill Burgwin.) His house, the "Hermitage" was built by John Burgwin, W.H.S.B.'s great grandfather; the original house burned in the 1880's.

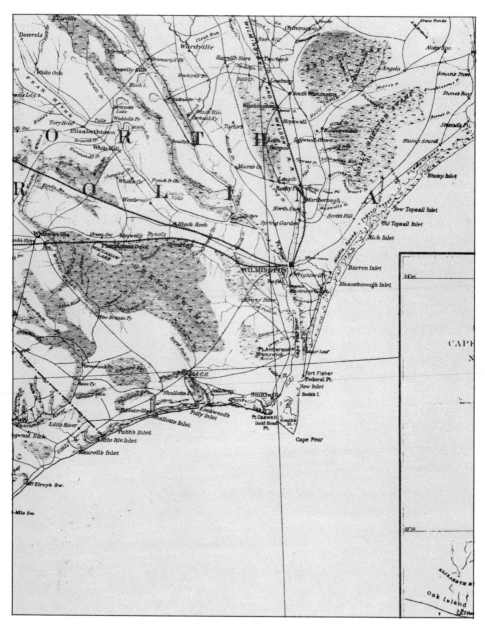

Map of North Carolina from Wilmington north toward Goldsboro showing the Wilmington & Weldon Railroad

O.R.A.: Plate CXXXIX

Friday February 27th 1863

Received permission to visit Wilmington and in town met my cousin Hazel who I promised to visit next week at his house. Heard General Ransom and Colonel Ransom were both promoted. Weather cloudy and misty and rained in the night.

Saturday February 28th 1863

Received three letters today. One from Mother dated January 22nd and [2]3rd; one from Harry dated 27th; and one from Dr. Watson of [?]Mectenburg City dated January 10th. Weather rained off and on all day but cleared up by morning so that there was no rain but was cloudy.

Sunday March 1st 1863

Remained in camp all day. Had preaching in the morning in the 49th [North Carolina] and evening in the 33rd [North Carolina] Regiments. Wrote out the furloughs for two of my men. The other two having returned from furlough. Weather fair. Wrote Captain Maxwell.

Monday March 2nd 1863

Received a letter from Father dated March 1st and one from Mother dated February 28th. Wrote my brother Harry. Went to the city to buy some stars for a coat for my brother but could not get any. Weather fair but windy.

Tuesday March 3rd 1863

Was inspected at 2:00 p.m. by the Inspector General of General [William H.C.] Whiting's Staff. He seemed pleased with the appearance of the regiment. Weather fair and pleasant. Sent home two men on furlough for seven days at home.

Wednesday March 4th 1863

Witnessed one of the battalions near our camp constructed on the river bank practice firing. Was much disappointed and mortified to see it so poorly done and the guns worked so badly. Wrote Father a short note. Weather fair but very disagreeable and windy.

Thursday March 5th 1863

General Ransom returned to camp from his furlough today. Weather cold but not as windy as yesterday. Tried to get leave to visit my cousin Hazel but was put off till Saturday. Had battalion drill in the afternoon.

Friday March 6th 1863

Received a letter from Father dated March 4th and one from Harry dated March 4th. Wrote Father and Harry. Weather fair and not much windy. Had company and battalion drill.

Saturday March 7th 1863

Received permission to go and see my cousin (Hazel Burgwyn) and return tomorrow evening. Stayed in town till 7:00 p.m. Then I took the train as far as New River where I walked a mile and a quarter back to his house the Hermitage and arrived there about 8:15 p.m. Wrote Colonel Ransom. Weather fair and high wind.

Sunday March 8th 1863

At 4:00 p.m. endeavored at Cousin Hazel's depot to take the train but it being behind time would not stop. I consequently had to wait till the next morning's train at 5:00 a.m. Weather fair and warm. Was very much taken with the appearance of the old house and grounds.

Monday March 9th 1863

Awoke at 4:30 a.m. and hurriedly walked to the depot at New River but again owing to the train being detained till 5:15 a.m. it would not stop. Returned to my cousin's and after breakfast at 8:30 a.m. I started in his buggy for camp which I reached at 11:30 a.m. [and] found orders for a review by General Longstreet; at 12:00 noon went out to be reviewed.

* * * *

Camp 35th Regiment North Carolina Troops
Near Wilmington March 9th 1863

Dear Mother,

I received your last and as soon as I was able went to town and made the desired enquiries the result of which is as follows: there is no white and black calico in town and the striped calico is from one dollar and three-quarters a yard to three dollars a yard and there are fine English cotton ladies stockings at one dollar and a half. If you wish me to get you anything let me know it and I will get them for you with pleasure.

On Saturday evening having obtained permission to go I visited Cousin Hazel who I found at home by himself in the bachelor style everything looking as if the hand of a women was very much needed but everything of any importance had been packed away and sent off. I was very much struck with the appearance of the place and house. The house is a long building with a center of two stories high flanked by two wings of only one story high. The house is painted white and the wings are covered with shingles naked as weather boarding. The house in all is, I believe, about 130 feet long and presents a very pretty view coming upon its front or rear. The grounds from the remains must have been very magnificent but are now very nearly totally obliterated but Cousin Hazel intends when the war ends to have these regenerated.

I found him very pleasant and am anxious to renew my visit.

You will have seen by my letter to Father that Harry is trying to get me on General [D.H.] Hill's staff which I am very desirous for and am anxiously awaiting the final decision. I can write no more. Many thanks again for your long and pleasant letters to Kenansville. Love to all.

Your affectionate son,
W.H.S. Burgwyn

* * * *

Tuesday March 10th 1863

Received orders at 9:30 a.m. to be ready to march immediately at 11:00 a.m. commenced our march through Wilmington and on the Plank Road for a distance of thirteen miles from Wilmington and halted at 4:30 p.m. Weather cloudy and drizzly.

Wednesday March 11th 1863

Stayed all day where we halted the night before. Weather rained hard in the morning but cleared up after dinner. Sent in an application for a furlough at 11:00 a.m. Received a letter from my brother dated March 9/63.

Thursday March 12th 1863

At 7:40 a.m. commenced our march towards Topsail Sound and marching about one and a half [miles] halted and pitched our tents and made ourselves as comfortable as possible. Was anxiously expecting my furlough but it did not come.

Friday March 13th 1863

Received my furlough at 7:00 p.m. but could not start for want of transportation till tomorrow morning. Had company and battalion drill. Weather fair but cold and windy.

Saturday March 14th 1863

Started at 7:00 a.m. on a wagon at 10:00 a.m. reached Wilmington. Saw cousin Hazel. Paid for my uniform today $175.00 and for a pair of boots $50.00 and hat $20.00. At 7:00 p.m. started on the train and at 1:00 a.m. next day reached Goldsboro. Weather fair.

Sunday March 15th 1863

Heard today Generals Longstreet and Hill were respectively attacking Washington and New Berne. Anxiously expecting news but could hear none of importance. At 1:30 p.m. started for Raleigh and arrived at 4:30 p.m. Weather fair but cold towards night and cloudy.

Monday March 16th 1863

Wrote an application to General Whiting to go on his staff. Heard by telegraph from Governor [Zebulon B.] Vance. Hill was repulsed. Paid a short visit to Mrs. Miller's.[8] Weather cloudy in the morning and cold but afterwards clear.

Tuesday March 17th 1863

Visited cousin Helen Johnston[9] and Bettie Warren[10] and Miss T. Haywood. Heard satisfactorily concerning Harry. Had Generals Gustavus W. Smith and [James G.] Martin to supper. Weather fair and pleasant.

---

[8] Frances Johnson Devereux Miller, a widow at this time, was the oldest sister of Major John Devereux, and daughter of Thomas Pollok Devereux and Katherine Ann Johnson of Connecticut.

[9] Helen Scrymgoeur Johnston was the sister of Betty Warren. Both were daughters of Reverend Dr. Samuel Iredell Johnston of Chowan and Bertie Counties in northeast North Carolina. Dr. Johnston was husband of Margaret Anne Burgwyn, third child of George William Bush (W.H.S.B.'s great uncle) and Maria Nash. She was a second cousin to W.H.S.B.

[10] Elizabeth Cotton Warren, the wife of Edward Warren, M.D., Surgeon of North Carolina forces. She was a second cousin of W.H.S.B.

Wednesday March 18th 1863

Called on Miss Helen Johnston and Misses Bettie [Elizabeth Earl] and Emmie [Emily Skinner] Johnson.[11] Took dinner at Dr. [Edward] Warren's.[12] Visiting Miss Bettie and Emma Johnson and Cousin [Margaret (Maggie)] Haywood.[13] Passed the evening at Mrs. Devereux's at the reading party. Weather cloudy and rained at night.

Thursday March 19th 1863

Called on Misses [Sue] Branch[14] and [Malvina Herman] Henry[15] in the morning and Cousin Kate Miller[16] in the afternoon. Had the two Miss Johnsons and Cousin Helen Johnston at supper to spend the evening. Weather misty and rained all day and sleet at night.

Friday March 20th 1863

Father received a letter from Harry written from camp eight miles from Greenville [North Carolina]. Weather sleeting all day and no prospect of its clearing up. Had some entertaining sport in shooting robins that were in great quantities around the house.

Saturday March 21st 1863

Weather trees covered with sleet and it sleeting all day. Called on Misses Johnson and Cousin Helen Johnston also on Aunt Emma. Mother received a letter from Harry dated ---- [*sic*].

Sunday March 22nd 1863

Did not go to church today owing to Mother's not going. Wrote Harry a letter recommending Lieutenant Peebles to the position of aide on his staff if the report of his promotion was true. Weather fair and cloudy and cool.

Monday March 23rd 1863

Called on Mrs. Richard Battle,[17] Miss Henry, Mrs. William Anderson,[18] and Mrs. Dr. Warren. Also on Miss Maggie Haywood to escort her to a society of ladies exclusively and a reading club. Weather cloudy but fair in the after part of the day.

---

[11] Daughters of Dr. Charles Earl Johnson and Emily Skinner of Raleigh; he was the founder of Edenton. Their sister, Mary, was married to George Burgwyn Johnson, son of Samuel I. Johnson, who was killed early in the war.

[12] Edward Warren, M.D., was Surgeon General of North Carolina Troops (1862-1865). He was the author of the wartime publication *Surgery for Field and Hospital.*

[13] Margaret Haywood, daughter of Senator William Henry Haywood, prominent Raleigh attorney, and Jane Graham. The Haywoods became related to W.H.S.B. by marriage after the war.

[14] Daughter of General Lawrence O'Bryan Branch, killed at Antietam, and Nancy Haywood Blount.

[15] Daughter of Louis DeBonaire Henry, North Carolina state legislator, and Margaret Haywood.

[16] Daughter of Frances Johnson Devereux and Henry Watkins Miller. Kate's mother was a sister of Major John Devereux.

[17] Mrs. Richard Henry Battle, Jr., (Anne Ruffin Ashe) was the daughter of Judge Thomas Samuel Ashe and Caroline Athelia Burgwyn, daughter of George William Bush Burgwyn and Maria Nash. She was a second cousin of W.H.S.B. Richard Battle, son of Governor Z. Vance's law professor at the University of North Carolina, served as the governor's private secretary, after having seen duty as First Lieutenant, Company I, 49th North Carolina Infantry.

Her brother, Samuel Theodore Ashe, married Margaret Devereux, a younger daughter of Major Theodore Devereux and Margaret Mordecai.

[18] Wife of Colonel William E. Anderson of Raleigh. She (Mary Louise Syme) was the daughter of John William Syme, editor of the Raleigh *Register*. Colonel Anderson was the brother of General George Burgwin Anderson and of Captain Robert Walker Anderson, second cousins of W.H.S.B.

Tuesday March 24th 1863

Called in the morning upon the Miss Mason,[19] Miss Lassin, and the Misses Littles. At 12:30 p.m. it commenced raining and continued so till night. Grandpa had a severe attack of giddiness this evening but it very soon passed off.

Wednesday March 25th 1863

Called on Miss Henry this morning. Went out to Camp Holmes on business but did not transact it owing to the person not being there who I wished to see. Harry sent his boy Kinchen up today. Weather rained a little no [illegible].

Thursday March 26th 1863

Called upon Miss Annie [Ann (Annie) Lane] Devereux[20] in the morning and a Miss Warren with Sister and on Miss Mary Haywood in the afternoon but neither were at home. Was at Emmie's to tea and met some ladies and gentlemen. Weather fair but windy.

Friday March 27th 1863

Today being the one set aside by Mr. [Jefferson] Davis for fasting, humiliation and prayer I went to church in the morning and evening. Father received a letter from General Whiting in reply to my application saying he could not at present say. Weather fair.

Saturday March 28th 1863

Called on Miss Mary Haywood in the morning and on Miss Sue Branch. Attended a reading party at Mrs. Branch's[21] at 4:00 p.m. Captain [Francis L.] Hawks [Jr.] and Major Blount called and took tea. Aunt Emmy and Uncle Tom [Thomas Pollok Burgwyn] also. Weather rainy.

— END OF BOOK ONE —

BOOK TWO: MARCH 29, 1863 - JANUARY 20, 1864[22]

Sunday March 29th 1863

Was much shocked at hearing of the sudden death of Mrs. Robert Strange[23] whose funeral took place in the afternoon from the church. Intended to start for camp at 12:00 midnight but put it off till tomorrow at 10:30 a.m. Weather cold but no rain.

---

[19] Probably grand-daughter of Reverend Richard Sharpe Mason of Christ Episcopal Church.

[20] Oldest daughter of John and Margaret Mordecai Devereaux, born October 10, 1843; half second cousin to W.H.S.B. According to family legend, she was engaged to Colonel Henry K. Burgwyn, Jr.; she never married after the war. (Margaret Burgwyn Cooley)

[21] Nancy Haywood Blount Branch, widow of General Lawrence O'B. Branch.

[22] The diary in "Book Two" was written in a book picked up at Fredericksburg in December, 1862 by Captain Burgwyn, who used it for his own diary. The few original entries were made by a member of the 13th New York Infantry.

[23] Wife of Robert Strange, who was a prominent Wilmington attorney and member of the North Carolina House of Commons.

Monday March 30th 1863

At 10:30 a.m. started for camp and at 2:30 p.m. reached Goldsboro where I found my regiment. Had the blues pretty bad. Weather at night commenced to rain a little and continued all night.

Tuesday March 31st 1863

Applied to go to town but could not get my pass signed. Wrote Mother and Harry and mailed a letter to him from Mother and Father. Visited a friend of mine, Robert Peebles in the 56th North Carolina Regiment. Weather cloudy and cold and windy.

Wednesday April 1st 1863

Was detailed as officer of the guard at 8:00 a.m. At evening dress parade an order from General Ransom was read curtailing the baggage and tent flies and I intended sending my trunk home tomorrow only reserving one suit of clothes. Weather fair but windy.

Thursday April 2nd 1863

Captain Maxwell and myself applied for permission to visit Goldsboro but only one could go and he went. Was sent in charge of the surplus baggage of the officers of the regiment to have it safely stored away at Goldsboro and while in town heard the brigade was ordered to Kinston and would leave the same night at 5:00 p.m. Lieutenant Colonel Jones marched the regiment in town expecting to leave at 6:00 p.m. but did not get off till 1:00 a.m. the next day. Wrote Mother and Colonel Ransom, the latter to recommend me to General Whiting. Weather fair and windy.

Friday April 3rd 1863

At 1:00 a.m. started on the train for Kinston which we reached at 3:00 a.m. Bivouacked for the night in a field near the town. About 7:30 a.m. Lieutenant Colonel Jones moved the regiment about one fourth mile to the place where it had camped eleven months ago and the company encamped on the very identical place it did eleven months previous. At 11:00 a.m. moved to a camp on low hills a mile from town. Weather about 4:00 p.m. turned very cold and high wind and cloudy lasted all day.

Saturday April 4th 1863

Had a chimney built but hardly was finished when we received orders to be ready to march tomorrow at 6:00 a.m. Weather early cold and windy but towards evening less windy and cold. Twenty-five conscripts arrived in the regiment this evening.

Sunday April 5th 1863

At 6:00 a.m. started in the directions of New Berne the 56th Regiment was also sent on picket in the direction of Greenville. At 10:00 a.m. with three companies of the regiment, Companies E, H, and I under command of Captain Maxwell arrived at our picket lines ten miles from Kinston and relieved three companies of the 24th Virginia Regiment. Have two posts of three men and one North Carolina officer at each post on a dirt road south of the railroad of three men on post and six men and one officer at another road south of the railroad. Slept very uncomfortably on the floor of a small hut with nothing to cover me but my overcoat, my blankets not yet having arrived. The men were all comfortably in shanties.

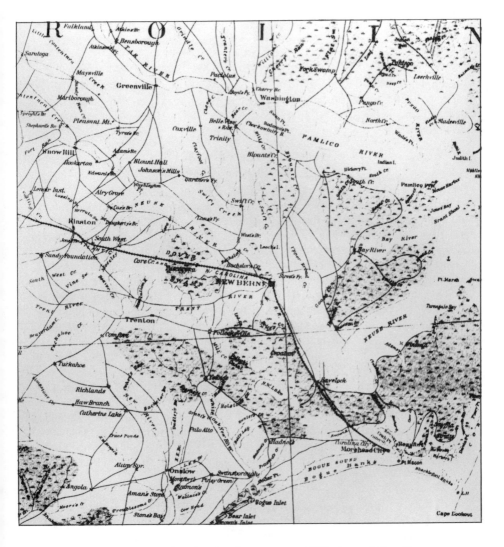

Map of North Carolina showing the area around Kinston and New Berne
O.R.A.: Plate CXXXVIII

Monday April 6th 1863

Was waked up at 4:00 a.m. and stood under arms till daybreak being the time most likely we would be attacked. In the morning was engaged in constructing a work of logs to defend our picket post on the Swamp Ford. Lieutenant [Thomas T.] Link, Company E superintended it in the afternoon. Received a letter from Mother dated April 4th. Weather fair in the morning but cloudy towards night very much like rain.

Tuesday April 7th 1863

Captain Maxwell received orders for Company E to report tomorrow at Wise Forks at 10:30 a.m. Wrote Mother. Made out a morning report for the command here and sent it [to] Colonel Jones by the guard staying here. Weather fair and pleasantly warm.

Wednesday April 8th 1863

Company E in compliance with orders received yesterday left this morning at 7:00 a.m. for Wise Forks. Wrote Father to [in] Raleigh. After dinner went out with a Mr. Evans the scout employed for this place for the purpose of seeing the country and as the men are suffering for something to eat owing to the cutting down of their provisions to one-fourth pound of meat per day also to kill a wild cow that are in the surrounding swamps. After marching about four miles we came upon two heifers, a yearling, and two calves. I managed to creep up to one heifer and shot her and then tried to kill some of the others but could not succeed. Neither the lieutenant or myself knew anything about [?]sticking cattle so we made a mess of it both in [?]sticking the heifer and in skinning her. But before we had finished skinning we got tired and came to camp and sent out some men to finish skinning her and bring her to camp. Weather fair and warm but cold night in the latter part of it.

Thursday April 9th 1863

Captain Maxwell received orders for Company F to hold itself in readiness to march tomorrow at 10:00 a.m. Captain Ellis Company F, his furlough being out returned to duty here. Heard the enemy were attacking Charleston, South Carolina and we Washington, North Carolina. My boy Pompey was taken sick with J [?jaundice] a [*sic*] and I sent him to the doctor at Wise Forks and returned about 3:00 p.m. with medicine. Weather fair and warm but frost in the morning.

Friday April 10th 1863

Company F was not ordered to march today as was expected. Nothing of any importance occurred to distract the monotony of outpost duty and the rising at 4:00 a.m. was punctually observed though it began to get very boring. Was much disappointed in not getting a letter from home but hope to get one tomorrow. Weather fair and warm very much like spring.

Saturday April 11th 1863

After dinner as the men were in want of meat I went out to kill a wild cow again but could not find one. Was much disappointed in not getting a letter from home today. Heard our forces had repulsed the enemy at Charleston on Tuesday and Wednesday sinking one monitor and disabling three more. Weather in the morning early foggy but warm and clear afterwards.

Sunday April 12th 1863

Remained in camp of picket guard all day. Wrote my grandfather to [in] Raleigh. In the morning went to the branch and took a good wash which made me feel much better. Captain Maxwell received orders for his company to cook one day's rations by 5:00 a.m. tomorrow. About sundown was attacked with the colic and till morning I suffered severely vomiting twice but it did not seem to relieve me. Took salt water and about a teaspoonful of sulphur and that seemed to relieve me a little but about 5:00 a.m. vomited a little and then went to sleep and awoke much better. Weather very warm and cloudy and fair by turns at night it thundered and rained.

Monday April 13th 1863

At 5:30 a.m. Captain Maxwell joined his company with Companies B and E and started in the direction of New Berne. I felt too sick to accompany them very much to my disappointment. It drizzled a little during the day. At about 12:00 p.m. Captain Maxwell returned with his company, the battalion having accomplished the object, i.e., putting a bridge across Core Creek. Towards evening felt much better though my bowels were very sore. Weather cleared up a little towards evening.

Tuesday April 14th 1863

My bowels felt much better though still sore. Companies E and B passed by on their way to regimental headquarters having passed the night before at Sandy Ridge. Some men from Company F stole four chickens from Mrs. Bucks last night and she having complained to Lieutenant Colonel Jones he ordered Captain Ellis to have her paid for them. Weather April showers.

Wednesday April 15th 1863

Received a letter from Mother dated April 13th saying she had been sick with chills and that the housekeeper also was very sick with pneumonia but that they were getting better. About 4:00 p.m. a courier arrived from Major Witherspoon saying the Yankees were advancing in heavy force up the railroad toward Core Creek. Captain Ellis commanding this post immediately sent a dispatch to Lieutenant Colonel Jones containing the news and he (Colonel Jones) sent in two companies B and E down to reinforce us. About 7:00 p.m. news came the enemy had fallen back and the two companies then went back to Wise Forks. Weather very rainy all day but cleared up at night. Wrote cousin Hazel Burgwyn.

Thursday April 16th 1863

Was in great hopes we would not be relieved today as we heard we would but at 2:00 p.m. two companies from the 49th [North Carolina Infantry] arrived to relieve us and at 4:20 p.m. we arrived at Wise Forks and remained there all night expecting we would go to Kinston tomorrow. Weather fair and cloudy but no rain.

Friday April 17th 1863

At 8:00 a.m. started with six companies of the regiment (the other four not having arrived from picket) and at 9:30 a.m. reached our camp one mile on the south of the Neuse River from Kinston. At 3:00 p.m. news having come that they were fighting at Core Creek our regiment received orders to go to Wise Forks and remained there. We found out there the Yankees in heavy force had advanced upon our men who only numbered one hundred and forty who held them in check an hour and five minutes and then fell back to Sandy Ridge about four miles. Casualties three killed and seven or eight wounded. The Yankees losses not known. Their number was four regiments. Weather fair and warm.

Saturday April 18th 1863

At about 1:00 a.m. Lieutenant Colonel Jones ordered the company to march down to the Gum Swamp and reinforce General Hill but I who slept in one of our ambulances did not know of it till about 7:00 a.m. but then walked down to where the company was. About 10:00 p.m. a dispatch arrived from Lieutenant Colonel Jones saying the enemy were advancing on the Neuse Road and consequently Lieutenant Colonel [John A.] Flemming of the 49th [North Carolina Infantry] in command at Sandy Ridge five miles below this post had to fall back to this place to prevent them from cutting him off. Company E of our regiment arrived about 11:30 p.m. to reinforce us. Received a letter from Grandpa dated April 16th. Weather fair and warm. Found out I was taking the itch but having washed in a strong solution of poke berry root which stung very much for a short time; awoke next morning almost well.

Sunday April 19th 1863

About 11:00 a.m. news came that the enemy were falling back on both roads (Neuse and Trent) and about 12:00 noon General Ransom and General [Beverly H.] Robertson with part of their staffs rode down to our pickets and there went back having as I imagine ordered Lieutenant Colonel Flemming to advance his command as far as Sandy Ridge. About 4:00 p.m. our three companies having been relieved by three companies of the 24th North Carolina Regiment we started for camp near Kinston which we reached at about 7:30 p.m. very tired. Weather fair and very warm.

Monday April 20th 1863

Remained all day in camp at 12:00 noon news came Lieutenant Colonel Flemming had had another attack and the Yankees charged him with cavalry. They fought one hour and twenty minutes, I believe, but do not know the casualties. The enemy drove our men a few hundred yards back but no farther. Weather very warm and fair but cloudy.

Tuesday April 21st 1863

At 9:00 a.m. Lieutenant Colonel Jones inspected the regiment but at 11:30 a.m. he came galloping up saying the regiment must march in fifteen minutes. Consequently in that time we started towards Kinston and took the road for Washington, North Carolina, and at 6:30 p.m. having marched in quick time reached our destination, "Covered" Bridge over the Contentnea Creek about thirteen miles from Kinston. Weather cloudy and cold and windy.

Wednesday April 22nd 1863

Sent my boy Pompey back to Kinston for my clothes I left there to be washed. Accompanied in the moving Lieutenant Barrows (Engineer Corps) to some batteries he was putting up on the Contentnea Creek. Wrote Mother. Weather cloudy and sunny at times; moderately warm.

Thursday April 23rd 1863

Our company was detailed with Companies E and K to work on some fortifications on the Neuse River about two and a half miles from camp but about 10:30 a.m. a storm came on and it rained in torrents for about three hours and then stopped and it also rained some about 4:00 a.m. Rained some more at night.

Friday April 24th 1863

Remained in camp all day. Cloudy all the evening but cleared up about night. Heard General Hill had arrived from Goldsboro at Kinston and that General Ransom was very sick with a fever.

Saturday April 25th 1863

About 12:00 noon obtained permission to be absent till tomorrow evening and having borrowed a horse from our quartermaster and started to visit General Pettigrew's brigade near Hookerton a distance of about thirteen miles. Found my brother (Colonel Burgwyn) at his camp he having just returned from a visit to Kinston. Found him well and looking very well. Weather fair and night cold. Received a letter from Mother dated April 23rd.

Sunday April 26th 1863

Wrote a letter yesterday night to Father about "Sultan"[24] and wrote one to Mother today after returning to our camp. Left Harry's regiment about 3:00 p.m. and reached ours at 5:30 p.m. Weather fair but cool and cold tonight.

Monday April 27th 1863

Our company and Company E was sent on fatigue duty and remained all day. Weather fair and hot all the day but rained some at night. Was invited to a picnic to take place tomorrow on the "Creek" about two miles from camp.

Tuesday April 28th 1863

Early I was awakened by the rain and was sorry to see it as I was afraid it would delay the picnic but about 11:00 a.m. it cleared up and we went and found a great many ladies. The company was composed entirely of country ladies and none of them pretty or entertaining. Had a very boring time and no dancing owing to ladies being mostly members of the church (Methodist or Baptist). At 9:15 p.m. received orders to march tomorrow at daybreak, that the Yankees were advancing and that they already had had a small fight; we heard the cannon. Weather cloudy and fair at times and rainy.

Wednesday April 29th 1863

At daybreak in pursuant to orders received yesterday, our regiment started for Kinston and at 11:30 a.m. reached its former camp in the east side of the Neuse River. Weather cloudy and fair and in the afternoon warm. My brother Harry's brigade having marched to Kinston today he called by and saw me a few minutes. Paid a visit to Bob Peebles in the 56th [North Carolina Infantry]. About dusk it clouded up and thundered and lightened and rained hard for a few minutes and then stopped. Wrote Aunt Emmy a long letter.

---

[24] W.H.S.B.'s horse which was at Thornbury.

Thursday April 30th 1863

Hearing there was a horse belonging to Dr. [E. A.] Thomas 56th North Carolina Infantry to be raffled off I took a chance and about 5:00 p.m. we all threw for him but Captain [Andrew J.] Miller, Quartermaster [of the] 25th North Carolina Infantry won him throwing in three throws with three dice 42. The tickets were at twenty-five dollars and after going to camp seeing the bill for reorganizing the staff of our army had passed I wrote Father a letter concerning it. Heard our pickets were firing with the enemy's at Gum Swamp. Weather fair and warm.

Friday May 1st 1863

Lieutenant Dixon started off at sunrise on a six day detail to go to Charlotte, North Carolina, to bring to the company eighteen recruits. Wrote Sister in the morning. Harry rode by for a minute and told me he was ordered off to Fredericksburg, Virginia, and would leave the same afternoon. I was very sorry to hear it. General Daniel's brigade came here today and camped below us a little way. Received a letter from Mother dated May 1st. Weather fair and warm. The ladies of Kinston gave a picnic today and had a Queen of May but I did not attend.

Saturday May 2nd 1863

Wrote my Grandfather and General W. H. C. Whiting, the latter in reference to his promise to appoint me in certain contingencies. Was excused from drill today owing to having a boil on my stomach which my pants hurt when walking. Weather fair and warm. General Daniel took command of Kinston and established headquarters there.

Sunday May 3rd 1863

Wrote Mother and read the lessons for the day in the Prayer Book and Bible. Received a letter from Grandpa dated May 3rd. Heard in the evening one of the two brigades (Ransom's or Daniel's) was ordered to Virginia but did not believe it.

Monday May 4th 1863

Remained in camp all day. Received some newspapers sent by Grandpa. Heard General Lee had by General Jackson getting in their rear completely routed General [Joseph] Hooker's army but that General Jackson was dangerously wounded. Weather fair and warm.

Tuesday May 5th 1863

Received a letter from General Whiting which was not as satisfactory as I would have wished it to have been. Heard Pettigrew's brigade had arrived as far as Hanover Junction by yesterday on their way to Fredericksburg. Weather fair and warm.

Wednesday May 6th 1863

Agreeable with orders received yesterday at 1:00 p.m. we started in company with Daniel's Brigade in the direction of New Berne and at 6:00 p.m. camped at Gum Swamp. Weather commenced raining at 1:00 p.m. and rained during the whole of the afternoon with one slight intermission very hard and at times as hard as I ever saw it did not clear off till about 12:00 midnight and then the sky did not clear up but it stopped raining.

Thursday May 7th 1863

At 8:00 a.m. started for Sandy Ridge and after marching through the worst road I ever saw full of water and black mud sometimes knee deep and constantly ankle deep we reached Sandy Ridge about 1:00 p.m. Remained there all day about dark. I was detailed to take charge of a picket guard of a dozen men and post myself three or four hundred yards below the encampment to stop any suspicious persons entering or leaving the camp. Daniel's Brigade about 8:45 p.m. passed by on their way back. The object of the expedition as I understand was to tear up the railroad and escort some refugees from New Berne that the Yankees had sent out of New Berne. Weather cloudy and cool.

Friday May 8th 1863

At 7:30 a.m. started for Kinston but when we came to Gum Swamp and had marched past it we were ordered to remain at Gum Swamp on picket. Our company was sent to the picket post on the ford and ordered to guard it all the time we remain here. Went out to a Mr. Hawkins and got a dinner. Some of Captain Maxwell's bed clothes were brought down on the commissary wagon and we made out very well for the night. Weather cloudy and cold all day.

Saturday May 9th 1863

Early in the morning sent Pompey to camp for some clothes; he returned about 3:00 p.m. and I wrote Mother and Harry and sent Harry's letter to Mother to send to him. Heard that we would be relieved tomorrow and hope it is so. Weather cloudy and cool in the morning but cleared up in the afternoon.

Sunday May 10th 1863

Received a letter from Mother dated May 7th. Was much disappointed in not being relieved today. Read the morning lesson in the Prayer Book but could not procure a Bible. Weather fair and warm; took a nice bath in the morning by having water poured over me.

Monday May 11th 1863

Remained in camp all day. Heard Colonel Ransom had arrived yesterday and intended to come down here but Colonel [Willliam J.] Clarke[25] [24th North Carolina Infantry] told him we would be relieved tomorrow. Was very sorrow to hear of General [Earl] Van Dorn's death and also of the cause of it was most mystifying to all Southerners.

Tuesday May 12th 1863

About 11:45 p.m. the relief from the 43rd North Carolina Infantry arrived and as soon as we could get off we started for camp which he reached about 4:00 p.m. Heard General [Edmund Kirby] Smith had whipped the enemy near New Orleans and that General Jackson's body had arrived in Richmond. Weather fair and hot.

---

[25] Clarke was the husband of Mary Bayard Devereux, sister of Major John Devereux and daughter of Thomas Pollok Devereux and Katherine Johnson.

Wednesday May 13th 1863

Passed almost all the day in the 56th North Carolina Infantry. Went swimming in the river in the afternoon but it was so cold could not swim much. Colonel Ransom appointed my friend Lieutenant Peebles (56th) [North Carolina] adjutant. Received some papers from Grandpa. Weather fair and hot. Colonel Ransom told me he had lost a letter given him by my Father to him for me.

Thursday May 14th 1863

Remained in camp all day. Was attacked with a severe headache in the afternoon but awoke next morning without it. Weather fair and warm but turned colder towards night and clouded up.

Friday May 15th 1863

Lieutenant Peebles having obtained a furlough to go home and get fitted out for his new position left today. Had company and battalion drill in the morning and afternoon. Received a letter from Father dated May 6th and 7th that he gave to Colonel Ransom for me but who having left it at home by mistake, Mrs. Ransom forwarded it to me.

Saturday May 16th 1863

Remained in camp all day. Wrote Mother and Father and sent it by Pompey early next morning who I sent home next day for a furlough for a week. Was disappointed in not getting a valise this afternoon by some men returning from furlough. Weather cloudy and fair at times a little rain at dark.

Sunday May 17th 1863

Sent Pompey home at daybreak to return Saturday. Wrote Mother having forgotten to give Pompey all my instructions. Weather fair and warm. Attended preaching in camp by the Reverend Mr. Russell of Fayetteville.

Monday May 18th 1863

Drilled our recruits in the morning but the afternoon was excused by the doctor on account of my bowels. Captain Maxwell sent three men on furlough. Weather fair and warm.

Tuesday May 19th 1863

Remained in camp all day. An order for the execution of a man for desertion in the 43rd North Carolina Regiment to take place at 12:00 noon tomorrow was published at dress parade and one regiment was detailed to execute the condemned. First Lieutenant [Henry W.] Humphrey, Company A, 35th North Carolina Regiment was detailed to command the executing party. Weather fair and warm.

Wednesday May 20th 1863

Went out with the regiment and brigade and Cooke's brigade to witness the execution of a man of the 43rd North Carolina Regiment condemned to be shot for desertion. It was a most painful sight and when after having prayed with his clergyman the front rank did not kill him and the rear rank then had to march up and shoot and they loaded again but it was unnecessary. Received a letter from Mother dated May 17th. Weather fair and warm.

Thursday May 21st 1863

At 2:00 p.m. the regiment was ordered on a working party to clear up a new camp about three-fourth [of a] mile off and about 4:00 p.m. we commenced to move and finished by night. Captain A. Obszwski, a Pole who after fighting for the "Liberty" of Poland and after the rebellion was crushed came to America in 1835 and is now going around with the different regiments in whom he can get a pass and having been able to get a pass in this regiment came here. Weather fair and warm.

Friday May 22nd 1863

About 8:30 a.m. news came that there was fighting at Gum Swamp and about 10:00 a.m. we started in that direction and were placed in the rifle pits at Jackson's Mill and as the enemy were expected to advance on us immediately I with twenty men was advanced as skirmishers but was called in in about an hour. The Yankees took six companies of the 56th [North Carolina Infantry] but Colonel [Paul F.] Faison escaped. About 5:00 p.m. we arrived [with]in about a mile and a half of Gum Swamp; we shelled the enemy in our pits at Gum Swamp. After shelling them out of the pits we pursued them as far as Sandy Ridge and halted for the night at about 10:00 p.m. At Gum Swamp the 27th [North Carolina Infantry] lost one man wounded in the leg by a shell that I know of. Weather fair and warm. I don't think I ever suffered more for thirst and fatigue.

Saturday May 23rd 1863

At 5:00 a.m. recommenced our march toward New Berne; at Core Creek five miles off we had a little artillery duel with the enemy getting one man in the 15th North Carolina Infantry wounded in the arm by a shell. At 6:00 p.m. having arrived near Batchelder's Creek opened with all our artillery (twenty pieces) but during the shelling the enemy advanced on our left and had a brisk skirmish with the 15th North Carolina Infantry which ended in our driving the enemy back. We then fell back three miles and halted for the night. The dust was almost suffocating and two or three men fainted and Captain [Stephen W.] Jones [46th North Carolina Infantry] had a slight sun stroke. Weather fair and warm.

Sunday May 24th 1863

Started for Kinston at 6:00 a.m. and about 9:00 a.m. reached Core Creek (five miles) stayed there till 6:00 p.m. My company and Company E were sent on picket. After a most severe march and a dreadfully dusty one we halted on the south side of Gum Swamp at 10:45 p.m. a distance of fifteen miles from our last night's bivouac. Weather fair and hot; the warmest day I think of this year.

Monday May 25th 1863

About 6:00 a.m. we started for Kinston and after one halt about a mile and a half off marched into camp about 9:00 a.m. Found all the tents of the men taken down and packed in the wagons. Lieutenant Peebles (Adjutant) returned to the regiment. Weather cloudy and so misty in the afternoon and rained at night.

Tuesday May 26th 1863

Remained in camp all day. Was much surprised that my boy Pompey did not return today since he was to return last Saturday evening. Recommenced my fencing lessons this morning. Weather cloudy and cool.

Wednesday May 27th 1863

About 9:00 a.m. heard we had to leave for Petersburg. The 25th [North Carolina] Regiment leaving first and our following. Captain Maxwell sent in his resignation today and had it approved by the Medical Examining Board.[26] Obtained permission to visit the plantation and stay a day. Weather fair and warm.

Thursday May 28th 1863

At 6:00 a.m. started in the train for Goldsboro. Arrived at about 8:00 a.m. and remained there till 1:30 p.m. and then started for Garysburg, Northampton County, North Carolina, but got off at Halifax and having obtained a horse from Mr. Peyton Hervay and a saddle from Mr. Henry Hervay I started for the plantation and reached it at 9:45 p.m. Sister awake but Mother was sick in bed with a severe sick headache. Father had gone to Raleigh. Weather fair and warm.

Friday May 29th 1863

Rode out in the morning with Mother in the open carriage. Was much pleased with the fine appearance of the crops and particularly the wheat. Weather rained at intervals and a little during the day. Was glad to see my horse "Sultan" had improved very much since I last saw him being much better. Became acquainted with Mr. Williamson (overseer). Sent back at 7:00 a.m. the horse I borrowed from Mr. Peyton Hervay of Halifax.

Saturday May 30th 1863

Started for Garysburg to overtake my regiment that I judged had passed in its way to Virginia but two and a half miles of Garysburg met [illegible] (Captain Gee's) boy who told me the regiment would not pass till tomorrow evening. Turned back and called on Colonel Ransom and am to send up to him tomorrow morning to see when the regiment will leave. Rode on horseback in the afternoon. Felt unwell with an attack of diarrhea. Weather fair and warm. Mother received a letter from Father saying he would be down on the next train.

Sunday May 31st 1863

Sent up early in accordance with promise to Colonel Ransom to find where I should leave but had to send up again in the afternoon as he did not know. Father arrived at 12:30 p.m. which I was very glad of indeed. Had my horse "Sultan" ridden and was much pleased with his appearance when under saddle. Rode out with Father and Mother in the open carriage in the afternoon. Felt much better, Aunt Bettie[27] having given me some medicine for my diarrhea. Weather rain and warm.

Monday June 1st 1863

Sent a boy in the morning to Colonel Ransom's to know when I should start and he sent word at 7:00 p.m. At 9:00 a.m. went with Father to Jackson; while there I called upon Mrs. [Louisa A.] Newsom[28] and had a pleasant visit. Returned about

---

[26] Captain Maxwell resigned on May 28, 1863, because of "general debility and want [of] physical stamina." His resignation would be accepted on June 23, 1863. Later he served as Colonel of the 85th Regiment North Carolina Militia. Lieutenant Dixon also resigned on May 27, 1863; no reason is given. (*N.C. Troops*, IX, p. 427.)

[27] Probably a house slave (Margaret Burgwyn Cooley).

[28] 1813-1888; member of The Church of the Savior in Jackson, North Carolina.

2:00 p.m. At 7:00 p.m. started by Garysburg but when I arrived at Colonel Ransom's I found I need not got there next morning. Returned home. Weather warm and fair.

Tuesday June 2nd 1863

At 7:00 a.m. started for Garysburg and was much disappointed in not seeing Colonel Ransom but at 9:45 a.m. took the train for Petersburg. Met our commissary Captain Gee. Arrived at 3:15 p.m. at Petersburg and found the regiment about three miles from the city. Received a letter from Harry dated May 30th also one from Mother and Father. Weather fair and warm.

Wednesday June 3rd 1863

Remained in camp all day. Colonel Ransom returned to camp from home. Heard we had been offered the position of guarding the country around here but do not know if Colonel Ransom intends to accept it. Wrote Mother and Harry and a letter in reply to one Captain Maxwell received from Lieutenant Charles L. Gibson 63rd [North Carolina] Regiment (Cavalry). Weather cloudy and cool and about 8:30 p.m. it commenced to rain and rained very hard for about one hour and then stopped. It also rained from about 3:00 to 7:00 a.m.

* * * *

Camp 35th North Carolina Regiment near
Petersburg, Virginia, June 3rd 1863

Dear Mother,

In ample time I arrived at Garysburg and as I expected did not find Colonel Ransom and he did not come at all. I thought I had remained as long at home as I ought to and therefore started by myself.

When I arrived at Petersburg 3:00 p.m. I was most agreeably surprised to find the regiment camped only about 3 miles from the city and Colonel Clark told me he thought it would remain here some time for the brigade is scattered to the four winds of heaven. The 25th and 56th at Richmond and the 24th and 49th at Blackwater and the 35th the only regiment of the brigade here.

I as I always do experienced most gratefully your foresight and kindness in the nice lunch you put up for me for after getting in the train I went to sleep and when I awoke up felt very hungry and Captain Gee (Commissary) who happened to be along being hungry I invited him to join me and it would have done your heart good to have heard his encomiums on the lunch.

While asleep as the train arrived at a station called Hicks Ford[29] there was a number of young ladies present who came to see their friends on the cars and among them was Miss Mildred Lee[30] your personification of all that is lovely and good in a woman. She I understand is staying at a Mr. Cooks at Hicks Ford. I was very sorry that I was asleep at the time.

---

[29] Present day Emporia, Virginia, on the Meherrin River, along the (then) Weldon and Petersburg Railroad.

[30] Youngest daughter of General Robert E. Lee. She attended St. Mary's College in Raleigh, North Carolina, in 1862 and 1863.

General Ransom has certainly been promoted and assigned to the command of North Carolina and General Hill of the Department of Southern Virginia and North Carolina.

I received a letter from Harry yesterday dated May 30th. He says "he thinks he will remain there unless General Lee advances into Maryland which he of course cannot tell about but that he imagines he does not intend to advance as he has just approved of a number of furloughs for officers and men of his regiment."

We had a most powerful rain from 3:00 to 7:00 a.m. today and it burst through my tent and inundated my bed which was nothing but a pool of water. How different from my last four or five night's resting place. I hope you had such a rain at home. I must close now. Give my love to all.

Your most affectionate son,
W.H.S. Burgwyn, Lieutenant

* * * *

Thursday June 4th 1863

Remained in camp all day. Was busily occupied in making out a descriptive roll and clothing account for the company. Had company drill in the a.m. Weather I think it rained at night but am not certain.

Friday June 5th 1863

Had company drill both in the a.m. and p.m. Weather fair in the day and warm but rained some at 8:00 p.m. Was still engaged in my descriptive roll and clothing account. Yesterday Lieutenant Kelly, Company C started for Amelia City [Virginia] with thirty men about to apprehend deserters from General Lee's Army that go that way in their retreat.

Saturday June 6th 1863

Lieutenant Colonel Jones and Adjutant Peebles went to a picnic about three miles off and enjoyed themselves much. Lieutenant Dixon and ten men from my company were sent on picket about two and a half miles near the river. The men were ordered to put up [illegible]. Weather fair and very warm but at night clouded up and seemed very much like rain but did not rain.

Sunday June 7th 1863

Attended preaching by the Reverend Mr. Russell of Fayetteville, North Carolina. Was disappointed in not receiving a letter from Mother. Heard it rumored that there had been another fight on the Rappahannock. Weather cloudy and fair and cloudy and cold night.

Monday June 8th 1863

Remained in camp all day. Had battalion and company drill. Nothing of any consequence occurred today. Weather fair and cool and cold in the night.

Tuesday June 9th 1863

Nothing of any consequence occurred today to distract the monotony of camp routine. Colonel Ransom went home in the night train. Weather fair and pleasant.

Wednesday June 10th 1863

Was much annoyed by a boil which hinders me from walking but drilled twice nevertheless. Received a letter from Mother dated June 9th. Weather fair and warm. A fatigue party of one hundred and fifty men and five officers under charge of Captain [Thomas J.] Blackwell was made.

Thursday June 11th 1863

Wrote Mother a letter this morning. My boil hurt me so much that I was not able to drill during the day. Weather cloudy and cool for June. Heard of the severe fight our cavalry had near Culpeper Court House and was very sorry to hear of the death of Colonel [Solomon] Williams[31] of the 2nd North Carolina Cavalry.

Friday June 12th 1863

The remainder of our brigade arrived today from Blackwater and continued on to Drewry's Bluff where they expect a fight. Two thousand men having landed below Fort Powhatan and six thousand at Mason's farm and two gunboats and two transports were going up the Chickahominy [River]. Weather fair and warm. Heard Pettigrew's Brigade is at Culpeper Court House.

Saturday June 13th 1863

Having obtained permission I started for Petersburg at 3:30 p.m. but on the way met a courier with a letter for Colonel Ransom and Adjutant Peebles; having opened it found we had to leave that evening for Fort Powhatan. At 6:00 p.m. started for Fort Powhatan; just as we started General [Micah] Jenkins' Brigade arrived at 10:00 p.m. Halted at a Church called [blank in original—probably Merchant's Hope Church] about two miles from camp. Wrote Grandpa in the morning. Weather fair and warm.

Sunday June 14th 1863

Started at about 5:00 a.m. and marched four miles farther and halted till 9:30 a.m. Then started back for camp and arrived at camp about 3:00 p.m. having marched eighteen miles. Weather cloudy.

Monday June 15th 1863

After morning dress parade went to town. While there heard Colonel Ransom had been promoted which was certainly so. Called on a Miss Jordan from Norfolk and heard some nice music. Took dinner at Jarratts Hotel which cost me $3.00. Weather fair and warm.

Tuesday June 16th 1863

Owing to a conversation I had with Lieutenant Dixon I determined to send in my resignation the next morning.[32] I succeeded in getting the officers to call upon General Ransom and congratulate him on his promotion and he answered us in a very feeling speech. Weather fair and warm. Dr. O'Hagan our surgeon in our behalf complimented General Ransom on his promotion.

---

[31] Son of Henry Guston Williams and Elizabeth Arrington.

[32] The reason for W.H.S.B.'s resignation is probably related to a dispute over his rank; see the letter of July 18, 1863.

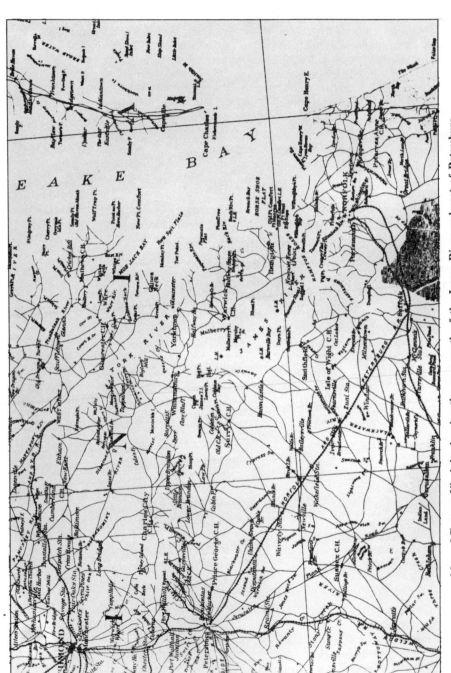

Map of Eastern Virginia showing the area south of the James River and east of Petersburg

O.R.A.: Plate CXXXVII

Wednesday June 17th 1863

In the morning sent in my resignation which Lieutenant Colonel Jones was kind enough to approve. General Ransom sent for me about 10:00 a.m. to come to him in town and when I came (having borrowed Lieutenant Peebles' horse) he only wanted to ask me why I resigned. At 8:00 p.m. I was sent in charge of my company on picket at a Mr. Beasley's two miles from camp. Wrote Father a letter telling him about my resignation. Weather fair and hot.

Thursday June 18th 1863

Started for City Point at 5:30 a.m. and about 9:00 a.m. reached City Point [33] a distance of about eight miles from Petersburg. At 8:00 p.m. it commenced to blow and shortly to rain and rained all night. Went in swimming in the afternoon.

Friday June 19th 1863

It rained till about 12:00 noon and then looked very much like rain though the sun sometimes made its appearance. Wrote my brother Harry. It having rained so hard in the day it was too wet to work on the fortifications in the morning but in the afternoon the right wing [of the 35th North Carolina Infantry] under Lieutenant Colonel [James T.] Johnson was sent to work on the works but a boat with a flag of truce having made its appearance they were sent back and were allowed to show themselves. It brought up about eighty sick and wounded. Cloudy.

Saturday June 20th 1863

The left wing being detailed to work on fortifications this morning. I in charge of my company was put to work on a redoubt. My Father arrived in Petersburg yesterday from home and came down on the train that brought the Yankee prisoners to be exchanged to see me. He was much put out at my resigning. He returned to Petersburg about 2:00 p.m. intending to go the same afternoon to Richmond and return on Monday.

Sunday June 21st 1863

Received orders at 3:00 a.m. to start off as soon as possible for Petersburg. We arrived at our old camps about 8:00 a.m. and found the 49th [North Carolina Infantry] just leaving going to Drewry's Bluff. We after resting a short time started to Petersburg but were stopped at the suburbs and sent back to our old camps. Weather cloudy and misty and about 4:30 p.m. it rained some and also rained a good deal at night. Received a letter yesterday that Father wrote me from Jarretts Hotel yesterday.

Monday June 22nd 1863

Received orders at 2:00 p.m. to start in an hour for Petersburg and as soon as the men could be got on the train after arriving at Petersburg we started for Drewry's Bluff. Arrived opposite Drewry's Bluff about 6:00 p.m. met there the trains from Richmond and saw my Father on it. He settled everything there he went to Richmond for. Weather fair and warm.

---

[33] Present day Hopewell, Virginia.

Tuesday June 23rd 1863

Before breakfast went to see Drewry's Bluff and was very much pleased with the fortifications and especially with an ironclad battery of those guns. Weather fair and warm.

Wednesday June 24th 1864

Remained in camp all day. Had battalion drill in the afternoon. Was very much pleased with what I saw. Weather in the afternoon a little rain and rained much in the night.

Thursday June 25th 1863

At 1:00 p.m. received orders to cook three days' rations and be ready to move at a moment's notice. At 6:00 p.m. started in the direction of Richmond taking the pontoon bridge road. At Rockets Hill took the Charles City Road and at 12:00 midnight arrived at the outer line of breastworks five miles from Richmond. Weather rained all day and night and the roads were dreadful. I think it was the worst march we ever had because we in the rear did not halt but once and then for only three minutes. Traveled about fourteen miles.

Friday June 26th 1863

Remained where we halted last night all day. Rumors were afloat that twenty-five thousand or thirty thousand Yankees had landed at White House and were marching on Richmond. Stopped drizzling about 11 a.m. and cleared up. It rained very hard for a short time during the night.

Saturday June 27th 1863

Obtained permission to visit the battle ground of "Seven Pines." I could only see some bones of Yankees who were buried so shallow that they had been dug up by the dogs. I visited the field where the 48th North Carolina Regiment charged five regiments of the enemy and drove them back and where our regiment stood picket one night and were surprised by the Yankees but finally drove them back. Weather cloudy but not rain.

Sunday June 28th 1863

About 6:00 a.m. we received orders to march immediately and as soon as we could get ready we started in the direction of the Williamsburg Road which from where we were on the Charles City Road and to where we halted on the Williamsburg Road about a quarter of a mile in rear of our breastworks was in a northwestern direction as far as I could judge. Remained here all day and put up our tent flies. Weather cloudy and like rain but no rain fell.

Monday June 29th 1863

Remained in camp on the Williamsburg Road. Drew a large quantity of clothing and issued them out. Paid a business visit to General Matt Ransom. Weather remained same during the day and night.

Tuesday June 30th 1863

Rained all the morning but at 12:00 noon it began to clear up. Nothing to do and felt very much disgusted with remaining here and also with the swampiness of the ground.

Wednesday July 1st 1863

The brigade started at 5:00 a.m. to throw down some Yankee entrenchments about three miles from camp. Each regiment worked half an hour at a time. Finished about 1:00 p.m. Remained there till 6:00 p.m. and then marched to camp. Weather fair and warm.

Thursday July 2nd 1863

The regiment started about day break and in advance of the brigade and marched to Bottom's Bridge about seven miles. The remainder of the brigade with Jenkins' and Cooke's brigades and two batteries under Major [James R.] Branch followed and it then became apparent that General Hill intended to fight the Yankees as they would not fight us. At 3:00 p.m. Jenkins' Brigade and our regiment advanced [a]cross the Bottom's Bridge over the Little Chickahominy. Cooke's Brigade followed about 5:00 p.m. As soon as Jenkins' Brigade arrived where the Yankees were they commenced skirmishing and about 6:30 p.m. our brigade and Cooke's having arrived we [started] the battle with our artillery but the enemy did not stand long only firing five or six shots and then retreated. We immediately followed but did not with our brigade follow them up more than one and a half miles but part of Jenkins' Brigade and Holcombe's Legion (Cavalry) and one piece of artillery followed them four miles. We returned to Bottom's Bridge by 12:30 p.m. The 24th [North Carolina] Regiment lost one man killed and Jenkins' Brigade three or four wounded. Weather fair and hot.

Friday July 3rd 1863

Our regiment did not go with the remainder of the troops back to camp but remained as pickets. Went in swimming in the afternoon in the Little Creek Chickahominy. Weather fair and very hot. Received a letter from Father dated June 28th.

Saturday July 4th 1863

Our regiment on fatigue duty in the morning to strengthen the entrenchments at Bottom's Bridge. Went about half mile from camp and got any quantity of good dewberries. Weather fair and hot. Heard General Lee was between Hooker and Washington City and [within] five miles of Washington City and that [General John B.] Magruder had taken New Orleans but do not believe either of the reports.

Sunday July 5th 1863

Remained in camp all day. Had preaching twice by the Reverend Mr. [Isaac G.] McLoughlin[34] of Charlotte, North Carolina, who came to see his son in my company. About 11:00 a.m. news came that the enemy had driven in our pickets at the cross roads about four miles from camp. Weather fair and very hot. Very much like rain.

---

[34] Clergyman of the Associated Reformed Presbyterian Church in Mecklenburg County, North Carolina.

Monday July 6th 1863

At 6:00 a.m. Colonel Jones with two hundred picked men started in accordance with orders from General Hill to drive in the enemy's pickets below the crossroads. At 9:30 we arrived in front of the enemy's picket post in a Mr. Talley's field about one and a half miles from our post at the crossroads. Colonel Jones had with him about fifty cavalry of Holcombe's Legion; as soon as the enemy saw us they charged us with about a dozen cavalry and as our regiment was placed where it had halted in the road in a deep cut up a hill the banks I should think fifteen feet high on either side and where the enemy came a shooting and making a tremendous noise and driving four of our cavalry before them who were sent out as decoys. It frightened the men very much and Colonel Jones galloping up to its head after some few missed orders gave the order to fall back and there was a tremendous scattering by the men trying to get up the bank out of the way of the cavalry but we soon formed at the foot of the hill and prepared to charge when Colonel Jones got orders that a strong body of the enemy were coming down the railroad and were turning his flank. We then fell back about on two miles leaving Captain [Robert E.] Petty [Company D] and about a dozen of his men on picket by mistake but they came in in about an hour. At 2:00 p.m. we came to our camp. Weather commenced a slight rain at 2:00 p.m. and continued till about 5:00 p.m. but when we came to camp found it had rained there much harder and longer.

Tuesday July 7th 1863

Weather rainy and misty all day and rained very hard at night. Our wagons, etc., arrived about 5:00 p.m. and well for us that they did arrive or we would have had a dreadful night. Heard the glorious news that Lee had captured forty thousand men of Meade's army and believe it to be true.

Wednesday July 8th 1863

Wrote Mother a letter this morning. Weather rained almost all day and about 10:00 a.m. it commenced in earnest and rained in torrents for about two hours. Heard the report of Lee capturing forty thousand Yankees confirmed but was much depressed though I do not credit the rumor that Vicksburg had fallen.

Thursday July 9th 1863

I was sent with my company on picket this morning at the railroad bridge over the Little Chickahominy to relieve Captain [Sanford G.] Howie, Company F. Was engaged in making out my muster and pay rolls for May and June. Began to believe Vicksburg has fallen in reality and am very much depressed about it. Had a most miserable night on account of the myriad of mosquitos. Weather fair and hot.

Friday July 10th 1863

Was engaged for a short time in my pay and muster rolls today. Weather cloudy but very warm. Had another miserable night on account of the mosquitos which were in greater numbers than I ever saw. Heard the sad intelligence that Vicksburg had certainly fallen and also heard General Lee had fallen back to Hagerstown, [Maryland], on account of provisions.

Saturday July 11th 1863

Was relieved this morning about 10:00 a.m. by Captain Blackwell's Company B. When I returned to camp found Captain [Joseph M.] Rogers had almost finished paying the regiment and I hastened to finish my pay rolls and was paid for my company $1,736.40. Weather cloudy and warm. Received a letter from Mother dated 7th.

Sunday July 12th 1863

About 2:00 p.m. news came we had to leave immediately and consequently as soon as we could get ready we got on the train at Meadow Station and arrived soon after in Richmond where we remained all night waiting for transportation. [?]Hood, General Ransom's courier, sent me word by a sick man that my brother Harry had been killed at Gettysburg, Virginia [Pennsylvania]. I could not bear to believe it and do not. I endeavored to find out something about it at Richmond in the Express Office but could not. It rained very hard from 2:00 p.m. to 4:00 p.m. and we were in it all. Wrote Mother a long letter but owing to the news I heard did not send it.

Monday July 13th 1863

At about 5:30 p.m. we took the passenger car for Petersburg. After getting off the train Major [John] Farrell Brigade Quartermaster told me the report of Harry's death was certainly incorrect and I immediately telegraphed Mother to that effect. Marched out to Dunn's Hill and camped opposite an old camp about one hundred and fifty yards. Weather rained almost all the afternoon but none at night.

Tuesday July 14th 1863

Obtained permission to visit Petersburg this morning and when I got there found that I could hope no longer that my dear beloved brother who I had just begun to appreciate for his good and noble qualities was [not] taken from us by the hands of hireling mercenaries.[35] I can hardly bear the thought of losing him and have no one to console with me. I am indeed wretched and to think that I yesterday telegraphed my dear Mother that he was not killed and to have today to let her know she must hope no longer is indeed hard to bear but had some consolation in writing her a letter. Weather rainy and cloudy. Rained sometimes very hard rained during the night.

Wednesday July 15th 1863

Wrote Father a letter this morning. Felt badly all day with pain in my bowels and my brother's death presses with a heavy load on my heart and I find difficulty believing or realizing it. Weather cloudy but sultry and very warm.

Thursday July 16th 1863

Obtained permission to visit Petersburg today. Called on a Mrs. Page[36] who was a particular friend of my late brother but she was not at home. Heard the reports of my brother's death were incorrect but such a report is ridiculous. Weather rained some during the day and cloudy.

---

[35] Colonel Henry K. Burgwyn, Jr., was killed July 1, 1863, at Gettysburg.

[36] Mrs. Caroline M. Page resided on Washington Street between Jefferson and Madison. She had entertained Henry K. Burgwyn, Jr., during his court martial duties earlier in the war. Not listed in the 1860 Petersburg *City Directory*, she may have been a refugee or parent of a soldier. She apparently was a friend of the Burgwyn family.

Friday July 17th 1863

Received a very consoling letter from my dear Mother dated July 14th; she happily seemed resigned to the heavy affliction. At 1:30 p.m. received orders to move to a new camp at Robinson farm near the Factory but when we got to the city we were immediately put on the train and sent to Drewry's Bluff. On arriving there we were put in the winter quarters put up by Daniel [and] are good [and] straight now. Wrote General Pettigrew a letter. Weather rainy and cloudy all the day.

Saturday July 18th 1863

Remained quietly here all day. Wrote Mother a letter in answer to the one I received yesterday. Saw in the New York *Herald* that General Pettigrew had been killed while defending the rear of General Lee's Army in recrossing the Potomac and all his brigade taken prisoner. Weather fair and warm.

* * * *

Camp 35th North Carolina Regiment at
Drewry's Bluff July 18th 1863

My dearest Mother,

Never have I been more fully conscious of the kindness of heaven for allowing me such dear parents than yesterday when I received your letter of the 14th instant. Oh how I longed to hear from home but I did not expect a letter so soon as I thought you would not able to write immediately but I have derived so much consolation from your letter and it is written in such a resigned state that it raises the load on my heart immeasurably.

I wish dear Father could have written a few lines for I want very much to hear from him and I know he feels poor Harry's loss so much that I am afraid it will make him sick and he has not so much assistance from God as you have, dear Mother, and it is therefore so much harder for him to bear up. But God has decreed that we should lose the beloved one and we should be thankful that he permitted Harry to die so peacefully and with so much resignation and who can doubt after such a peaceful death but that he was received into God's own abode. I hope by this time you and Father have received my two letters written from Petersburg which we left immediately after I received your letter and we came here by the cars.

Immediately after receiving your letter I sat down to write you but orders came to leave and I then determined to write an application to General Pettigrew as I would have time to do that but while on the cars from Petersburg here I saw in the "New York Herald" that Pettigrew was killed defending the rear of Lee's army while crossing the Potomac and that his brigade were all captured and also that General Pettigrew's body was in the Yankee's hands; though it was in a Yankee paper I doubt not it is true as it was an official dispatch from General Meade to General Halleck. This is indeed an hour of sadness and gloom but we will emerge from it soon and more to be feared than ever.

Enclosed I sent you a copy of a note I received from a Mrs. C.M. Page at whose house Harry stayed when he was on Court Martial [duty] last winter in Petersburg to show you how much he was admired and loved by all those who knew him. He is spoken of on all occasions and by all with the highest consideration. I wrote you a letter from "Bottom's Bridge, Little Chickahominy River" proposing to get a position in the North Carolina Troops but I addressed the letter to Garysburg and as you do not mention it I suppose you have not received it.

After much deliberation I have thought if I could get a position in the North Carolina Troops as lieutenant colonel or even major my position would be much improved and it would be an easier way to get out of present difficulties. Bob Peebles has written to his brother to get him a position and General Ransom told him he would try and get him a majority and that he (General Ransom) had just as soon have a position in the North Carolina Troops as his present one if it were of the same rank. I shall take no farther steps in the matter till Father writes me his opinions on the subject. If I could get such a position I would always be near you and Father and would possibly be able to do something for myself while there is no possibility to do so here. If Father will agree to my trying to get the position I will get General Ransom and Matt Ransom's recommendation. My present position is still undecided. General Ransom calls me captain and Colonel Jones, lieutenant. General Ransom told me he ordered Colonel Jones to let me go up as it was foolishness in him to endeavor to prevent me from going up and I consider myself as captain though I would not have you address me as such yet. General Ransom day before yesterday asked me how I would like captaincy of a company of sharpshooters. I told him very much. He then said he had written recommending me to the Secretary of War to be attached to his brigade. I do not wish to trouble you and Father with my details but I write them as I think I ought to inform you of everything concerning myself and you have always been most ready and willing to do all you can for me and such details have never been considered by you as troublesome.

I am truly sorry to hear Colonel Hughes is in a dying condition from his wounds. Poor fellow may God let him live for his father's and mother's sake. By all means send me a copy of Captain [Joseph J.] Young's letter. I want to know how dear Harry spent his last moments on this earth and where they have buried him for we must bring him where kind friends will always be near him, and who may by their tears pay a fitting mark of affection for him who when living was the center of our hopes and love. Recollect that when I write you dear Mother I write Father. Tell him may he stand up under the heavy blow and that I and the rest of the children will endeavor to make up for the loss of poor Harry and try to imitate him in our unvarying obedience to his wishes.

Goodbye dearest Mother and thank our Father you are resigned.

Love to all,
W.H.S. Burgwyn

* * * *

Sunday July 19th 1863

Received a letter from Mother dated July 17th. The Yankees' gunboats turned back and there are no more now this side of City Point. Weather fair and very hot.

Monday July 20th 1863

Had company and battalion drill but I did not attend. Wrote Father a letter. Weather fair and very warm. Received order at 9:00 p.m. to be ready to move tomorrow at 4:00 a.m.

Tuesday July 21st 1863

At 4:00 a.m. we got ready to move and marched down the railroad opposite our camp. Took the train for Petersburg. Marched from Petersburg to our old camp at Dunn's farm. Received a letter from Father dated July 17th. Weather fair and very hot.

Wednesday July 22nd 1863

Remained in camp all the morning. At 3:00 p.m. received a note from Bob Peebles who was in town that caused me immediately to go to town. Called on Mrs. C.M. Page after tea and passed a very pleasant two hours. Returned to camp about 11:45 p.m. Weather fair and very hot. Wrote Father a letter.

Thursday July 23rd 1863

Got permission to visit the city again on important private business that I did not finish yesterday. Wrote Mother a short note to send me by express my uniform. Returned to camp about 6:45 p.m. Mrs. C.M. Page called to see me as she was riding on horseback in this direction and presented me with a handsome bouquet.

Friday July 24th 1863

Attended company drill in the morning. Received an invitation from Mrs. Limuel Peebles[37] to spend the coming evening with her but I had previously accepted an invitation from Mrs. C.M. Page. About 7:00 p.m. presented myself at Mrs. Page's. Had supper about 8:00 p.m. Passed a very pleasant evening. Colonel [Leroy M.] McAfee and Captain [Cicero] Durham, 49th North Carolina Regiment, were there. About 11:00 p.m. Captain Petty and myself started for camp. Weather fair and very hot.

Saturday July 25th 1863

About 8:00 a.m. was detailed to go on a picket and relieve Captain [Philip J.] Johnson Company K on the Jerusalem [Plank] Road about three miles distant from camp. Passed a wretched night owing to having washing [*sic*] in a strong tea of poke [berry] root to cure me of the ground tick and which tea was so very severe gave me a terrible headache. Weather fair and very hot.

Sunday July 26th 1863

Remained on picket all day. Was very much tormented by the ground tick and washed again in poke tea which made me suffer very much and I do not think was of much avail. Weather fair and very hot. Sent yesterday Lieutenant Dixon and Private P.B. Hodges on recruiting service and Corporal A. Grier Hunter and Private I. C. [?Cornelius D.] Earnhardt and J.L. Shaffer on furlough.

Monday July 27th 1863

I was relieved by company A. About 3:00 p.m. orders came to be ready to move at a moment's notice and at 7:00 p.m. orders came to move. We went to Petersburg and took the mail train for Weldon. Weather at 11:00 a.m. took to raining and rained very hard during most of the afternoon. Received a letter from Father dated July 25th.

---

[37] Resided at the corner of Tabb and Union.

Tuesday July 28th 1863

Was sent early in the morning by General Matt Ransom with five of my men on a scouting expedition and I was to mount them at my Father's and Uncle's. At 3:00 p.m. my men having arrived and I after considerable difficulty obtained the horses and accouterments and having given them a good dinner we started for Boone's Crossroads about four miles when there heard heavy artillery firing at Boone's Mill but not thinking it of any consequence started for Jackson when I heard General Ransom was but in two miles of I found that the enemy had taken possession of Jackson and were fighting our men at Boone's Mill. I then returned by way of Boone's Crossroads to my father's and after sending out a picket to find out the news at our picket post at Faisons' Mill and they reporting everything quiet I had supper cooked and went to sleep. Weather.

Wednesday July 29th 1863

Started at 2:00 a.m. to report to General Ransom who I found at his house. Took breakfast with him and then accompanied him till he sent me with my squad; took a dispatch to Colonel C. Clarke near Garysburg. On returning found the general gone and intended to follow him but heard a report that there were twenty-five drunken Yankees at a Mr. Dorsey Deloach's Mill a mile off. Sent a dispatch to General Ransom asking him to send me some more men and I would capture them. He had none to send me but I started after the Yankees with my three and a picket of Griffin's Cavalry of five men. Found the Yankees between six and seven hundred strong at Deloach's Mill. I then reported to General Ransom and went home to feed my horses and men. Weather cloudy and rainy. I rode today at least fifty miles and was *very* much exhausted and sore.

Thursday July 30th 1863

Joined General Ransom at Boone's Mill about 9:00 a.m. He handed me a dispatch from my Father saying he had arrived at Garysburg last night and to send up the buggy for him this morning. Sent one of my men back to Mr. Williamson[38] with a note to send the buggy. At 11:00 a.m. went out with some of [Colonel Joel R.] Griffin's men and of Captain Barham's men on a scout to Deloach's Mill and when I arrived there found the enemy had retreated after burning the mill and bridge. Reported back to General Ransom. Met my Father while at dinner at Mr. Newsom's. Returned with Father in the buggy to plantation my men accompanying me. Weather cloudy and a little rain.

Friday July 31st 1863

After breakfast and in accordance with orders from General Ransom dismissed my men and sent them to their companies. I returned to camp about 5:00 p.m. and found them on the road to Garysburg five miles from home. Took supper at Bob Peebles. Weather fair and hot.

Saturday August 1st 1863

Took breakfast with Bob Peebles and stayed with him till about 10:00 a.m. when we heard the brigade was ordered to Garysburg. He (Bob Peebles) carried me to Garysburg in his buggy. Slept with my men. Weather was hot and fair.

---

[38] Overseer for Henry K. Burgwyn, Sr., on Thornbury Plantation.

Sunday August 2nd 1863

Took dinner with General Person and after dinner my buggy having brought me some vegetables I obtained permission to go home. Gave a watermelon to my men and some cucumbers and visited some of my friends. Arrived at home about 7:00 a.m. Found Father very well. Weather very hot and fair.

Monday August 3rd 1863

Went deer hunting with my friend Bob Peebles and Dr. [Andrew] Peebles[39] his brother but unfortunately did not get any deer. Stayed home all day. Received a letter yesterday from Sister dated August 1st. Weather fair and very hot.

Tuesday August 4th 1863

Stayed home all day. Rode out with Father in the buggy in the morning and afternoon. Received a note by our mail boy from Colonel Jones ordering me to report for duty at once as I had no officers for duty in the company. Weather very hot and fair. This day twelve months ago I was elected First Lieutenant of Company H, 35th North Carolina Regiment.

Wednesday August 5th 1863

About 9:00 a.m. started for camp; found the regiment about one-half mile from Garysburg. Had battalion drill in the afternoon. After drill obtained permission to visit Weldon and returned at 9:00 p.m. Weather fair and very hot.

Thursday August 6th 1863

Remained in camp all day. Had company drill in the morning and battalion drill in the afternoon. Weather very hot and fair.

Friday August 7th 1863

Had two drills as customary. Today obtained permission to go home tomorrow to remain till Sunday afternoon and sent my boy Pompey to bring the buggy up for me. Weather very hot but cloudy and rained a little during the day.

Saturday August 8th 1863

At daybreak Colonel Jones received orders for us to go to Rocky Mount [North Carolina] and about 8:00 a.m. we took the train at Garysburg for Rocky [Mount] which we reached about 12:00 noon, a distance of thirty-five miles. Bivouacked almost one half mile from the town where the 52nd and 47th North Carolina Regiments of Pettigrew's brigade camped last year. Weather very hot and rain.

Sunday August 9th 1863

Remained quietly in camp all day. Went in swimming in the Tar River in the afternoon but found the river very muddy. Weather fair and very hot. Our camp was in a most awfully hot pinery where no air could reach us.

---

[39] Andrew Peebles, older brother of Bob Peebles, lived in Northampton County.

Monday August 10th 1863

Adjutant Peebles arrived this morning from Raleigh where he went to get some uniform cloth for the officers of the regiment but he could not succeed. Moved the regiment at 5:00 p.m. to a cool grove of oaks about one half mile north of the town near by the railroad. Went in swimming again but was more disgusted than ever with the dirtiness of the water. Weather fair and very hot.

Tuesday August 11th 1863

About 4:00 p.m. a train arrived from Goldsboro and the Captain said for the purpose of bringing our regiment to Weldon and to carry back the 49th [North Carolina] Regiment to Tarboro. Colonel Jones tho[ugh] he did not receive any orders as the telegraph wires at Rocky Mount were out of fix. Determined to go to Weldon and at 7:15 p.m. we started and reached Weldon about 10:30 p.m. Stayed all night at Weldon. Weather fair and very hot.

Wednesday August 12th 1863

Moved early in the morning to a camp on the Raleigh & Gaston Railroad about two and a half miles from Weldon but almost immediately returned to Weldon and marched towards Garysburg to our old camp one half mile from the town. Weather fair and very hot in the day but rained; at night it clouded up and had a severe thunder storm. Wrote Mother a short letter.

* * * *

Camp 35th North Carolina Regiment (Infantry)
at Garysburg August 12, 1863

My Dear Mother,

We have just returned from Rocky Mount where we have been for the last three days and am truly glad to camp here again.

Father left here last Saturday for Richmond and was to return yesterday but did not but I expect him here today and as I have obtained permission to go home this afternoon I expect to go home with him.

It has been, dear Mother, awfully hot this week and the only consolation I have is in the supposition that as warm weather agrees with you so much better than cold this hot weather will be of benefit to you.

I was anxious to be detailed a few days ago to go to Raleigh to get some government cloth for the officers of the regiment but Bob Peebles was detailed to go as he had some business to attend to. I want very much to go up and see you all if only for a day but it seems I cannot get an opportunity. I was very glad Father gave "Hawk Eye"[40] to George, poor fellow; if dear Harry's death has been of benefit to him it is a severe way of accomplishing his good but God in His great wisdom may have ordained that Harry should be killed to make a change in George and improve his character. I am truly thankful that you must have received great consolation in seeing how universally he was loved and respected by all who knew dear Harry and with the knowledge that he died willingly and resigned and I know if you were certain all of us could be required to die and with a full belief we would go to heaven

---

[40] Henry K. Burgwyn, Jr.s, horse.

you would be contented if we were to be killed for what is a few days spent here compared with eternity in heaven.

Good-bye dear Mother. I will write more from [the] Plantation when I see Father and hear the news.

Love to all.

Your most affectionate son,
W.H.S. Burgwyn

* * * *

Thursday August 13th 1863

Obtained permission from Colonel Jones to go home today. My boy Pompey having arrived about 10:30 a.m. with the buggy. I started for home in time to take dinner at 1:30 p.m. Weather rained some during the morning but none in the afternoon but very hard about night time and lasted half the night.

Friday August 14th 1863

Remained home all day. Rode and threw down twice my horse "Sultan" and was very much pleased with him. Rode on horseback with Father in the morning and in the buggy in the afternoon. Received a note by our mail carrier from Adjutant Peebles saying I could remain at home till tomorrow morning but that the regiment had received marching orders and that we could not leave to go deer hunting on Saturday as we contemplated. Weather cloudy but very sultry.

Saturday August 15th 1863

Started for camp about 9:30 a.m. and reached it at 11:30 a.m. Found that our orders to leave would not have to go in effect. Received a letter from Mother dated August 12th. Weather very hot and fair.

Sunday August 16th 1863

Having borrowed an ambulance and harness from Dr. O'Hagan and permission from Colonel Jones, Major [Simon B.] Taylor, Adjutant Peebles, and myself started to church at Elam but finding there would be no church there we went to Adjutant Peebles', six miles and took dinner and returned at 6:00 p.m. Met Father coming up in the buggy to see General Ransom and he promised to join us at Adjutant Peebles' at dinner. He failed to do so.

Monday August 17th 1863

Remained in camp all day. Had drill morning and evening. Weather very hot and fair. Obtained permission from Colonel Jones to go deer hunting tomorrow with Adjutant Peebles and Major Taylor.

Tuesday August 18th 1863

Hunted all day and about 5:00 p.m. a deer running by Adjutant Peebles' stand. He killed it. I came home to dinner, but found Father had gone to Halifax. He returned about 5:00 p.m. and brought with him Commodore [William F.] Lynch, Confederate States Navy. We all returned to camp after supper. Weather cloudy and not hot.

Wednesday August 19th 1863

On arriving at camp yesterday night. Found Colonel Jones had gone home on a furlough. Had two drills. Weather cool and night very cool. Had a chill last week.

Thursday August 20th 1863

Was detailed to take charge of the working parties that were to work on the fortifications at Weldon. Had detail of one hundred men from the 24th [North Carolina] Regiment. Knocked off about 6:00 p.m. and I rode home my horse "Sultan." Pompey rode up to Garysburg to bring the mail. Weather a little cloudy and not hot.

Friday August 21st 1863

Returned to Weldon at 8:00 a.m. from home rode up in the buggy. The detail today was from the 49th [North Carolina Infantry]. I returned home again tonight. Weather fair and hot.

Saturday August 22nd 1863

Returned by 8:00 a.m. today. Found a detail from 35th [North Carolina Infantry] which did not do much working owing to the extensive heat. Father left at 4:00 p.m. for Raleigh. Returned at 6:00 p.m. home and found Lieutenants [W.G.] Bender and Brown of Engineer Corps at the house at Father's request and offer.

Sunday August 23rd 1863

Remained home all day. Wrote Mother. Weather fair and hot.

Monday August 24th 1863

Started for Weldon at 6:00 a.m. Lieutenants Brown and Bender also went but not in my company as I had to ride fast. Returned home in the afternoon at 7:00 p.m.

Tuesday August 25th 1863

Returned again to Weldon and after working on a redoubt at Weldon returned home at 7:00 p.m. Weather cloudy but warm.

Wednesday August 26th 1863

Went to Weldon and returned home in the afternoon. Weather cloudy a little and warm.

Thursday August 27th 1863

Rained in a drizzly fashion all the morning and I did not go to Weldon till 2:00 p.m. when it had cleared up but found it had rained very little at Weldon. Returned home at night.

Friday August 28th 1863

Returned to Weldon at 8:00 a.m. and did not come home at night but gave orders to Pompey to come for me tomorrow morning. Weather cloudy and cool.

Saturday August 29th 1863

Having finished work at 2:00 p.m. I started for home and arrived at 4:00 p.m. Weather cloudy and cool.

Sunday August 30th 1863

Lieutenants J. Waverly Johnson, volunteer aide de camp and P[owell] C. Johnson, Engineer Corps, attached to General Ransom, came down about 10:00 a.m. to spend the day. I expected them yesterday evening but they stayed all night at General Ransom's; sent Mrs. Ransom some fruit. Wrote Mother. Weather cloudy and cool.

Monday August 31st 1863

We three started for Weldon at 6:00 a.m. intending to call for General Ransom on our way but when we got there he detained us till it commenced raining and it rained continually till about 12:00 noon when we three and Dr. Means, aide to General Ransom, started for Weldon, General Ransom having gone before us in a carriage. Weather rained off and on all day and night.

Tuesday September 1st 1863

Worked all day on the works as usual. Weather cloudy but warm.

Wednesday September 2nd 1863

At work all day in the fortifications. Weather cloudy but warm.

Thursday September 3rd 1863

At work in the fortifications. Received a letter by Pompey from Father [blank in original] Weather little cloudy and warm.

Friday September 4th 1863

At work in the fortifications. Lieutenants J.W. and P.C. Johnson went to Petersburg and Richmond at 9:15 p.m. intending to return Monday or Tuesday. Weather fair and warm.

Saturday September 5th 1863

Worked in the works till 12:00 noon and then knocked off. Received a letter from Mother dated September 3rd. Started for home at 12:30 p.m. Weather fair and very warm.

Sunday September 6th 1863

Went [to] church in the buggy and took Lieutenant Brown with me. Was much pleased with Mr. Lightbourne's sermon. Returned immediately after church broke up. Weather fair and warm. Wrote Mother.

Monday September 7th 1863

Started for Weldon at 6:00 a.m. Found no detail at work, Captain [John Cargill] Pegram[41] having failed to order one. Had one ordered and we started to work at 11:00 a.m. Weather rained and hailed at 5:00 p.m. very heavily for about a half hour.

Tuesday September 8th 1863

At work all day on works. Josh, in obedience to orders, rode "Sultan" my stud horse up to Weldon for General Ransom to see but he was not to be found. Weather fair and warm.

Wednesday September 9th 1863

At work all day but at 5:30 p.m. went home in the buggy. I had ordered Pompey to bring up for me. Wrote Mother. Weather fair and hot.

Thursday September 10th 1863

Returned to Weldon at 8:00 a.m. Worked all day on works. Weather cool and cloudy.

Friday September 11th 1863

Finished the redoubt I was engaged on at Weldon and that being all I had to do at Weldon I started for home intending to commence on Monday at Faisons' Mill. I took a Mr. Ried, a famous overseer here, with me. Called on my way hence at Bob Peebles to make arrangements to go deer hunting tomorrow.

Saturday September 12th 1863

At 5:45 a.m. started to go deer hunting. Rendezvoused about one and a half miles from house. Hunted all day and though Dr. Peebles and I shot at a deer we did not kill any. Heard yesterday that two of our Negroes, Alfred and Elsey, had run off. Alfred returned but Elsey did not. Weather fair and very warm.

Sunday September 13th 1863

Stayed home all day. Wrote Mother and asked her to come down and spend a week or two down here with me. Weather in the morning fair but in the afternoon rainy and a little in the night.

Monday September 14th 1863

Went out after breakfast to see if the Negroes had come but found they had not but Lieutenant Olds, Engineers, arrived about 8:00 p.m. with the Negroes. Weather rained about one and a half hours in the afternoon.

Tuesday September 15th 1863

Put the Negroes on the work to be constructed on the hills this side of Faisons' Mill and on the right hand side joining to Jackson. Weather fair and warm.

[41] Son of Robert B. Pegram and Lucy Cargill. Robert Pegram was a captain in the United States Navy and later in the Confederate States Navy. John Pegram graduated from V.M.I. in 1858, served as Asst. Adj. General for General Matt Ransom, and was killed on June 16, 1864.

Wednesday September 16th 1863

At work all day on the works. Received a note from Father dated September 15th. Weather fair and warm.

Thursday September 17th 1863

At work all day on the entrenchments. Sent a detail to go to Raleigh to get some engineering implements but the detail was disapproved by General Ransom. Received a letter from Mother dated respectively August 31st, September 8th and 14th, and one from Sister dated September 6th, and one from Captain Donnan[42] dated September 14th written in reply to a letter I wrote concerning him to Mayor W.W. Townes, mayor of Petersburg.

Friday September 18th 1863

At work at intervals on the works owing to the state of the weather which varied constantly. Wrote Mother.

Saturday September 19th 1863

At work most of all of the afternoon but in the morning it rained all the time. Received a letter from Father dated September 15th. Weather turned very cool. Elsey who ran off returned tonight.

Sunday September 20th 1863

Remained at home all day for which I got a scolding from my clergyman because I did not go to church. Wrote Father. Weather cool and windy but fair.

Monday September 21st 1863

At work all day on the works. Weather cool but fair. I think we had a little frost this morning.

Tuesday September 22nd 1863

At work all day on the works. Weather fair and moderately cool.

Wednesday September 23rd 1863

At work all day on the works. Wrote Captain Donnan at Petersburg. Weather fair and warm.

Thursday September 24th 1863

At work all day on the works. Received an invitation to go to a ball at Weldon. Weather fair and moderately warm.

Friday September 25th 1863

Received yesterday a letter from Father and Mother dated September 23rd. At work all day on works. Weather toward night very much like rain did rain some.

---

[42] Either Alexander M. Donnon or James M. Donnon, brothers and Petersburg lawyers.

Saturday September 26th 1863

At work all day on works. Weather fair and in the morning windy.

Sunday September 27th 1863

At work part of the day on the works and rested in the afternoon. Weather very cool. Wrote Father.

Monday September 28th 1863

At work all day on works. Weather fair and warm. Received a letter from Father dated September 23rd enclosing $150.00.

Tuesday September 29th 1863

At work all day at works. Received a letter from Father dated September 28th. Weather fair and warm.

Wednesday September 30th 1863

At work all day on works. Weather fair and warm.

Thursday October 1st 1863

At work all day on works. Sent up the carriage buggy and a two horse wagon for Mother and Father to Garysburg at 3:00 a.m. Weather fair and warm but cloudy towards night. Was very much disappointed in their not coming. Received a letter from Mother dated September 30th and Father dated September 21st.

Friday October 2nd 1863

At work all day on works. Received a letter from Mr. Lightbourne dated September 30th. Wrote Mother. Weather fair and warm.

Saturday October 3rd 1863

At work all day on works. Weather fair and warm.

Sunday October 4th 1863

Wrote Father and sent home a drawing of our works at Faisons' Mill. Weather fair and warm.

Monday October 5th 1863

Received a telegram and letter from Mother dated 3rd instant saying she would be down on Tuesday the 6th. At work all day. Weather fair and warm.

* * * *

Thornbury Plantation
October 5th 1863

My dear Father,
 I send you the enclosed drawing of our works at Faisons' Mill made very hastily by me and the angles, etc. I took with my eye and though the drawing is not as

W.H.S. Burgwyn's map of fortifications at Faisons' Mill, North Carolina

accurate as if it had been done with a compass and chain I think it a very accurate profile. [Map, opposite] Williamson had just finished his sugar press but has not got it up as it needs some little more work on it to make it press easily. He will have it at work I think by this afternoon. It seems a very good press and will I no doubt work well. [Diagram with original letter] It consists of three rollers worked by the middle roller by cogs mortised in the middle roller viz [illustration] and the middle roller turned by the beam "B" to which a horse is attached. The cane to be put between the middle roller and either outside one and the juice runs down into a trough cut into the beam "C" which also is the receptacle of the ends of the three rollers from the trenches in, beam "C": the juice runs into the tubs on the ports you may intend to receive it. I speak and describe the press so indistinctly because I imagine you know how one is built.

We are now entirely out of candles and if you and Mother come down you will not find any light so you had better bring some down with you. The commissary neither at Weldon or Garysburg have any candles. I have got ten pounds of sugar from the commissary at Garysburg; we have used none of your [illegible] since we have been here. Tell Mother I am hoping [illegible] Gary will find it convenient to make her as short as possible as I do not expect to be here more than two weeks. I don't know what the hands are doing as I am too much occupied at the work to go over the plantation.

With much love to all, I am in haste

Your most affectionate son
W.H.S. Burgwyn

* * * *

Tuesday October 6th 1863

Sent up for Mother and Father who arrived about 12:00 noon. At work all day on works. Weather fair and warm.

Wednesday October 7th 1863

At work all day on works. My Father and Mr. [blank in original] came out to see the works and were very much pleased with them. Weather fair and warm.

Thursday October 8th 1863

At work all day on works. Weather rained a little in the morning but some in the afternoon. Was glad it cleared up for we intend sending to Garysburg tomorrow morning for Sister and Miss Devereux who were coming on a visit. Was very much gratified to hear that Miss Devereux was coming to spend some time with Sister.

Friday October 9th 1863

At work all day on works sent up for Sister and Miss Devereux who arrived about 12:00 noon. Weather fair and warm.

Saturday October 10th 1863

At work all day on works. Weather fair and warm. Mother and Father went to Jackson today. My brother George arrived from Chapel Hill today having left to process a statement that he was not eighteen years of age.

Sunday October 11th 1863

Lieutenant Olds and myself rode out with my sister and Miss Devereux in the morning and in the afternoon we walked out. Weather fair and warm.

Monday October 12th 1863

At work all day on works. Lieutenant Olds and myself accompanied my sister and Mrs. Devereux on a ride to Boone's Mill. Weather fair and warm.

Tuesday October 13th 1863

At work all day on works. Weather cloudy and rained at night. Expect to finish tomorrow the work at Faisons' Mill and then go to work near Garysburg where the Murfreesboro Road crossed the railroad eight miles from Garysburg. My brother George returned to Chapel Hill.

Wednesday October 14th 1863

At work all day on works but did not quite finish them. Weather cloudy a little; a little rain I think at night.

Thursday October 15th 1863

Finished our work easily this morning and waited till about 2:00 p.m. for the wagons that General Ransom was to send us to transport the baggage of the hands to our new place of work. Weather cloudy but rained at night.

Friday October 16th 1863

Lieutenant Olds went to Murfreesboro Road to lay off the work and arrange the hands. I did not accompany him as it was not necessary. Weather rained almost all the morning but cleared up afterwards.

Saturday October 17th 1863

Lieutenant Olds returned to breakfast. He did not think it necessary for me to go to the Murfreesboro Road today so he and I rode our horses back with my sister and Miss Devereux instead rode to the hillside where our former house stood.[43] Weather fair and warm.

Sunday October 18th 1863

We all went to church today, Father and Mother in the carriage and Lieutenant Olds drove Sister in the buggy and I Miss Devereux in a buggy returned to dinner. Had a very good lesson. Weather fair and warm.

Monday October 19th 1863

About 10:00 a.m. started for the works on the Murfreesboro Road and after losing my way through a place called Gumberry I arrived at 12:30 p.m. Stayed all night with Sergeant Newsum. Weather early rainy but cleared off.

---

[43] Hillside Plantation, built in 1840, burned in 1849. It was in this house that George P. Burgwyn, W.H.S.B.'s brother, was born.

Tuesday October 20th 1863

At the works till 3:00 p.m. when I started home for the purpose of seeing Father before he left for Augusta. Weather fair and warm.

Wednesday October 21st 1863

Started for Murfreesboro Road at 9:30 a.m. Lieutenant Olds accompanying me. Took dinner with Sergeant Newsum and after dinner went in search of a house to board at and got board at a Mr. William Garriss' about two miles from the works. Left them all well at home. Weather fair and warm.

Thursday October 22nd 1863

At work all day in works. Lieutenant Olds went to Weldon where he saw the family on their return to Raleigh. Weather fair and much cooler. He (Lieutenant Olds) obtained two weeks forage for two horses from the quartermaster at Weldon, Mr. Garriss not being able to feed our horses.

Friday October 23rd 1863

At work all day on works. Lieutenant Olds went to Boone's Mill to attend to hands there. Weather a little cloudy and warm.

Saturday October 24th 1863

Rained all morning so I could not go out to the works but cleared up afterwards and I started for home stopping on my way at the works to see Sergeant Newsum. At Mr. Peebles' met my friend Adjutant Peebles and those other officers from the brigade who were going deer hunting and they persuaded me to go with them which I did for one drive but not killing a deer I kept on going.

Sunday October 25th 1863

Stayed all day at home. Weather cloudy and cool but no rain.

Monday October 26th 1863

Returned to Murfreesboro Road. Weather cloudy and cold. Received a letter from Mother dated 25th.

Tuesday October 27th 1863

At work all day on works. Weather cloudy and fair and cold. Sent Sergeant [?]Whitmise and private Martin after runaway free Negroes.

Wednesday October 28th 1863

At work all day in works. Received a letter from Sister written from Wilmington, North Carolina, dated October 22nd. Weather fair and beautiful day.

Thursday October 29th 1863

At work all day in works. Weather fair and cool.

Friday October 30th 1863

At work all day on works. Weather fair and warm.

Saturday October 31st 1863

At work all day on works but all the slaves hence not to return and thirty-eight free Negroes who had farms and families to return in two weeks. Returned to plantation about 3:30 p.m.

Sunday November 1st 1863

Went to church at Jackson. Wrote Mother a letter. Weather fair but windy and cold.

Monday November 2nd 1863

Started for works about 9:00 a.m. Weather fair and warm.

Tuesday November 3rd 1863

At work all day on works. Weather fair and warm. Two hundred and fifty men from the 25th and 35th North Carolina Regiments arrived from General Ransom's Brigade to do fatigue duty or on constructing the works.

Wednesday November 4th 1863

At work all day on works. Weather fair and warm.

Thursday November 5th 1863

At work all day on works. Weather fair and warm.

Friday November 6th 1863

At work all day on works. Weather fair but windy.

Saturday November 7th 1863

About one half hour to day break I was awakened by General Ransom in person who ordered me to take the Negroes and go immediately to Parker's Mill on the Margarettsville Road and blockade the road as it was reported the enemy were advancing from Winton, North Carolina. The troops returned to Weldon and the 25th [North Carolina] Regiment was sent to Mr. Garriss' and the 35th [North Carolina Infantry] to Parris Cross Roads two miles from Garysburg. In the afternoon I reported to General Ransom at Jackson as he ordered me to see that the road was blockaded up and then I went home. Weather fair and warm.

Sunday November 8th 1863

Found on my arrival yesterday that Mr. Read had just arrived from Garysburg who came here to pay me a visit. Stayed at home. Received a letter from Mother yesterday night dated November 6th.

Monday November 9th 1863

Started for the works about 9:30 a.m. About 3:00 p.m. hearing General Ransom with the 25th and 35th North Carolina Regiments intending going down to Winton and driving the enemy off. I started to overtake him and accompanying the brigade down. Overtook the brigade thirteen miles below Jackson. Weather fair and cool. Passed the night with my friend Adjutant Peebles, 35th North Carolina Regiment.

Tuesday November 10th 1863

News having come that the enemy has left Winton. General Ransom returned to Weldon and P[etersburg Railroad] to the fortifications. On arriving at my boarding house I found a letter from Mother stating my Father had had an attack of paralysis after dinner. I went to Weldon and having obtained permission to visit Raleigh for two days to see my Father from Captain Pegram, Assistant Adjutant General, I left about 4:00 p.m. Reached Raleigh about 12:00 p.m. and found my Father had improved a good deal since he was attacked. Weather fair and cool.

Wednesday November 11th 1863

Called on Miss Annie Devereux and took tea at her house. My father was much better today. Saw my grandfather and uncle and aunt and Cousin Kate [Katherine Mary MacRae]. Weather fair and cool.

Thursday November 12th 1863

Called on Cousin Fannie [Frances Devereux] Polk and her brother Captain [Alexander] Hamilton Polk.[44] My Father improved much today. Left Raleigh to return to Weldon at 12:00 p.m. and accompanied Miss Annie Devereux and her cousin Miss Margaret Mordecai as far as Garysburg. Passed a moderately comfortable night. Weather fair and warm.

Friday November 13th 1863

Arrived at Weldon about 8:30 a.m. Started from Weldon for Garysburg. Found a carriage and horses to take me home which came up for my Father who expected to be able to come over to the plantation today. Arrived at plantation about 11:45 a.m. Wrote Father in the afternoon. Weather fair and warm.

Saturday November 14th 1863

Remained at home all day. Went squirrel hunting in the morning and afternoon and in the afternoon was accompanied by the Reverend Mr. Lightbourne. Weather fair and very warm; at about 4:00 p.m. it clouded up and rained heavily for a short time.

Sunday November 15th 1863

Remained all day at home and did not consequently go to church. Wrote Mother. Weather cloudy and cool.

Monday November 16th 1863

Remained all day at home. Went squirrel hunting with Mr. Lightbourne in the afternoon. Weather fair and moderate but colder towards night.

Tuesday November 17th 1863

Intended going to works today but the weather was so threatening I did not go. Weather cloudy and with the appearance of rain or snow and I think it was too cold for snow but cleared up towards night and a clear night.

---

[44] These were two of the eight children of Lt. Gen. Leonidas Polk and Frances Anne Devereux. Frances M. Polk was the sister of Thomas Pollok Devereux and George Devereux. Francis Devereux Polk and Alexander Hamilton Polk were second cousins to W.H.S.B.

Wednesday November 18th 1863

Started for the works at 9:30 a.m. Found every thing quiet and orderly at the works. Weather fair and warm. Received a letter from Mr. John Reid dated November 1st.

Thursday November 19th 1863

At the works all day. Two hundred and fifty soldiers, half from the 25th and the other from the 35th North Carolina Regiments came down to the works to assist in throwing up breastworks. Weather fair and warm.

Friday November 20th 1863

At work till 2:30 p.m. when I started for the plantation as I had promised the Reverend Mr. Lightbourne intending to go hunting for squirrels next day. Weather fair and warm.

Saturday November 21st 1863

About day break went out squirrel hunting and after breakfast went with Mr. Lightbourne duck hunting in the afternoon went squirrel hunting again. Weather cloudy and very warm and rained during the night.

Sunday November 22nd 1863

At home all day. Went to our chapel [on Thornbury plantation] in the night with our clergyman the Reverend Frederick Lightbourne. Received a letter from Mother by Caroline [?Caroline Reid] who arrived in the afternoon at 6:00 p.m. from Raleigh dated the 21st instant also one from Mr. Reid dated 10th instant who sent his horse down to be taken care of till his return from the South. Weather cloudy and very much like rain; rained during the night.

Monday November 23rd 1863

At home all day on account of the rain which fell at intervals all day but not heavily. Wrote Mother yesterday and Mr. Reid.

Tuesday November 24th 1863

At home all day on account of the weather which was misty all day and rained most of the morning.

Wednesday November 25th 1863

Started for works about 9:00 a.m. found everything going on well. Weather cloudy and warm.

Thursday November 26th 1863

At works all day. Weather fair but cloudy.

Friday November 27th 1863

At works till 2:00 p.m. when Lieutenant Olds and myself started for home when about [a] mile from home met our carriage which was returning from Garysburg with Mother and the children. Father having remained in Raleigh waiting for Mr. Blackwell his colleague. Weather fair but warm and commenced Saturday to rain about dark.

Saturday November 28th 1863

In the afternoon Captain Gee of General Ransom's Staff came to see me and Lieutenant Olds as the general wished some works put up on the Margarettsville Road orders having come for him to be ready to march to Petersburg at any moment and he wished to finish some works on all the roads before he should leave. Weather rained all day till late in the afternoon.

Sunday November 29th 1863

Went to see General Ransom at his house as I promised Captain Gee yesterday. Found the General at home who told me my regiment had already left Garysburg for Petersburg and that I should leave tomorrow evening to join it. I was extremely sorry to hear it. Weather rained all the morning but cleared up in the afternoon.

Monday November 30th 1863

Agreeable with my instructions I received yesterday evening I started for Weldon at 4:00 p.m. to take the train to Petersburg. Met Father in Weldon which I was very glad of indeed. Left Weldon at 9:00 p.m. for Petersburg and after a moderately pleasant ride reached Petersburg at about 3:30 a.m. next day. Weather very cold and clear.

Tuesday December 1st 1863

Remained in the city of Petersburg till about 2:00 p.m. when I started for the regiment camped about two miles from the city of [on] the City Point road. Found the regiment pretty well situated in woods where they got plenty of wood to burn. Weather cold and a little windy.

Wednesday December 2nd 1863

Received permission from Colonel Jones to return to Weldon to see General Ransom on business and got the conductor of the train to put me on the train as I could not get on unless I had a pass and I could not obtain one unless my permit was countersigned by General [George] Pickett and I could not wait to get it done. Arrived at Weldon about 3:00 p.m. and immediately saw General Ransom who said I should be attached to his staff for the present. Telegraphed Colonel Jones as he had requested me that General Ransom said he should leave for Petersburg tomorrow or the next day.

Thursday December 3rd 1863

Remained at home all day as he had requested; General Ransom said he should leave for Petersburg tomorrow or next day. Borrowed a horse from Captain Venable, quartermaster, and rode home. The family was much surprised to see me. Weather fair and moderate.

Friday December 4th 1863

Remained at home all day having found out that General Ransom would not leave. Weather rained some.

Saturday December 5th 1863

Remained at home all day as I did not think the general would leave. Weather rained some and turned off cool.

Sunday December 6th 1863

Accompanied Mother and Father and the family to church at Jackson. Weather cold and clear.

Monday December 7th 1863

Started with the Reverend Mr. Lightbourne in the afternoon to call upon Mr. and Mrs. Ransom but met my brother George who had been to Weldon and who said General Ransom had left for Hamilton that there was a skirmish down in that section of the country with the enemy. The 24th North Carolina Regiment (Ransom's Brigade) be the troops engaged. I immediately returned home intending to get ready to join General Ransom next day. Weather cold and cloudy and some rain in the morning.

Tuesday December 8th 1863

Waited at home till my brother George could return from Garysburg and tell me whether General Ransom had returned or not. George returned about 4:00 p.m. and said General Ransom was expected to return tonight from Hamilton. Weather cloudy but no rain.

Wednesday December 9th 1863

Went about 9:00 a.m. to General Ransom's house to see him. Found him at home and he told me he should not now have to leave Weldon that General [Thomas L.] Clingman[45] would go to Petersburg in his stead and that I might stay at home till he sent me word to go to Weldon. Weather cloudy.

Thursday December 10th 1863

Accompanied Mother, Sister, and cousin Katie [MacRae] and George to Jackson to be present at the burial of Virginius Copland a friend of mine who lived in Jackson and was killed near Culpeper Court House. It was a very melancholy sight and I sympathized heartily with his affected parents. Weather cloudy but moderate.

Friday December 11th 1863

Remained at home all day. Weather fair and moderate.

Saturday December 12th 1863

Remained at home all day. Weather rained hard in the night.

Sunday December 13th 1863

Had service at home the clergyman (Mr. Lightbourne) being about at Warrenton, North Carolina. Weather rained during the night.

Monday December 14th 1863

Remained at home all day. Weather fair and very windy.

---

[45] Thomas Lanier Clingman was a close friend of H.K.B., Sr., and this relationship would be helpful to W.H.S.B. in the future.

Clingman was a lawyer in western North Carolina, which he represented in the state legislature. He served in the United States House of Representatives and Senate. A secessionist, he served as Colonel of the 25th North Carolina Infantry and in May, 1862, he became a brigade commander.

Tuesday December 15th 1863

Remained at home all day. Mr. Lightbourne and the Reverend [Fordyce M.] Hubbard, D.D.,[46] a professor at our University who came to pay my Father a visit arrived. Weather fair and warm.

Wednesday December 16th 1863

At home all day. My Mother and Father and Dr. Hubbard drove to Jackson. Lieutenants Olds and Bender (Engineers) took dinner but had to return to the fortifications near Weldon. Heard of a most disgraceful and cowardly murder perpetrated by a citizen Dan Jacobs on a Mr. Edwards, hotel keeper in Jackson, North Carolina. Weather fair and warm but cloudy towards night and rained pretty hard during the night.

Thursday December 17th 1863

At home all day. Weather cloudy and rained some.

Friday December 18th 1863

Father and Sister started for Richmond about 7:00 a.m. on a visit and business combined but he left [illegible] business papers behind and George, my brother, brought them to him by the 9:00 p.m. o'clock train. Weather moderate and a little rain in the early part of the morning but cleared off cold.

Saturday December 19th 1863

My brother George returned from Petersburg this afternoon and brought me word from General Ransom that I should meet him tomorrow morning in Weldon with my horse, etc., to accompany him to Elizabeth City on a raid. Weather cold and windy.

Sunday December 20th 1863

Started for Weldon in the buggy at 7:30 a.m. having sent Pompey before with my horse to Weldon. General Ransom did not leave as he intended; the enemy he intended to meet having returned to their camps. General Ransom gave me a strong recommendation[47] to General Clingman for the position of Inspector General of his

---

[46] Hubbard, a New England-educated lawyer, served at Christ Episcopal Church in New Bern, and later on the faculty of the University of North Carolina.

[47]   Headquarters Weldon, N.C.
                                                  December 20, 1863

Brig. Genl. T.L. Clingman,
    Sir.
        Having learned from you that you desired to have an Inspector appointed for your Brigade permit me to recommend to you Capt. W.H.S. Burgwyn Co. "H" 35th N.C. Infy.
        Capt. Burgwyn is a gentleman & soldier of high intelligence of approved gallantry and a very good military education. He has served under me with very great satisfaction and I say with pleasure that I know no young officer of superior virtue. I advise you if you will allow it with entire sincerity to take him on your staff you will find him always everything that he ought to be. I dislike to spare him but for very good cause he desires a staff position.
                                I am Genl. very truly yours.
                                    M.W. Ransom
                                    Brig. Genl.
[Courtesy of Margaret B. Cooley, Jackson, North Carolina]

brigade and I telegraphed Father to Richmond to see General Clingman and make application for the position. I returned home about 4:30 p.m. Weather windy and very cold.

Monday December 21st 1863

Wrote Father and General Clingman and enclosed in General Clingman's letter the letter of recommendation of General Ransom. Remained at home all day. Weather cold and cloudy.

Tuesday December 22nd 1863

Remained at home all day. Weather cool but fair. The river had been up for a day or two but commenced falling; yesterday it was only a moderately high freshet.

Wednesday December 23rd 1863

My cousin Kate MacRae and the Reverend F.M. Hubbard who had been staying with us a few days left today for Raleigh. Weather cool and little cloudy.

Thursday December 24th 1863

At home all day and in the evening assisted my Mother in decking the house in Christmas style. Mother received a letter from Sister saying send for them to Garysburg tomorrow and next day. Weather cold about freezing.

Friday December 25th 1863

Accompanied my Mother and two youngest brothers [John Alveston Burgwyn and Collinson Pierrepont Edwards Burgwyn] to church today and for the *first* time attended the communion table. Was much disappointed in Father's not coming home today. The Negroes need to break in upon their Christmas holidays to get ice but they will receive another day to make up for it. How differently I spent this Christmas from the last and the only thing that saddened the day was that my poor brother Harry had been killed and could not be with us as was hoped last Christmas. Weather moderate and sun.

Saturday December 26th 1863

Father arrived about 4:30 p.m. and looked as if his trip had improved him. Weather moderated towards night and turned quite warm.

Sunday December 27th 1863

Did not go to church today as it was the Sunday for service at Jackson but we had service in the drawing room. Weather warm and little cloudy and towards night a little rain and rained during the evening.

Monday December 28th 1863

Rained some during the day. Went hunting in the morning.

Tuesday December 29th 1863

At home all day. Weather fair and pleasant.

Wednesday December 30th 1863

Went hunting in the afternoon. Weather fair and pleasant but rained hard during the night.

Thursday December 31st 1863

Rained all day with a little interruption. Weather mild.

Friday January 1st 1864

Wrote General Ransom an application for leave of absence for two days to see General Clingman at Petersburg, Virginia, for the purpose of pursuing in person my application for a position on his staff but General Ransom was not at Weldon having gone up the railroad on a visit. Weather in the afternoon turned very windy and cool also windy in the morning.

Saturday January 2nd 1864

There being a pretty high freshet went hunting in the morning in a canoe on the river and where its waters had overflowed its banks. Weather cold and windy. Wrote General Clingman a letter asking him to return me General Ransom's letter of recommendation.

Sunday January 3rd 1864

Went to church with Mother and the little Mordecai. Father not going on account of the weather which was cold but fair and moderated very much in the after-part of the day. Sent Pompey to General Ransom's house to ask him to please reply to my note of the 1st instant and as he sent back word I might go so I determined to start Monday morning.

Monday January 4th 1864

Started from here about 6:45 a.m. and reached Weldon just in time to get on the train before it left, I having to go to it to get a passport. Arrived at Petersburg about 3:00 p.m. and immediately hired a horse and rode to General Clingman's head-quarters at Dunn's [illegible]. My interview was as satisfactory as I could expect under the circumstances. Passed the night at Jarretts Hotel. Weather moderate but cloudy.

Tuesday January 5th 1864

Started on my return at 9:30 a.m. Met in Petersburg Captain J.M. Rogers, our quartermaster, and in the cars Lieutenant [Robert Walker] Anderson[48] a cousin who was going home on a ten days furlough from the Rapidan. Reached Garysburg at about 3:00 p.m. and home about 4:30 p.m. Weather rained a little in the morning but cleared up in the afternoon.

Wednesday January 6th 1864

At home all day. Wrote my Aunt Emily a letter. Weather towards night it began to sleet but during the night it rained a little.

Thursday January 7th 1864

Cold all day; in the afternoon commenced to sleet and started to sleet and sleeted heavily much all night. Went hunting for turkeys in the afternoon.

Friday January 8th 1864

Not quite so cold today. Thermometer about from 25°-29°; a little snow in the morning but cleared up towards night and a pretty clear night.

---

[48] Brother of General George B. Anderson, and second cousin of W.H.S.B. He had married Rebecca Cameron in 1863 and would be killed at Spotsylvania Court House in May, 1864.

Saturday January 9th 1864

Endeavored to skate on the mill pond today but the ice was not strong enough. The plantation hands were busy all day getting ice. Weather fair but cold.

Sunday January 10th 1864

Found the ice some thicker this morning. Attend with the family the plantation chapel. Weather cloudy in the afternoon and cold.

Monday January 11th 1864

Skated some on the mill pond at the peach orchard flat. Went on business for Father to Halifax about six miles distant. Received a letter from General Clingman dated 9th instant which induced Father to determine upon going to Richmond and I wrote General Ransom an application to go with him. Weather cloudy but not so cold.

Tuesday January 12th 1864

My brother George went to Weldon to get my Father and my passports and my permission to go to Richmond and we left on the 10:00 a.m. train for Richmond. Arrived at Petersburg about 3:00 p.m. and met General Clingman at the depot agreeable to a telegram sent him by Father. Started for Richmond about 4:30 p.m. and arrived about 7:00 p.m. Tried to get lodging at the Spottswood [Hotel] but could not as it was full and put up at the American [Hotel]. Weather cloudy and moderate.

Wednesday January 13th 1864

Reported myself at General [John H.] Winder's office (commander of the police of Military commander) but my permission not being countersigned by General Pickett (Department Commander) I was ordered back to Weldon. Started for Petersburg as 4:45 p.m. and arrived about 7:15 p.m. Remained all night in the city at Jarratts Hotel. Weather misty.

Thursday January 14th 1864

Started for Garysburg at 4:14 a.m. leaving Father in Petersburg to come out tomorrow morning. Arrived at Garysburg about 12:15 p.m. just as Captain Barham's Company of Cavalry were having a tournament. As there was no carriage for me at Garysburg I stayed at Colonel John Long's with my friend John Long.[49] Attended the party given by the riders of the tournament and had a moderately good time considering almost all the ladies were Methodist and did not dance. Weather misty and rainy.

Friday January 15th 1864

Agreeable to my orders my boy Pompey went up for me about 9:00 a.m. in the buggy and I set off for home. Father came in the 3:00 p.m. train. Weather fair and very delightful.

---

[49] John Joseph Long, Jr., lived with his parents at "Longwood" near Garysburg. The house has fallen but remains and can be seen from the highway. (Margaret Burgwyn Cooley) He was the grandson of Colonel Nicholas Long (see August 9, 1862). The Long and Burgwyn families would be related after the war. In 1869 John Joseph Long, Jr., married Sallie Ridley of Southampton County, Virginia; she was the first cousin of Emma Wright Ridley and would later marry W.H.S.B.'s younger brother, George.

John Joseph Long, Jr.'s sister, Ellen Williams Long, married General Junius Daniel.

Saturday January 16th 1864

Wrote General Ransom about my visit to Richmond. Weather fair.

Sunday January 17th 1864

Attended church at Jackson with the family. Had a little headache and cold to-day. Weather fair but clouded up at night. Received a letter from Mrs. John Reid dated January 15th.

Monday January 18th 1864

Weather rained almost all day was busy at work on a trunk. My brother George started at 9:00 a.m. for Petersburg to carry a Negro boy to be sold for stealing.

Tuesday January 19th 1864

Was busy all day on my trunk. George brought me word from General Ransom that General Clingman wanted me to go at once to Petersburg and act on his staff and I start tomorrow. Weather windy and cool and turned cold towards night.

Wednesday January 20th 1864

Did not start for Petersburg as I intended to owing to not being able to get ready. Intend to start tomorrow morning. Weather fair and pleasant. At work all day on my trunk but finished it at night.

— END OF BOOK TWO —

CHAPTER 4

BOOK THREE: JANUARY 21, 1864 - SEPTEMBER 28, 1864

Thursday, January 21st 1864

Started about 7:30 a.m. for Garysburg to take the train for Petersburg which place I reached about 3:00 p.m. Happened to see Major Gage, Commissary of the brigade, who hauled my baggage and me to General Clingman's headquarters. Found on arriving at General Clingman's quarters that the papers from General Head-quarters, Army of Tennessee had not as yet arrived in Richmond and I therefore determined to go to Richmond and see about it on Saturday morning at 5:00 a.m. Weather fair and pleasant.

Friday January 22nd 1864

Was visited by Captain Edward White, Assistant Adjutant General (who was commissioned to invite some gentlemen to a party given by a Miss Major). Had a most agreeable time indeed. The party broke up about 10:00 o'clock a.m. next day and I went to Jarratts Hotel and remained there till about 4:30 a.m. and started for the depot to take the train for Richmond where I was going to see about my appointment as Assistant Adjutant General to Clingman's Brigade. Weather fair and moderate.

Saturday January 23rd 1864

Remained in the city all day. Went to the Adjutant Generals Office to see about General [Thomas C.] Hindman's application for Captain White and also to see about an application made by General Clingman to get aide-de-camp Captain [Frederick R.] Blake appointed Inspector General. The papers in reference to Captain White had only arrived the day previous and no action had as yet been taken on them but they reported to tell me about General Clingman's application when if any action had been taken or what. Accompanied Lieutenant [Thomas Waverly] Johnson,[1] a friend I came with from Petersburg, to a cousin [uncle] of his, Mr. (Colonel) [Marmaduke] Johnson.[2] Weather fair and pleasant.

---

[1] Thomas Waverly Johnson was the son of William Ransom Johnson, II, and Ariadne Elvira Branch. Ariadne Elvira Branch was the daughter of David Henry Branch and Mary Branch, his niece. David Branch was the brother of Thomas Branch; both brothers lived in Petersburg. The Branch brothers were the sons of Thomas Branch of "Willow Hill" in Chesterfield County, and Mary Patteson.

[2] Son of William Ransom Johnson, I, the "Napoleon of the Turf" in Petersburg.

**Brigadier General Thomas L. Clingman (center), Captain W.H.S. Burgwyn (left),
and First Lieutenant Henry S. Puryear (right)**

Clark, *Histories*, IV:481

Sunday January 24th 1864

Owing to some information that I heard at Colonel Johnson's last night (that a particularly intimate lady friend was in the city) I determined to remain in the city all day to see her. Called at Dr. Barney's and took dinner with him after accompanying him to the Episcopal Church [of] St. Paul's, Dr. [Charles] Minnegerode pastor. After some trouble about dusk found my lady friend, Miss Margaret Stuart,[3] and her sister Mrs. Captain Randolph.[4] Passed a very pleasant time and about church time returned to the hotel and retired. Weather fair and pleasant.

Monday January 25th 1864

Started about 6:00 a.m. for Petersburg. On arriving went immediately to see a friend of mine, a Mr. John Reid, to see if he had sold my horse "Sultan" as I left word for him to do last Friday night. Found he had not and I then had him advertised to be sold on Wednesday next. Tried very hard to buy a horse but could

---

[3] Margaret Stuart was the daughter of Dr. Richard Stuart, a cousin of Robert E. Lee's.
[4] Mary Ada Stuart.

not find one to suit me. Took dinner at Mr. Reid's brother's home, a Captain Gary Reid. On arriving at camp found an invitation from the Misses Branch to spend the evening at their house and meet a few friends. Had a most pleasant evening till about 11:00 p.m. when news came to General Clingman that the enemy were burning up a farm (Lower Brandon) about twenty-five miles below on the river and for him to take one of his regiments and drive them off and start as soon as possible. Weather fair and pleasant.

Tuesday January 26th 1864

The General, Captain White, Captain Blake and myself started about 6:00 a.m. for Lower Brandon. About seven miles from Lower Brandon the General sent Captain Blake and myself ahead to see how much destruction the Yankees had committed but we had not been there more than half an hour when the general and Captain White arrived. We returned about five miles to Brandon Church and camped for the night. Was very much exasperated at the great destruction the Yankees committed at the farm. They destroyed everything in the house and all the barns and corn, etc., etc. Weather fair and very pleasant.

Wednesday January 27th 1864

Started on our return about 6:00 a.m. and about 12:00 noon reached camp a distance of over twenty miles. Immediately after dinner Captain White and myself went in town I to accompany a lady in a walk but not arriving in time I went to see Captain George Reid about my horse "Sultan" who was not sold today as I ordered owing to not having enough offered for him. Went with Captain White to take tea with Miss Miller and Miss Bettie [Rosalama] Branch[5] and passed a very pleasant afternoon. Received a letter from my Mother dated January 26th enclosing one from my Aunt Emily dated January 21st and a note from my Father who had been in town yesterday but had gone to Richmond early in morning. He returned from Richmond this evening. Weather fair and pleasant.

Thursday January 28th 1864

Went in town early this morning to see my Father before he left for Garysburg on the 9:00 a.m. train. Had some conversation with him and on his recommendation went to see a horse and the horse pleased me so much that I immediately bought him. Called on in the morning Mrs. Page and her daughter Miss Major whose party I was at a few nights ago. Returned from the city about 2:00 p.m. after having called twice at Mr. William Johnson[6] to see his son Waverly Johnson but was unable to see him. About 7:00 p.m. orders came from Major [Charles] Pickett, Assistant Adjutant General of this department ordering General Clingman to be in town with his brigade at 8:00 a.m. tomorrow. Sent my boy Pompey home with my horse as I was unable to sell him at a good price. Weather most delightful and warm.

---

[5] Daughter of Thomas Branch and Sarah Pried Reid. (Also see January 23, 1864, and February 11, 1864.)

[6] William Ransom Johnson was the son of William R. Johnson and Mary Evans. He was a tobacconist for William R. Johnson and Bro., on the southwest corner of High and Cross; resided on South End Heights.

Friday January 29th 1864

Started at 7:00 a.m. for Petersburg to take the train for Weldon. Before starting Captain White and myself called upon Miss Major and Miss Mollie and Miss Bettie Branch. Started at 10:00 a.m. for Weldon which we reached about 7:00 p.m. Remained there till 10:00 p.m. and then started for Goldsboro. Weather fair and pleasant.

Saturday January 30th 1864

Arrived in Goldsboro about 2:00 p.m. Took dinner at Griswald Hotel and was much surprised at the good fare they gave me. About 3:30 p.m. started for Kinston which we reached about 6:00 p.m. Bivouacked about four miles from Kinston on the Dover Road. Weather fair and pleasant.

Sunday January 31st 1864

Started about sunrise for New Berne as we had by this time found out that we were going to attack New Berne. General [Robert F.] Hoke's Brigade marched in advance. Marched to within about ten miles of New Berne. Halted for the night. Weather fair and pleasant moderately cold.

Monday February 1st 1864

About 2:00 a.m. we recommenced our march so as to arrive at New Berne about daybreak or sunrise. About 3:15 a.m. we attacked the enemy outposts at Batchelder's Creek and lost Colonel [Henry M.] Shaw of the 8th North Carolina, one of the very best colonels in service, though we only had about a hundred and fifty men at the crossing owing to the dense fog and mist and did not force a crossing. At about 7:00 a.m. General Hoke immediately on crossing pushed his men forward as fast as they could go intending to reach the railroad in time to cut it and also cut off the enemy's camp at Deep Gully and a train with all included cars attached but the troops being very much exhausted they only came in view of the train so it passed with the iron clad car and about four hundred Yankees. Our brigade was there put in advance and we marched down the country road till we came in view of New Berne. General Clingman's brigade followed after General Hoke's but at Batchelder's Creek he marched cross the country to the railroad to cut off the enemy's force camp[ed] at Deep Gully. After arriving in sight of New Berne we remained quiet for some time but about 2:00 p.m. we moved about a mile from the road to the right and made a demonstration in front of a body of cavalry that were maneuvering on the Trent Road so arrived in above one-half mile from there and formed in line of battle as they had the appearance of preparing to charge us which they attempted but the fire of our skirmishers alone drove them back. They then fired some five or six shots from a light field piece one of which shots a shell exploded and three shrapnel balls and a piece of the shell struck General Clingman but having hit the sand before striking home he was only bruised. About 5:00 p.m. we returned to the railroad three miles from New Berne and bivouacked for the night. General [Seth M.] Barton commenced his attack on Brice's Creek at 12:00 noon but we heard very little firing and anxiously awaited his attack on New Berne after destroying the railroad communication [with Morehead City, route of Federal communication] as was the plan. Weather fair and pleasant till almost 3:00 a.m. next day when it rained a little.

Tuesday February 2nd 1864

Did not attack New Berne but awaited for General Barton to make some attack on New Berne from his side of the Trent River but as he never did attack New Berne on account of being unable to take the works on the opposite side of Brice's Creek to where he was. General Pickett after communicating with General Barton through Captain [Robert A.] Bright of his staff who crossed the river and back the same day ordered us to fall back and about 2:00 a.m. next day we fell back to the Kinston side of the Core Creek about thirteen miles from New Berne. Night before last [Commander] Colonel [John T.] Wood with some boats attacked most gallantly a Yankee gunboat [four-gun steamer *Underwriter*] in the Neuse and boarded her and burnt her right under the guns of New Berne. Weather fair and pleasant.

Wednesday February 3rd 1864

Remained all day in bivouac a mile this side of Core Creek that is from the time we arrived almost 8:00 a.m. Weather fair but very windy.

Thursday February 4th 1864

Remained on watch in the direction of Kinston about sunrise our brigade being next to Kinston in line of march. Reached Kinston about 3:00 p.m. and were very anxious to go on immediately to Petersburg but transportation could not be furnished immediately and General Ransom's Brigade was to leave first. My boy Pompey returned to me from home bringing two letters from my Mother and Sister. Weather fair and pleasant.

Friday February 5th 1864

Remained in camp all day, transportation not being as yet furnished for General Ransom's Brigade. Sent my boy Pompey home to meet me in Weldon with a new horse in exchange for my present one who is rather old. Wrote my Mother by Pompey. Weather fair and pleasant.

Saturday February 7th [6th] 1864

Remained in camp all day. Part of General Ransom's Brigade did manage to get off today. Weather fair and pleasant.

Sunday February 7th 1864

Marched into town as we marched to be near the train when she arrived and were in hopes that she would arrive during the day but General Clingman was informed in the afternoon that the train would not arrive till late in the night. Bivouacked for the night about [a] mile and [a] half from the railroad in a woods behind a Mr. Washington's house. Weather fair and pleasant.

Monday February 8th 1864

Started about 5:30 a.m. and did not delay on the road longer than was indispensably necessary till all reached Weldon about 2:00 p.m. and we remained the[re] till 9:00 p.m. Found on arriving in Weldon that the enemy were reported advancing on Richmond and that part of General Ransom's Brigade had gone as far as Petersburg but before we left Weldon the news was contradicted or rather the Yankees went back to their starting place. Left Weldon about 7:30 p.m. and reached Petersburg at 5:00 a.m. the next day. Went immediately to camp at Dunn's house. Weather fair but cold night and as we had no fire in the camp suffered very much from cold.

Tuesday February 9th 1864

Went in town for an hour in the morning with Captain Blake aide-de-camp and in the morning took tea at Mr. [Thomas] Branch's[7] with Captain White and General Clingman. Returned to camp about 11:00 p.m. Weather fair and pleasant.

Wednesday February 10th 1864

In accordance with my promise I took dinner at Mr. Branch's and after dinner accompanied Miss Bettie Branch to prayer meeting at the Presbyterian Church and after the service took a very pleasant walk with her. Returned and took tea at her father's with General Clingman and Captain Blake. Returned to camp about 11:00 p.m. Weather fair and very pleasant.

Thursday February 11th 1864

Remained in camp all the morning so I let Captain DuHaume have my horse to ride into the city. Major [Alfred M.] Erwin and myself accompanied Miss Bettie Branch to tea at her brother's Lieutenant Colonel James Branch[8] of the artillery. Returned to camp about 1:30 p.m. Weather fair and pleasant. Wrote Father today. General Clingman and Captain White went to Richmond this evening on private business.

Friday February 12th 1864

Agreeable to promise I called on Miss Pattie Branch[9] to get her to introduce me to some of her lady friends. We called on a Misses Cabaniss,[10] Bolling,[11] DeVoss,[12] Golden, and Robinson[13] and had a most agreeable morning indeed. In the evening after supper at Mr. Thomas Branch's accompanied the ladies to a social gathering at Miss Major's. General Clingman and Captain White returned in time to attend at Miss Major's. Called on in the morning Miss Major and Miss Peterson, a lady staying with her. Returned to camp about 12:00 noon. Weather fair and pleasant.

---

[7] Thomas Branch was the son of Thomas Branch of "Willow Hill" of Chesterfield County. He was an owner of Thomas Branch and Sons, wholesale grocers and commission merchants, 8 Old Street, resided between Liberty and Oak. He was important in financial affairs and in the Methodist Church. He had served as mayor of Petersburg from 1842-1843. He was a Unionist delegate to the Virginia Convention of 1861.

[8] Lieutenant Colonel James Read Branch, oldest son of Thomas Branch, resided on High near Market Street.

[9] Pattie Branch was the daughter of Daniel Henry Branch, brother of Thomas Branch, and Martha Patteson Branch.

[10] Possibly daughter of Charles J. Cabaniss, a Petersburg lawyer.

[11] Mary Tabb Bolling, the daughter of George Washington Bolling, would marry W.H.F. Lee in November, 1867.

[12] Possibly the daughter of P.J. DeVoss, shipper of tobacco who resided on Franklin between Orleans and Jefferson.

[13] Mary Robinson, daughter of Thomas Robinson, M.D.

Saturday February 13th 1864

Major Erwin and myself under chaperonage of Miss Bettie Branch called on a number of Miss Branch's lady friends, viz., Misses Ford,[14] Branch's, Curray, Spottswood,[15] Johnson and passed a very agreeable morning. Wrote my Father in the morning. Tuesday Mr. John Reid came out to see me bringing me a fine turkey out from home to me and also a letter from my Father dated 10th instant. Weather fair and pleasant.

Sunday February 14th 1864

Accompanied Miss Pattie Branch to the Episcopal Church in the morning and after church took dinner with Mrs. Colonel Branch and met General and Mrs. Pickett after dinner. I called at Mrs. Thomas Branch and after tea escorted Miss Lelia [Emily Read] Branch[16] to church. Returned to camp about 10:00 p.m. Weather fair but cloudy and consequently disagreeable. General Roger A. Pryor now a private in a cavalry company called at Colonel Branch's as we were at dinner right before we had finished.[17]

Monday February 15th 1864

Called on Miss Pattie Branch to make an engagement with her to call on a Miss Robinson after tea. Called on Miss Heath and Cabiniss and Miss Major and Peterson. Took dinner at Mr. George Reid's[18] and after dinner called on Miss Major and Bettie Branch as I had promised to take a walk with Miss Bettie Branch in the afternoon of today but as commenced to snow at 2:30 p.m. I could not fulfill the engagement. Remained and took tea and left about 11:00 p.m. Enjoyed myself very much indeed. Stopped snowing about dusk but rained for a short time afterwards.

Tuesday February 16th 1864

Went in the city in the morning and called upon Miss Mary Robinson and Miss Mary Johnson[19] and Miss Pattie [Martha Patteson] Branch.[20] Received a letter from Father enclosing a short one from Mother dated 15th instant. Wrote Mother in the morning and in the afternoon Father. Had a very handsome Valentine sent me today through a lady friend but have not been able to discover who sent it. Took tea at Mrs. May Scott's[21] and had the pleasure of meeting Lieutenant Haws (Provost Marshal) and his lady. Had a most pleasant evening; returned to camp about 12:00 p.m. Weather very windy in the after part of the day and turned very cold.

---

[14] Possibly the daughter of George E. Ford, bookseller and stationer, who resided on the upper floor of 54 Sycamore.

[15] Possibly daughter of William F. Spottswood, apothecary, who resided on Liberty near Harrison.

[16] Daughter of Thomas Branch.

[17] Pryor had served in the United States Congress and had commanded a division in the Army of Northern Virginia. He was without command following reorganization of the army and resigned on August 18, 1863. He had enlisted as a private in Major General Fitzhugh Lee's cavalry.

[18] George Reid, a commission and shipping merchant (Scott and Reid), resided on Sycamore opposite Tabb.

[19] Mary Johnson was the daughter of William Ransom Johnson, brother of Waverly Johnson.

[20] Martha Branch was the daughter of David H. Branch.

[21] Possibly wife of Frederick R. Scott, of Thomas Branch and Sons, who resided on Liberty between Harrison and Byrne or wife of J.V. Scott, of Scott and Reid, who resided on Franklin between Jefferson and Adams.

Wednesday February 17th 1864

In the evening Captain Blake and myself called at Mr. [George Bernard] Major's and took tea with the ladies. Met General Clingman at his house. Received a letter from Father dated 16th instant. Returned to camp about 11:00 p.m. Weather extremely cold and wind high.

Thursday February 18th 1864

Called upon Misses Heath, Cabaniss, Bolling, Spottswood, Joynes[22] and [?]Marge Mary Page. Found only Miss Page, Cabaniss and Heath at home. In the evening Captain White and myself took tea at Mr. Thomas Branch's. Returned to camp about 12:00 p.m. Weather colder than I think it has been this year.

Friday February 19th 1864

Agreeable to an engagement made last night with Miss Bettie Branch I accompanied her on a visit to a sick protege of hers on the heights. Took dinner at Lieutenant Colonel Branch's and had a most delightful evening. Weather fair but cold, though not so cold as yesterday.

Saturday February 20th 1864

In company with Miss Pattie Branch called upon Misses Bolling, Joynes, DeVoss, and Meade[23] but found them all not at home except Miss Joynes and Miss DeVoss who was unwell. Returned to camp to dinner and returned to Petersburg in the evening and took tea at Mr. Thomas Branch's. Returned to camp about 11:00 p.m. Received a letter from Sister from Raleigh dated 17th instant. Weather fair and much warmer.

Sunday February 21st 1864

Escorted Misses Mollie and Bettie Branch to the M. E. Church and heard a very good sermon from a Mr. Wheelwright. Took dinner at Mr. Thomas Branch accompanied Miss Bettie Branch to the Presbyterian Church in the afternoon and heard an eloquent sermon from Mr. Miller. Took tea at Mr. Major's and accompanied Miss Major to church. Orders came last night from General Pickett to General Clingman to make his headquarters at Ivor Station and leave his two regiments here but General Clingman made an application for a leave of absence for two weeks and delayed going till he could hear from it. After calling at Mr. Branch's on our way back from Mr. Major's we reached camp about 12:00 p.m. Called on Miss Mary Johnson and Miss Pattie Branch to bid them good-bye. Weather fair and pleasant.

Monday February 22nd 1864

Accompanied Miss Bettie Branch on a visiting expedition. Called on Miss Bolling but found her not at home and also upon Miss Harrison who was at home. General Clingman heard from his application for leave of absence which was granted him. Wrote Waverly Johnson about getting me some government cloth. Accompanied Miss Pattie Branch to Dr. [Thomas] Emmett Robinson's[24] and took tea there and passed the evening. Enjoyed myself very much. Returned to camp about 12:00 p.m. Weather cloudy but warm.

---

[22] Daughter of Judge William T. Joynes.

[23] Marion Meade was the daughter of Richard K. Meade who resided on the corner of Perry and Washington. He had previously served in the House of Representatives and as United States ambassador to Brazil.

[24] Thomas Emmett Robinson, M.D., resided on the corner of Second and Bollingbrook.

Tuesday February 23rd 1864

In the morning (before dinner) called upon Misses Bettie and Mollie Branch and Miss Mary Johnson and Victoria Branch[25] but found them out and Miss Bettie Page but she was not at home nor either of the Misses [Marion and Indiana] Meade. After dinner returned to Petersburg and passed the evening at Mr. W.R. Johnson's. Received a letter from Mother and Father dated 22nd instant. Weather fair and pleasant. Wrote Mother today.

Wednesday February 24th 1864

Called upon the Misses Branch in the morning and also to Major Erwin to call upon Miss Mary Robinson. Took dinner at Mrs. C.M. Page and walked with Miss Mary Johnson in the evening; agreeable to an appointment took tea at Mr. T. Branch's and met two Misses Henkle, refugees from Baltimore, just arrived from there. Returned to camp about 12:00 p.m. Weather cloudy but warm.

Thursday February 25th 1864

Called upon Miss Giles, a refugee from St. Louis and staying at Mr. T. Branch's. Called on Miss Robinson and took dinner there. Escorted Miss Giles and Bettie Branch to the Episcopal Church for evening service. Escorted Miss Mollie Branch to a lecture delivered by Reverend Mr. [James A.] Duncan,[26] Methodist minister in Richmond; was much pleased with the lecture. Returned to camp about 12:00 p.m. Weather fair but cloudy.

Friday February 26th 1864

Called on Miss Henkles in company with Captains White and [Cyrus W.] Grandy and also Miss Mary Robinson and I spent a few minutes at Mr. Thomas Branch's. Escorted Miss Bettie Branch and Miss Giles from church. Spent the evening at Mrs. C.M. Page's and had a very pleasant time. Returned to camp about 10:45 p.m. Weather fair but exceedingly disagreeable on account of wind.

Saturday February 27th 1864

In company with Major Erwin called upon the Misses Branch and Miss Giles and also upon Miss Spottswood. Alone I called upon the Misses Meade but found only one at home (Miss Marion). Called at Colonel Branch's but Miss Pattie[27] was sick in bed. After dinner returned to Petersburg in company with Captain White and we accompanied Miss Bettie Branch and Miss Giles in a walk. Took tea and escorted Miss Giles to the theater to hear General R.A. Pryor deliver an address on the times. Was very much disappointed but was glad to hear he was not himself this evening. Returned to camp about 12:00 p.m. Wrote Father. Weather fair and very pleasant.

Sunday February 28th 1864

In the morning accompanied Miss Mary Johnson to the Episcopal Church. Took dinner at Mr. Thomas Branch's and escorted Miss Lilia Branch to church in the after-

---

[25] Victoria Branch was the daughter of David Henry Branch.

[26] Duncan was minister of the Broad Street Baptist Church and regarded as a dynamic pulpit orator.

[27] Martha Louise Patteson, Colonel James R. Branch's wife.

noon at Mr. [Churchill] Gibson's church [Grace Episcopal Church on High Street]. Took tea at Dr. Emmett Robinson's and escorted Miss Mary Robinson to [St. Pauls Episcopal] church in the evening; heard a most delightful sermon in the evening from Mr. [William H.] Platt.[28] Weather fair and little windy. Returned to camp at 12:00 p.m.

Monday February 29th 1864

Remained in camp till about 6:00 p.m. on account of the weather which began to drizzle about 9:30 a.m. and continued so all day. Took tea at Mr. Thomas Branch's and returned to camp about 12:00 p.m. Met at Mr. Branch's Miss Thomas. Received a letter from Captain Rogers, quartermaster of the 35th North Carolina Regiment enclosing a certificate [of] when I was last paid.

Tuesday March 1st 1864

In the morning Major Erwin and myself called at Mr. Branch's and I leaving him there called on Miss Tabb Bolling; found her at home and passed a pleasant time during the visit. Received a letter from Sister dated 28th ultimo. After dinner Major Erwin and myself went to the city and took tea and passed the evening at Dr. Robinson's. Weather rainy and windy all day. Wrote Mother today.

Wednesday March 2nd 1864

In the morning called on Misses Peterson and Majors but they were out and also called at Mr. Branch's. Paid a visit to a Miss Haskill who I met some time since at the Majors. Had a very pleasant walk in the afternoon with Miss Mary Robinson. Passed the evening at Mr. T. Branch's. Wrote Mother again. Weather fair and very pleasant.

Thursday March 3rd 1864

Did not go into the city in the morning. About 1:00 p.m. I heard that the enemy had approached near Richmond in heavy force and in about a quarter of a hour Colonel [Hector M.] McKethan commanding the line regiments returned saying he had been ordered by General Pickett to take his command immediately to the Richmond Depot and that if any of the staff felt so disposed he would be pleased to have them accompany him. As Major Erwin and Captain White were in town, I awaited for their return so we all should go in together. We started for Petersburg at 4:30 p.m. and after saying goodbye to a few friends left for Richmond at 5:30 p.m. which we reached at about 10:30 p.m. Reported at General [Arnold] Elzey's headquarters but could get no information of the whereabouts of the brigade so we put our horses in a livery stable and went to the Spottswood Hotel.

Friday March 4th 1864

After breakfast we heard the enemy had gone and in fact it was telegraphed not to send the brigade but it did not arrive in time. I started about 11:30 a.m. before the rest of the staff and reached Petersburg at 4:30 p.m. and after leaving a note for Miss Bettie Branch asking her to let me accompany her to the lecture I went to camp. Received a letter from Mother dated March 2nd. About 7:00 p.m. rode into

---

[28] William H. Platt would later marry Indiana Meade.

the city and escorted Miss Bettie to the lecture by the Reverend Mr. Henkle refugee from Baltimore. The lecture was nothing but a collection of facts in reference to the Negro. Weather yesterday fair and pleasant and also fair today but a little windy.

Saturday March 5th 1864

In the morning called on Miss Mary Robinson and at Mr. Branch's. Got an order from Captain Stack ordnance officer to have a bit made at the Ordnance Department. Returned to camp for dinner and called at Mr. Branch's in the evening for a short time and then at Dr. Robinson's. Returned to camp about 10:00 p.m. Weather rained during the day but cleared up in the afternoon about 4:00 p.m.

Sunday March 6th 1864

Heard positively today that we would leave for Ivor Station tomorrow morning, a thing which we have been fearing for some time as it was ordered some time since and General Clingman's furlough only delayed it. Intended to escort Miss Robinson to church today but arrived after she started. Returned to Camp for dinner and Captain White and myself returned to the city about 4:30 p.m. and said goodbye to Miss Pattie Branch and Miss Johnson and the ladies at her house and then we spent the evening at Mr. Branch's. Captain White escorted Miss Bettie Branch to church and a Lieutenant Battles [escorted] Miss Giles. Miss Mollie and myself did not attend any church. As we were riding out of the city about 11:00 p.m. for camp Lieutenant Colonel James Branch met Captain White and told him General Pickett had ordered him (Colonel Branch) to order General Clingman to remain till further orders in view of the fact that Colonel John V. Jordan [31st North Carolina Infantry] had fallen back to Ivor Station. We were all very much grateful at the revoking of the orders. Weather fair and pleasant.

Monday March 7th 1864

Accompanied Miss Bettie Branch on a visiting tour to invite some lady friends to a party at her house in honor of Miss Giles. Returned to camp to dinner and agreeable to an appointment accompanied Miss Giles on a ride on horseback borrowing Lieutenant [Henry S.] Puryear's (aide) mare for Miss Giles to ride. Had a pleasant ride. Took tea at Mr. Johnson's and spent the evening and enjoyed myself very much a Mr. [?]Leuroni and Miss Robinson called during the evening and Captain [Edward R.] Baird, General Pickett's staff. Returned to camp about 11:00 p.m. Weather fair but clouded up in the afternoon.

Tuesday March 8th 1864

Owing to the rain did not go in town in the morning. About 1:00 p.m. received a note from Father saying he was at Jarratts Hotel and to come in and see him. Immediately I went in and spent the time with him till 4:00 p.m. when he went to Richmond. After he left called on Misses Robinson, Page and sisters, Spottswood and Peterson and Major. Called at 8:00 p.m. for Miss Mary Johnson to escort her to the party at Mr. Thomas Branch's but did not reach Mr. Branch's till about 4:00 p.m. Enjoyed myself very much at the party and saw some very beautiful ladies. About thirty persons were present I should judge. Left about 1:00 a.m. and after escorting Miss Johnson home came directly to camp. Weather rained all morning but in the afternoon no rain and cleared up somewhat.

Wednesday March 9th 1864

Called upon the Misses Branch and Miss Giles and also upon Miss Robinson and Miss Tabb Bolling but they were not at home. And also called at Mrs. Mary Page and saw Miss Lucy but her sister Bettie was not at home. Returned to camp to dinner and returned in the afternoon with two horses to take a ride with Miss Bettie Branch but she could not get a habit and we took a walk. My Father returned from Richmond at about 7:30 p.m. and I remained with him till he returned to bed which he did very soon as he was very tired. Spent the remainder of the evening at Mr. Branch's and returned to camp about 11:00 p.m. Telegraphed my Father to Richmond but he did not receive it. Weather fair and warm but clouded up in the evening.

Thursday March 10th 1864

Owing to the rain I did not go in town till after dinner about 4:00 p.m. and called upon Miss Robinson and at Mr. Thomas Branch. Returned to Jarratts Hotel to see my Father at 7:00 p.m. but he not being at home I returned [and] spent the evening at Mr. Branch's. About 11:00 p.m. returned to Jarratts and my Father arrived soon after. Returned to camp about 11:30 p.m. Weather rained all day with short intervals but about 11:00 a.m. cleared up.

Friday March 11th 1864

In the morning went in the city and called on Miss Robinson but she was confined to her room with a chill. Called at Mr. Branch's. Returned to camp and about 8:00 p.m. started for the city to keep an engagement with Miss Pattie Branch to go call at Mr. [Judge William T.] Joynes' and spend the evening. Did not go to Mr. Joynes' but spent the evening at Mr. [George W.] Bolling's.[29] On our way back called at Mr. Branch's to concert arrangements to go to Richmond with Miss Giles though she was not visible it was determined that I should call for her at 4:00 a.m. next day. About 11:00 p.m. went to Jarratts Hotel and slept till about 4:00 a.m. when I had to rise to go to Richmond. Weather fair and pleasant.

Saturday March 12th 1864

At 4:15 a.m. called for Miss Giles and we walked to the depot. Was very sleepy so I slept from Petersburg to Richmond. Arrived in Richmond about 7:30 a.m. and after escorting Miss Giles to her uncle's house I went and breakfasted at the Spottswood Hotel. Met General Clingman there who had gone to Richmond the evening previous. About 10:00 a.m. went to [Julian] Vannerson's Photograph Gallery at 11:30 a.m. agreeable to an appointment Miss Giles met me there. Had my carte de visite taken but it could not be finished till late in the evening so they promised to send it to me at Petersburg. About 4:40 p.m. we started for Petersburg and reached it about 7:30 p.m. Took supper at Mr. Branch's and remained there till about 11:00 p.m. meeting Captain McGaan and during the evening Miss Joynes and a friend of hers, a Dr. Scarborough, called for a short time also a Lieutenant Eleason (Artillery). Weather fair and very pleasant. Returned to camp about 11:00 p.m.

---

[29] George Washington Bolling was a Petersburg attorney whose office was in the Exchange Building and who resided on the northwest corner of Liberty and Sycamore at "Poplar Lawn." He was the father of Mary Tabb Bolling.

His brother Robert B. Bolling was a successful Petersburg planter who had visited at Thornbury before the Civil War. Robert was the owner of Center Hill and had served as mayor of Petersburg from 1839-1840.

**War-time photograph of
Captain William H.S. Burgwyn**
Clark, *Histories*, IV:481

Sunday March 13th 1864

Agreeable to an engagement I escorted Miss Giles to church at St. Paul's in the morning. Took dinner at Mr. George Reid's and supper at Mr. Branch and escorted Miss Bettie Branch to church and the Washington Street M. E. Church. Returned to camp about 12:00 p.m. Weather fair and very pleasant. General Bragg and Pickett came on yesterday evening's train from Richmond, I forgot to state.

Monday March 14th 1864

Escorted Miss Bettie Branch on a horseback ride in the morning. Started about 10:00 a.m. and returned about 12:00 noon. Enjoyed myself very much. Returned to camp to dinner and came back to the city about 4:30 p.m. expecting to take a buggy ride with Miss Mollie Branch but she could not obtain the horses. Took tea at Mr. Dr. Robinson's and escorted Miss Mary to the lecture given by a Reverend Hall, Washington Artillery, on the "Historical Significance of the Lutheran Revolution." Was rather pleased with the lecture. Returned to camp about 11:00 p.m. Was introduced to Dr. Emmitt Robinson. Weather fair in the morning but lowering at night.

Tuesday March 15th 1864

Agreeable to promise I escorted Miss Mary Robinson to ride on horseback though I had much difficulty in getting her to go but enjoyed myself extremely during the ride and made an agreement to accompany Miss Mary Johnson and Miss Mary

Robinson on a horseback ride tomorrow morning. Took dinner at Jarratts Hotel and at 3:45 p.m. called for Miss Joynes to go to [St. Pauls Episcopal] church as previously arranged. After church paid a visit to Mr. Platt in his study and had an agreeable visit. Took tea at Dr. Robinson's and passed the evening in Dr. Robinson's room which was a particular favor and I don't know when I have passed a more pleasant evening. Wrote Mother a short letter. Weather fair in the fore part of the day but about 4:00 p.m. turned cloudy and cold and about 7:00 a.m. it snowed a little but cleared up before day. Returned to camp about 12:00 p.m.

Wednesday March 16th 1864

In the morning about 11:30 a.m. I called for Miss Robinson to walk with her to Mr. W.R. Johnson to start on the horseback ride from there. Rode for about an hour and was surprised to see how well Miss Mary Johnson rode and how much improved from her yesterday's ride Miss Mary Robinson was. Dined at Mr. Branch's and escorted Miss Bettie to church and took tea and spent the evening at Dr. Robinson's with Major Erwin, Captain White, Miss Mary Johnson and Miss Osborne.[30] Wrote Lieutenant Waverly Johnson at Weldon, North Carolina. Weather cold and cloudy.

Thursday March 17th 1864

Had a pleasant ride on horseback with Miss Bettie Branch; rode through the country. Returned to camp to dinner and spent the evening at Mr. Branch's with General Clingman and Captain White and two or three ladies other than the ladies at the house. Weather fair and very pleasant.

Friday March 18th 1864

Remained at camp all the morning; about 4:30 p.m. rode to the city to take a ride on horseback with Miss Mary Johnson but the wind was too high to ride on horseback. Took tea at Mr. Branch's and escorted Miss Mollie Branch to a lecture delivered by the Reverend Edwards from Richmond. After the lecture went to Mr. Johnson's as I had been invited and met Misses Giles. Bettie Branch and Major Erwin and Captains White and Blake and [blank in original]. Returned to camp about 12:00 p.m.

Saturday March 19th 1864

In the morning about 10:00 a.m. rode on horseback with Miss Bettie Branch; had a most delightful ride. Returned to camp to dinner in the afternoon about 5:30 p.m. Miss Mollie Branch having obtained her brother John's[31] pair of horses we drove out in the buggy and enjoyed ourselves very much. Passed part of the evening at Judge Joynes' with Miss Pattie Branch and part of the evening at the Branch's. Returned to camp about 11:30 p.m. Received a letter from Mother dated [blank in original] instant. Weather beautiful and warm.

---

[30] Possibly the daughter of Edmund H. Osborne, owner of a Petersburg tobacco factory.

[31] John Patteson Branch, son of Thomas Branch, was a lieutenant in the Confederate Army.

Sunday March 20th 1864

Escorted Miss Mary Johnson to church in the morning returned to camp to dinner. Mr. Platt was very earnest in the sermon. Took tea at Dr. Robinson's and escorted Miss Mary to church. Mr. Platt was again very earnest in his sermon exhorting the young soldiers to be confirmed. Returned to camp about 11:00 p.m. Weather fair and very delightful but turned cool at night.

Monday March 21st 1864

Remained in camp all the morning after dinner went into the city and called on Miss Tabb Bolling but she was not at home. Took tea at Mr. Branch's and escorted Miss Bettie Branch to the lecture at the Baptist Church on Washington Street but as neither General Pryor or Mr. Edwards (the lecturer) did not arrive [sic] we did not enter the church but returned home. About 11:00 p.m. returned to camp. Weather cold and cloudy. Wrote Mother today.

Tuesday March 22nd 1864

About 12:00 noon I was very much surprised to see it snowing though the weather for a day or two had been much like it. About 1:00 p.m. orders came to General Clingman to hold himself in readiness to move with his two regiments tonight or tomorrow morning. About 6:00 p.m. Captain White and myself went into the city, I to say goodbye to some friends. Called first at Mr. W. R. Johnson's and finally at Mr. Branch's. Returned to camp about 12:30 a.m. through a heavy fall of snow and the wind blowing a severe gale. Weather commenced snowing a blowing about 12:00 noon and continued all day and night.

Wednesday March 23rd 1864

Agreeable to promise I sent my horse in town about 8:30 a.m. to make up a sleigh ride and I came in about 11:00 a.m. After I got to town I found that Captain McGann had drawn some already but had not as yet driven the ladies out so as soon as they could get ready, Misses Mollie and Bettie Branch, Thomas, and Major [were] escorted by Captain McGann, Nellie [Emily Read] Branch and her brother Melville [Irby Branch] and accompanied by a soldier to assist in drawing we started and had a very pleasant ride for about an hour and a half. After we returned I took charge of the sleigh and called for Miss Bolling and Miss Mary Johnson and Miss Robinson. The two first named ladies went but Miss Robinson said she could not. Miss Bettie Branch was also kind enough to agree to ride with me again. As I came out of Miss Bolling's gate with Miss Tabb we met General Jenkins who accompanied us on the ride. We rode very pleasantly for about a half hour but as the snow was melting very fast and the horses getting tired, I, after we had got as far as Blandford [Church], turned down a street to go home again and came directly upon a steep hill and in turning round broke the tongue of the sleigh. The ladies escorted by General Jenkins walked home while I remained to get the sleigh home. After many ineffectual attempts to get the horses to pull the sleigh home I hired a cart to do so. As soon as I got the sleigh to Colonel Branch's stables and after calling at Mr. Branch to see if my horse was there as I had left him there, I rode to camp at 4:30 p.m. Did not go to the city any more. Weather a little warm and the snow melted very much.

Thursday March 24th 1864

Called at Mr. Branch's and found Miss Bettie very well though she had had a severe cold the night before owing to her walk. Called to see how Miss Bolling was and also called at Mr. Johnson's and Dr. Robinson's. Miss Johnson suffered very much the night before from neuralgia but was much better today. Returned to camp to dinner and at 7:00 p.m. went into the city with General Clingman. Took tea and spent the evening at Mr. Branch's. Was guilty of a very unfortunate and unpleasant [illegible] which I regret not to have been as I know what the result would be if I should do what I did. Weather cloudy and fair and the snow melted very much.

Friday March 25th 1864

Went to church in the morning called at Mr. T. Branch's but found Miss Bettie unwell. Called at Mr. Johnson's. Returned to camp to dinner intending to return to the city in the evening and spend it at Dr. Robinson's but the weather was so bad I did not leave camp. Received a letter from Father and Mother dated 24th. Wrote Sister a letter. Weather cloudy in the morning and about 5:00 p.m. commenced raining and rained almost all night.

Saturday March 26th 1864

In the morning called at Mr. Branch's, Mr. Jenkin's, Colonel Branch's, Dr. Robinson's and Mr. Bollings. Found all at home but Miss Tabb Bolling was very sorry to hear that Miss Mollie Branch was confined to her room from indisposition. Returned to camp to dinner. Took tea at Dr. Robinson's and then Miss Mary Robinson and myself called at Miss Mary Johnson's. Met Captain White and a Mr. Symington there. Returned to camp about 11:30 p.m. Weather fair and windy in the day but at dusk it sprinkled a little.

Sunday, March 27th 1864

Agreeable to engagement escorted Miss Mary Robinson to Church in the morning and though I had intended to remain and dine in the city on second thought I determined I would not and having come up with an ambulance rode the remainder of the distance. Took tea at Colonel Branch's and escorted Miss Pattie to church. Returned to camp about 10:00 p.m. Weather cloudy and fair and little cloudy.

Monday, March 28th 1864

Went in the city about 10:00 a.m. intending to ride with Miss Bettie Branch but she could not get a saddle. Called on Miss Pattie Branch and Miss Giles also on Miss Robinson and Miss Johnson. After dinner returned to the city about 4:30 p.m. to ride with Miss Mary Johnson. Major Erwin and Captain White also rode with ladies. Took tea at Mr. Johnson's and escorted Miss Mary to the lecture by a Mr. Scule D. Vene, Professor of Modern Languages at the University. After the lecture Miss Mary Johnson went to Dr. Robinson's and remained till 11:15 p.m. Weather fair and warm but clouded up a little about dusk.

Tuesday March 29th 1864

In the morning called upon Misses Bettie and Mollie Branch and on Miss Joynes at Colonel Branch's in company with Major Erwin and then upon Miss Robinson alone. Received an invitation in company with some others of the staff to spend the evening at Colonel Branch's to meet some ladies and the ladies at the house. Returned to camp to dinner. Commenced raining about 3:30 p.m. and rained very hard during the remainder of the afternoon but about 6:00 p.m. Captain White and myself rode into the city through the rain to keep the invitation. Went first at Mr. Thomas Branch's [and] took tea and as the rain had ceased prevailed upon Miss Bettie to go with me to Colonel Branch's. Arrived late about 9:30 p.m. Remained till about 11:30 p.m. and about 12:30 p.m. we returned to camp. Weather commenced raining about 3:30 p.m. and rained hard till 8:00 p.m. then stopped.

Wednesday March 30th 1864

Did not go in the city till after dinner and about 5:30 p.m. Called at Dr. Robinson and took a walk with Miss Mary and took tea there about 8:30 p.m. Weather cloudy and windy at intervals and so inclement looking that I could not keep an engagement with Miss Bettie Branch to go to ride. Wrote Father, too.

Thursday March 31st 1864

Went to the city in the morning and called upon Miss Branch at Colonel Branch's and also upon Miss Mary Johnson. Returned to camp about 2:30 p.m. and after dinner returned to the city to keep an engagement with Miss Giles to go to ride. After returning from the ride went to Mr. Johnson's to escort Miss Johnson to Dr. Robinson's to spend the evening but she was too unwell to go so after tea about 9:00 p.m. I went and enjoyed myself very much. Weather cloudy but moderately warm.

Friday April 1st 1864

Went in to the city in the morning and called upon Miss Robinson and Mr. Thomas Branch but found the Miss Branches not at home. Agreeable to engagement I called on Miss Page in company with Miss Pattie Branch. Afterward called on the Misses Branch and saw Miss Mollie. Returned to dinner and returned to the city to take ride with Miss Robinson and enjoyed the ride extremely. Took tea and spent the evening at Dr. Robinson's and returned to camp about 11:00 p.m. Weather very April-like but at about dark it rained pretty steadily and about 12 [a.m.] it rained hard and all night.

Saturday April 2nd 1864

About 8:00 p.m. it commenced to snow and I think the flakes were larger than any I had ever seen and the atmosphere was more transparent than I had ever seen it before on such an occasion. You were enabled to see the flakes up in the air at least two hundred and fifty or three hundred feet. About 12:00 noon it discontinued to snow and rain and about 6:00 p.m. I went in the city. Called on Miss Bolling but she was not at home. Escorted Miss Bettie Branch to Colonel Branch's and took tea and spent the evening there. Returned to camp about 11:30 p.m.

Sunday April 3rd 1864

Went to church in the morning and escorted Miss Mary Johnson home. Returned to camp to dinner. My horse "Beverly" from some reason or other sprained himself a little and I determined to send Pompey home tomorrow morning for another horse.

Took tea at Mr. T. Branch's and escorted Miss Bettie to her church W. M. E. Church. Returned to camp about 10:15 p.m. Weather cloudy and little cool. Received a letter from Father dated 29th ultimo and one from Sister dated 2nd instant. Wrote Father a letter and Mother a few lines to send by Pompey tomorrow.

Monday April 4th 1864

Sent Pompey home for a horse on the 10:30 a.m. train. Went in the city about 11:00 a.m. and after calling at Mrs. C. Page called at Dr. Robinson's remained to dinner and till about 4:30 p.m. when I called to see Mr. Platt, Episcopal Minister. Had a very pleasant time with him. Called on Miss Bettie and Mollie Branch and remained about three-fourth hour and then returned to Dr. Robinson's as I had promised. Spent almost all evening in the Doctor's room and was very glad to see him so much better. Taking everything into consideration it was decidedly the most pleasant day I have passed since I have come to Petersburg. Weather commenced to rain about 12:00 noon and continued raining a little all day and night. Returned to camp about 12:00 p.m.

Tuesday April 5th 1864

Rained incessantly till about dark consequently I did not go to the city till about 6:00 p.m. Took tea and passed the evening at Dr. Robinson's in company with Major Erwin. Returned to camp about 11:15 p.m.

Wednesday April 6th 1864

Called on the Misses Branch but they were not at home. Also upon Miss Johnson and Miss Pattie Branch and on Miss Robinson; found them all at home. Returned to camp for dinner and had a turkey which Pompey brought from home this morning, he having returned very unexpectedly and without the horse I sent him for. Took tea and spent the evening at Mr. Johnson's. Left about 10:00 p.m. and spent an hour and half at Dr. Robinson's. Weather fair and moderately warm. Wrote Father and received a letter from him by Pompey.

Thursday April 7th 1864

Called on Mrs. Mary Page and Miss Bettie and Mollie Branch and at Dr. Robinson's. Returned to camp to dinner and then returned to the city to take a ride with Mrs. Mary Page as previously engaged. Took tea at Mr. Branch's and spent a very pleasant evening. Returned to camp about 11:15 p.m.

Friday April 8th 1864

Went into the city in the morning and attended St. Paul's Church. Heard a very good sermon from Mr. Platt. Returned to camp after church and feasted on bread and about 6:00 p.m. went to the city. Took tea and spent all the evening at Dr. Robinson's except a short time after tea that I spent at Colonel Branch's where I went to see Miss Pattie Branch to find out from her if she would go down the country tomorrow as she had determined to do. Weather fair and warm but clouded up after dark. Returned to camp about 10:45 p.m.

Saturday April 9th 1864

Owing to the rain did not go in the city till about 5:30 p.m. and after calling at Mr. Branch's took tea and spent the evening at Mr. Johnson. Met Waverly Johnson who had been sent up by General Ransom on business. Received a letter from Captain Peterson at Weldon dated 8th instant saying my Father had bought me a horse and to send for it. Returned to camp about 11:00 p.m. Weather rained all day after 11:00 a.m.

Sunday April 10th 1864

Escorted Miss Pattie Branch to Church in the morning. About 4:30 p.m. called at Mr. Branch's to see Miss Bettie and had the pleasure of meeting Colonel and Mrs. [Arthur S.] Cunningham. Took Miss Mary [Robinson] to church. Was confirmed by Bishop [John] Johns [Coadjutor Bishop of the Episcopal Diocese of Virginia]. Returned to camp about 12:45 a.m. Weather rained some in the afternoon (thunder storm on a small scale) and rained during the night.

Monday April 11th 1864

Having obtained my leave of absence I started for Garysburg at 10:30 a.m. and reached Garysburg about 4:14 p.m. Waited till about dark for the carriage which had gone to Weldon bridge to meet Father who was to come from Raleigh but who did not. Reached home about 8:00 p.m. and was glad to find the family all well. Weather rained some little during the day.

Tuesday April 12th 1864

After accompanying Mother on a walk I commenced on a pair of gloves and worked on them till dinner and most of the afternoon finished one and a half. Father arrived about the same time I did yesterday and was looking very well which I was very glad. Weather rained some during the afternoon.

Wednesday April 13th 1864

After riding out over the plantation with Father (and rode the nice young horse he bought me) I about 5:30 p.m. started after turkeys accompanied by Robert (coachman) but after a fatiguing paddling over the low grounds for turkeys returned home about 8:30 p.m. without any game. Worked some on my other glove today. Weather fair and no rain and perfectly delightful.

Thursday April 14th 1864

Rode out with Father in the morning and met my brother George who was returning from the Clarkeville Junction where he had been to see about storing some cotton. After dinner Mr. John Reid, his brother George and Mr. Lee arrived. Went out with the [illegible] to to look for some turkeys but did not see any. They could not remain to tea as expected but left just before. Weather fair and pleasant.

Friday April 15th 1864

Rode out with father in the morning. Weather clouded up in the afternoon and rained a little.

Saturday April 16th 1864

Rode out with Father in the morning and about 1:30 p.m. had all the Negroes up to find out who stole all of his wine he had hid under a barn to keep it from the Yankees in case they should ever get to the plantation. After dinner started to look for deer or turkeys but could see none. Weather rained all the morning till about 11:30 and rained a little the latter part of the evening.

Sunday April 17th 1864

Did not go to church to Jackson but Mother and Father did and [younger brothers] Allie [John Alveston Burgwyn] and Collin [Collinson Pierrepont Edwards Burgwyn]. Had some ice cream in honor of myself for dinner today. Sent Pompey with a note to Mr. John Reid asking him to take a deer hunt tomorrow and also to bring some eggs and fowel at Uncle Tom's plantation [Occoneechee Wigwam]. Weather fair and very pleasant.

Monday April 18th 1864

Rode out with Father in the morning. Started to meet the cars for Petersburg at 5:30 p.m. a cart taking my valise and bag of potatoes, this box of provisions for the Miss [blank in original]. At 7:30 a.m. left Garysburg for Petersburg which I reached about 2:00 p.m. The cars were crowded with soldiers and no other passengers were permitted by the government for sixty days. Weather fair and warm but clouded up and looked very much like rain late in the afternoon.

Tuesday April 19th 1864

On walking down the street about 9:00 a.m. met Major Erwin who told me the general staff had gone to Ivor Station. Was not surprised to find that they had gone as I expected they would be. Called on Miss Robinson and at Colonel Branch's also on Miss Johnson and Mr. Thomas Branch. Rode out to camp in a wagon that carried out my boxes and about 5:00 p.m. returned to Petersburg to keep an engagement to walk with Miss Bettie Branch. After taking the walk took tea and spent the evening at Dr. Robinson's with Miss Pattie Branch who I escorted there and home again. Major Erwin also spent part of the evening at Dr. Robinson's. Returned to camp about 12:00 p.m. Weather fair.

Wednesday April 20th 1864

After taking breakfast at Doctor Robinson's Major Erwin and myself started for Ivor Station about 9:15 a.m. which we reached about 1:00 p.m. Found that General Clingman was on his return from Suffolk and he arrived about 4:00 p.m. Weather windy but fair. General Clingman found or saw nothing of interest on his march to Suffolk.

Thursday April 21st 1864

Wrote Mother in the morning. Passed a disagreeable day from enuui and in the afternoon had a rather severe pain in the stomach. General Pickett telegraphed General Clingman that General Hoke had taken Plymouth and 2,500 prisoners and sunk two gunboats [U.S.S. *Bombshell* and U.S.S. *Southfield*]. Weather fair but little windy.

Friday April 22nd 1864

In accordance with a previous determination, viz., that he would go to Petersburg today if he did not receive any cautionary orders, General Clingman and staff started for the city about 2:00 p.m. and arrived at 6:00 p.m. When opposite our headquarters I left the train and walked to camp and after changing my traveling apparel I went to the city. Took tea and spent the evening at Mr. Thomas Branch's. Returned to camp at 11:45 p.m. Weather fair and very delightful.

Saturday April 23rd 1864

Called upon Miss Robinson and Misses Branch and also to see Captain McGann who was wounded in the attack on Plymouth. Found him getting on as well as could be expected. Returned to camp to dinner and again to the city about 7:00 p.m. Took tea and remained till about 8:45 p.m. at Dr. Robinson's and then went to see Miss Bettie Branch. Returned to camp about 10:45 p.m. Weather fair and pleasant. Wrote Mother.

Sunday April 24th 1864

Escorted Miss Pattie Branch to church and took dinner with her. Accompanied Mrs. Jas. Branch[32] to call on Captain McGann but could not see him as the surgeon would not permit it. Heard from General Clingman about 4:30 p.m. that we were ordered to Ivor Station tomorrow morning. Called to see the Misses Branch and say goodbye and then agreeable to engagement took tea and spent the evening at Dr. Robinson's. Weather fair and warm till about 5:30 p.m. when it rained an April shower and rained some during the fore part of the night.

Monday April 25th 1864

Did not go to Ivor as expected but remained as Majors Erwin and Gays could not get their business arranged in time. Visited Misses Robinson and Johnson and the Misses Branch. Rode in the afternoon with Miss Bettie Branch but as her saddle gist broke we took but a short ride. Took tea and spent part of the evening at Mr. Branch's and the remainder at Dr. Robinson's. Weather fair.

Tuesday April 26th 1864

Called on Miss Robinson and the Misses Branch and Miss Joynes but did not find the last three at home. Also called on Miss Pattie Branch. Rode with Miss Branch and enjoyed myself very much. Took tea and spent the evening with her. Wrote my brother George. Weather little cloudy.

Wednesday April 27th 1864

Started for Ivor Station, Suffolk and Petersburg Railroad. Arrived about 12:30 p.m. Had a tent put up near the railroad for my quarters. Received a letter from Mother dated April 26th. Weather little cool and turned cool towards night.

---

[32] Wife of Lieutenant Colonel James R. Branch.

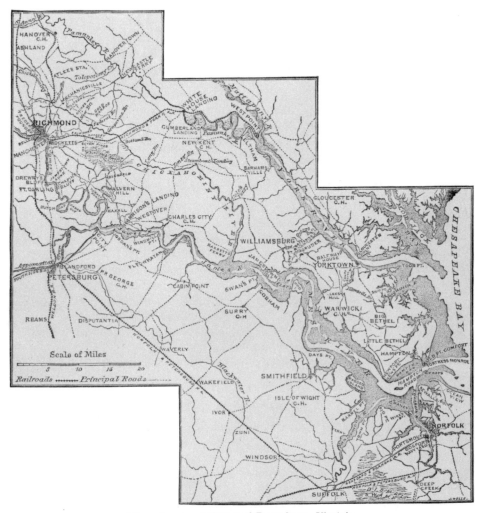

Map of area southeast of Petersburg, Virginia

Battles and Leaders, II:167

Wednesday April 28th 1864

About 7:00 a.m. started with General Clingman and Colonel [James D.] Radcliffe to visit the picket post. First post, Blackwater Bridge Captain Clements headquarters of Colonel [Valentine H.] Taliaferro's Cavalry Regiment (7th Confederate Cavalry). Blackwater Bridge from Ivor ten miles, Captain C. [?Clements] commanded about forty men and one commissioned officer. Second post, Elys ford, four men and one non-commissioned officer, about three miles from Blackwater Bridge. Third post, Joyners Bridge, Lieutenant [N.H.] Fennell, Captain [L.L.] Keith,[33] and Colonel Radcliffe's Regiment (61st North Carolina) one sergeant and nine men distant from Elys ford, the way we went by a Mr. Brown's at whose place we dined, six miles. Fourth post, Lawrence Ford, two and a half miles from Joyners Bridge, Captain Keith, in command with about twenty men. Fifth post, Spivey's Ford, four men and one noncommissioned officer, about 10 miles from Lawrence Ford, from Spivey's Ford returned to Ivor at about 8:00 a.m. about seven miles from Spivey's Ford. Weather cloudy and a little cool.

Friday April 29th 1864

Started again with General Clingman and Colonel Radcliffe. First post, Broadwater Ferry, four miles from Ivor, one sergeant and fourteen men from Colonel Taliaferro's Regiment. Second post, one sergeant and five men one mile from Broadwater Ferry. Third post, one sergeant and six men, on Smithfield road three miles from Blackwater Ferry. Fourth post, Smithfield but no pickets on the way. Dined at a Colonel Thomas', very hospitable gentleman. South from Ivor sixteen miles. Fifth post, Wilson's, Mill Lieutenant Cross, three non-commissioned officers and thirteen men from [illegible] about two miles. Sixth post, Rock Wharf, Lieutenant Moody and about fifteen men of his corps (Signal Corps). Colonel Taliaferro 3 [*sic*] post also at Rock Wharf, one commissioned officer, three non-commissioned officers, and twenty men. Rock Wharf from Smithfield ten miles. Passed the night at Colonel Reed's three miles from Rock Wharf. Weather little windy and little cloudy.

Saturday April 30th 1864

Started about 7:00 a.m. from Colonel Reed's. First post, Burwell's Bay four miles from Rock Wharf. One corporal and six men. Second post, Bacon Castle headquarters of Colonel Taliaferro's command. Captain Morse, Company A, four commissioned officers, six [non-commissioned officers] and thirty-seven men. Captain Phillips, Company K, one commissioned [officer], zero [non-commissioned officers], and thirty-three men. Lieutenant Matthews detachment of one company [of] mountain howitzers three pieces, one commissioned officer, zero [non-commissioned officers], and thirty men. Distant from Rock Wharf ten miles on the way from Bacon Castle to Ivor. A courier met the General with two telegrams from General Pickett ordering him to make a reconnaissance below Suffolk to find the enemy's strength at Portsmouth and Norfolk. Reached Ivor going by [?]Preston Ferry, a distance of about twenty miles from Bacon Castle about 9:00 p.m. Weather fair but rained a little towards dusk.

---

[33] Company G, 61st North Carolina Infantry.

Sunday May 1st 1864

Started with General Clingman to overtake the troops which had marched five miles below Broadwater Bridge. Start 5:00 a.m. overtook the command which consisted of about one hundred cavalry under Lieutenant Colonel [Thomas D.] Claiborne [7th Confederate Cavalry], one regiment infantry under Colonel McKethan, and one battery [of] artillery Captain [Nathaniel A.] Sturdivant at Providence Church about six miles from Suffolk and twenty [miles] from Ivor. Started for Suffolk at 11:00 a.m. After remaining at Suffolk till about 5:00 p.m. the general ordered the troops to return, that is artillery and infantry. The staff left about 6:00 p.m. followed by the cavalry. Had a very little skirmish with the Yankee picket at a run one and a half miles below Suffolk where they had their advance picket post and drove them off. Halted for the night about eight miles from Suffolk. Weather rained pretty regularly till about 2:00 p.m. Dined in Suffolk with a Mr. Riddick.

Monday May 2nd 1864

At 6:15 a.m. started for Ivor. Breakfasted at Windsor and then obtaining permission I rode in the front of the troops to arrive in Ivor in time to write some letters; had time to write Father, Captain Blake, and Lieutenant DuHaume. Accompanied by Major [Giles W.] Cooke of General Beauregard's staff and one of his Europeans arrived from Petersburg. Major Cooke came to inspect the picket posts on the Blackwater line. Weather [was] a very April day but [it] did not rain but about 5:30 p.m.; it clouded up for about three-fourth hours it blew and rained a very hurricane.

Tuesday May 3rd 1864

Wrote Misses Pattie Branch and Mary Robinson and Bettie Branch. Heard by today's papers good news from all quarters though of no fight between Lee and Grant. Went fishing in a mill pond about three miles off in the afternoon but caught nothing. Weather fair and little warm and windy.

Wednesday May 4th 1864

Went fishing again and at the same place in the morning but caught nothing. About 12:30 p.m. telegraph came from General Picket ordering General Clingman and one regiment to come to Petersburg immediately. About 6:00 p.m. the train having arrived we started for Petersburg which we reached about 8:00 p.m. Moved out shortly after arriving in Petersburg to our old headquarters at Dunn's farm. Weather fair and warm. Heard that the enemy had landed in heavy force at Bermuda Hundred with the intention of marching on Petersburg or Drewry's Bluff.

Thursday May 5th [6th] 1864

About 9:00 a.m. General Clingman started with one regiment [51st North Carolina Infantry] and some artillery (Captain Owen's Company [Washington Artillery]) to take position on the turnpike (and Fort Clifton) roads on which the enemy were reported advancing on. Halted about two and a half miles from Petersburg distributing the force on both roads. About 5:00 p.m. part of General [Johnson] Hagood's Brigade [21st South Carolina and part of the 25th South Carolina] arrived

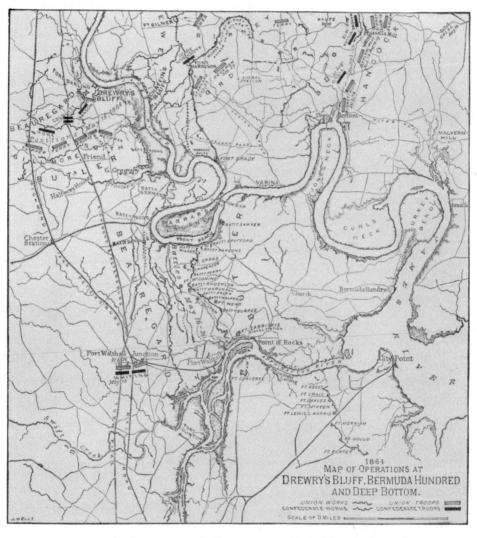

**Map of Bermuda Hundred Peninsula, Drewry's Bluff, and positions of
the Union and Confederate lines subsequent to June, 1864**

and were put on the railroad to Port Walthall Junction about five miles off where they met the enemy and had a severe fight with them. Two regiments only confronted their whole force about two brigades [Brigadier General Charles A. Heckman's brigade]. Weather fair and warm. The result of the fight was almost a drawn one.

Friday May 6th [7th] 1864

General Bushrod Johnson (Tennessee) having arrived with his brigade from Richmond and making a junction with General Hagood to fight the enemy who attacked them about 10:00 a.m. but after a severe fight were forced to give up the possession of the railroad to the enemy and after dark he (General Johnson) retired to Swift Creek about three miles. Our brigade remained inactive guarding the Fort Clifton road and acting as reserve. Weather fair and warm.

Saturday May 7th [8th] 1864

About 10:00 a.m. General Clingman received orders to go with his staff but leave his regiment (51st North Carolina) behind and take charge of the lines east of the city. About dark reports came in from all quarters that the enemy had made their appearance in three miles of the breastworks on several roads leading to Petersburg. The report caused us some anxiety but we heard that reinforcements were arriving from Weldon and that Hoke's old brigade had already arrived. Weather fair and warm. Having heard several reports that the enemy were advancing in heavy force up the City Point Road, I went down to see and came upon our advanced pickets under Colonel Scott who were slowly retiring in front of a large body of Yankees who were advancing with their skirmishers in front. After return of fire some time slowly in their front the enemy sent some cavalry ahead which unexpectedly charged us who, as there were not more than eight and as only three were armed with rifles and the enemy about twenty or more, we fled so as to keep a respectable distance ahead of them but after they had charged us once not thinking they would do so again we went along slowly and they came upon us so suddenly that they got within some two hundred yards before we perceived them. They followed us so rapidly that they ran into our line of pickets who fired into them wounding one horse which I afterwards, about fifteen minutes going out to reconnoiter, came upon and captured a saddle. Wrote, etc.

Sunday May 8th, 1864

[no entry]

Monday May 9th 1864

In accordance with orders General Clingman with part of his brigade and Hoke's Brigade and Sturdivant's Artillery made a reconnaissance towards City Point and started about 2:00 p.m. At two and a half miles from City Point came on the enemy's picket which after observing for some time we turned back and reached our headquarters about 9:00 p.m. Weather fair and warm.

Tuesday May 10th 1864

About 10:00 a.m. on returning from a ride along the works with General Clingman he received an order to report with his brigade on the Richmond Turnpike to General Hoke. After unavoidable delays the brigade left Petersburg about 5:30 p.m.

to join General Hoke. In the time the brigade was being collected I took dinner in company with General Clingman, [and] Captain White at Mr. Thomas Branch and after dinner called on Miss Robinson and about 6:00 p.m. started with the general and staff to overtake the brigade. Stopped for the night about six miles from Petersburg and joining General [Montgomery] Corse's Brigade. Weather about 6:15 p.m. commenced to blow and rain and rained hard for some time but about 9:00 p.m. stopped.

Wednesday May 11th 1864

Started about 5:00 a.m. but after the division had left came up with it about the Halfway House. Shortly after arriving at the Halfway House news came that the enemy were approaching and General Hoke formed his troops in line of battle. Shortly after our brigade moved to the rear to occupy the front line of breastworks around Drewry's Bluff and took position on the right of General Johnson. General Ransom's Brigade had some smart skirmishing with the enemy after we left and Major [Thomas P.] Branch[34] of General Robert Ransom's staff in command of some cavalry fired on them with some artillery and dismounted cavalry. Weather commenced to rain about 6:00 a.m. and rained about all day and some times as hard as I ever saw it rain.

Thursday May 12th [13th] 1864

About 2:30 [a.m.] General [Matthew] Ransom who had moved to the extreme right of the breastworks was suddenly surprised by the enemy who completely flanked him forcing his men to jump on the other side of the works and fight. He lost Captain Durham acting on his staff but Quartermaster [of the] 49th North Carolina Regiment seriously wounded and Lieutenant [Waverly] Johnson on his [Matthew Ransom's] staff painfully wounded. Then we fell back about one mile and formed parallel with the Turnpike and about three-fourth miles from it. Weather rained off and on all day but not heavily. Our brigade was smartly engaged all day skirmishing.[35]

Friday May 13th 1864

About 2:00 a.m. our lines fell back to the inner line of entrenchments around Drewry's Bluff about three-fourths mile in rear of the first. Our brigade suffered some today losing some men in skirmishing with the enemy who had the advantage of a thick woods to approach our sharpshooters with carbines about 4:00 p.m. were driven back to within one hundred and fifty yards of the breastworks. Weather rained pretty heavily during the day.

Saturday May 14th 1864

The [Clingman's] brigade skirmished all day with the enemy and lost considerably about one-fourth killed and wounded of those that were engaged. The enemy fired some artillery but did not injure us much. I forgot to state yesterday that General Beauregard arrived at Drewry's Bluff about 2:00 a.m. with General [Alfred H.] Colquitt's Brigade and Colonel [John A.] Baker's [3rd North Carolina] Cavalry Regiment. Our picket lines having been driven back during the day they were advanced some one hundred and fifty yards and pits dug for the men. Weather rained some in the afternoon and during the night.

---

[34] Thomas P. Branch was the son of Thomas Branch of Petersburg.
[35] Events described as happening on May 12 actually occurred on May 13. During periods of increased activity, W.H.S.B. wrote his diary several days after the fact.

Sunday May 15th 1864

Engaged all day in skirmishing with the enemy but did not lose as many as the day before, owing to the rifle pits. About 8:00 a.m. orders came from General Beauregard saying he intended attacking the enemy early next morning. Weather fair and warm.

Monday May 16th 1864

About daybreak General Robert Ransom on our extreme left opened the fight with his division and succeeded in driving the enemy before him and capturing many prisoners and some artillery. General Johnson then engaged the enemy driving them before him till he reached our outer line we evacuated on the morning of the 13th. General Hoke then attacked the enemy with our and General Corse's Brigade about 9:00 a.m. At the word "charge" our two regiments, the 51st and 31st [North Carolina] Regiments (the 8th and 61st being temporarily detached) and in concert with Corse's Brigade, but which shortly after the charge commenced faced to the right to meet the enemy on their flank, sprang upon the parapet and with a yell started for the enemy. As soon as the word "charge" was given I sprang upon the parapet, waved my hat and yelled with all my might as soon as I could cross the ditch in front. I ran ahead of the regiment, waved my hat, and called on the men to follow and nobly did they come though the enemy's sharpshooters fired as fast as possible from rifles that shot seven times in succession and though the line was considerably disorganized from crossing the ditch and going through the thick underbrush not a man faltered. About three hundred yards from our breastworks and fearing that the enemy fire and the bad ground might throw them into confusion, I seized the colors of the 51st North Carolina Regiment and called on the men to follow. Running in advance I came in about a three hundred yards to the enemy's first line of rifle pits or breastworks made of rails, logs, etc. Mounting them and waving the colors I jumped on the other side and pushed forward closely followed by the men with their color bearer and their colonel at their head. About fifty yards from the first line a number of Yankees were behind pits firing at our men with most deadly aim. As soon as they perceived me four aimed their pieces at me but I falling down at the time, partly from sheer exhaustion and to prevent them from shooting me, their balls missed me but one passed through my hat brim. Rising again and with a shout I ran past the pits and the Yankees surrendered by crowds. I had just time then to hand the colors to a color bearer when I fell down almost fainting and a severe fit of vomiting seized me but which by the time the regiment had got somewhat into line passed off and seeing a piece of artillery about two hundred and fifty yards off fired on our line I again seized the colors and called on the men to charge the battery. With a yell that must have made the Yankees quake, we started passed by the gun and kept on in full speed to charge the enemy's main line of battle, about four hundred yards off posted behind rifle pits and garrisoned by at least two brigades. Giving the colors to the color bearer I ran in advance and took off my hat and waved it over my head cheering as loud as I could but which was not very loud as I was as hoarse as a raven. The first to reach the works, I fell down again exhausted but rising up again as the men commenced to mount the works; I climbed over them and started after the flying enemy but immediately in our front and on either flank the enemy were in tremendous odds and they opened on us with fearful slaughter, that is if they had not fired too high.

Faced by the great force in front and on both flanks and with no support we fell back first to the last works we charged and then to the next and to the last of their breastworks; not being able to rally the men there we fell back to within about two hundred yards of our breastworks. After forming in line General Clingman saw the men were so thoroughly exhausted they could not oppose the enemy if they advanced so he fell back to the rifle pits. There we remained till about 2:00 p.m. when we moved forward and occupied our former position in the outer line [at the original Confederate lines] the enemy having in the mean time retreated. About 5:00 p.m. General Johnson with his brigade and ours marched in pursuit of the enemy along the road and halted for the night in one-half mile of the enemy who were in the woods south of the Halfway House and immediately in our front. The 51st [North Carolina] lost during the day about one hundred and nineteen men and the 31st [North Carolina] about seventy. Weather fair and warm. The enemy left large quantities of ordinance stores and commissary stores besides those they destroyed. We captured some three thousand prisoners, Brigadier General [Charles A.] Heckman and staff, and some six [five] pieces of artillery, four [three] [20-pound] Parrotts and two Napoleons.

Tuesday May 17th 1864

About 3:00 a.m. formed line of battle about three-fourths mile from where we halted last night and about three-fourths of a mile from turnpike to support a battery of artillery which opened upon a woods where it was supposed the enemy were but after shelling a half hour found the enemy had absconded. About 12:00 noon having come in contact with the enemy's pickets about six or seven miles from Bermuda Hundred and placed directly cross the country from the James to the Appomattox River we halted and formed in line of battle and sent forward our skirmishers and remained all day till about 1:00 a.m. when a sharp fire took place between our pickets and the enemy's but it soon ceased. Wrote Mother a letter. Weather fair and warm.

Wednesday May 18th 1864

Remained fronting the enemy all day; had some skirmishing with the enemy. Wrote Miss Bettie Branch thanking her in behalf of the general and staff for a box she and Miss Mollie sent us by Lieutenant [Henry S.] Puryear. Weather fair and warm but an April shower abut 12:00 noon.

Thursday May 19th 1864

About 4:00 p.m. moved our lines forward about a mile occupying the lines the enemy were driven from during the day. Wrote Miss Mary Robinson and sent it by Captain [Cyrus W.] Grandy (Quartermaster of the 8th North Carolina Regiment). Had some sharp skirmishing with the enemy. Weather fair and warm. Received a letter from Father dated 16th instant which gave me great pleasure to receive and one from my brother George dated 6th instant.

Friday May 20th 1864

Had some severe skirmishing with the Yankees[36] and I think General Ransom's Brigade lost over two hundred men charging some Yankee rifle pits. Weather fair and warm.

---

[36] Engagement at Ware Bottom Church.

Saturday May 21st 1864

Very quiet comparatively all day along the lines. Wrote Father a letter. Walked back to where the wagons were with Captain White after supper a distance of about two miles. Returned at 9:30 p.m. About 12:00 p.m. a sharp fire occurred between our pickets and the enemy's and some artillery firing occurred but soon ceased. Received a note from Miss Robinson which was exceedingly acceptable. Weather fair and warm.

Sunday May 22nd 1864

Very quiet again along the front. Our men and the enemy busily engaged in throwing up and strengthening their rifle pits. A Yankee gunboat fired some shells at us but did not damage or hurt anybody that I know of. Wrote Father yesterday. Weather fair and very warm and also little cloudy about 3:00 p.m.

Monday May 23nd 1864

Very quiet again along the lines. The Yankee gunboats shelled us some today wounding some three or four men. Wrote Miss Robinson yesterday; sent it to the city today. About 12:00 p.m. considerable firing took place between our skirmishers and enemy's. Weather fair and warm. (Yesterday walked again back to the rear where the wagons were. Received a letter from Father dated 21st instant.)

Tuesday May 24th 1864

After breakfast visited the wagons; again took a good bath in a clean running stream nearby. Wrote Father today. Received a note from Miss Robinson. Weather fair and warm but rained hard during the night.

Wednesday May 25th 1864

Very quiet all day. Nothing stirring of any importance. Received a note from Miss Bettie Branch. Returned to the wagons and passed the night there having obtained permission to go to Petersburg tomorrow. Weather fair and warm but rained some during the night.

Thursday May 26th 1864

Started for Petersburg in company with Captain Grandy and Major Erwin about 7:00 a.m. Met Mr. John Reid in the streets on his way to Weldon. Sent a message home by him to correct a letter he wrote them saying our brigade had gone to Lee's army. Called first on Miss Bettie Branch and Miss Robinson and Miss Johnson and saw her brother Waverly. Took dinner at Mr. Thomas Branch's. After dinner called on Miss Major and Miss Bolling. Then rode out in Mr. Branch's carriage in company with Miss Mollie and Bettie Branch and Captain McGann and visited two officers of the brigade that were wounded and staying at the General Hospital. Spent the evening at Dr. Robinson's and passed the night there occupying of Dr. Pettigrew's room. Weather rained considerable during the early part of the morning but cleared up afterwards.

Friday May 27th 1864

Started for the brigade about 4:30 a.m. Found them in *status quo ante* when I left. Received a letter from Father dated 25th instant enclosing one from Sister and one from my little brother Collie. Wrote Father a letter and sent it by the mail carrier to Petersburg to the care of McIlwaine Son & Company. Weather fair and warm but clouded up towards night. Very quiet all day with some little shelling from the Yankees and a few responses from one of our guns.

Saturday May 28th 1864

Very quiet all day. Wrote a note to the Robinsons in reference to taking care of my trunk, etc., and sent Pompey in the city with it. Weather in the afternoon clouded up and rained some about dark.

Sunday May 28th 1864

Not a gun fired all day from the enemy and but one from our side. Returned to the wagons and read the morning lesson in the Bible and Prayer Book. Weather cool for this time of the year and not very clear.

Monday May 29th 1864

Heard heavy guns in the morning and was informed by Captain Cooper, General Hoke's staff, that General Lee had moved up five miles last night from Mechanicsville to Atlee Station with the intention of attacking General [Ulysses S.] Grant this morning and that the guns we heard were from there in all probability. Returned in company with Captain White to the wagons in the afternoon and took a good wash. Sent Pompey to the city today to get some clothes he left there on the 28th to get washed. Weather fair but little windy.

Tuesday May 31st 1864

About dark yesterday afternoon orders came from General Hoke[37] to be in readiness to move tomorrow morning at day break but about 2:00 a.m. today marching orders came and the brigade moved at once to Chester Station to take the train for Richmond in company with the remainder of the division. Was taken very sick about dark last evening with a severe attack of cholera morbus and suffered internally all night and instead of accompanying the troops on the train rode in an ambulance to Richmond which we reached about 12:00 noon. Having bought some paper wrote Father a letter to Petersburg in care of McIlwaine Sons and Co.; about 3:00 p.m. having heard the brigade had gone to Mechanicsville I started in the ambulance for the place about five miles from Richmond. After being there some time found the brigade had gone in the direction of Cold Harbor. On arriving at Gaines' Mill about four or five miles from Cold Harbor about 8:00 p.m. heard the brigade had been in an engagement with the enemy and been flanked and forced to retreat and that Captain White, A. A. G., had been wounded. Captain Blake, A. A. G., who had joined me at Mechanicsville and myself immediately started for the brigade about a mile and [a] half distant I feeling very badly and excessively weak. About half mile from Gaines' Mill found Captain White who was painfully wounded in the back by

---

[37] Clingman's Brigade had been assigned to Hoke's Division on May 15 prior to the assault the following day. It would remain assigned to Hoke for the remainder of Burgwyn's active service with it.

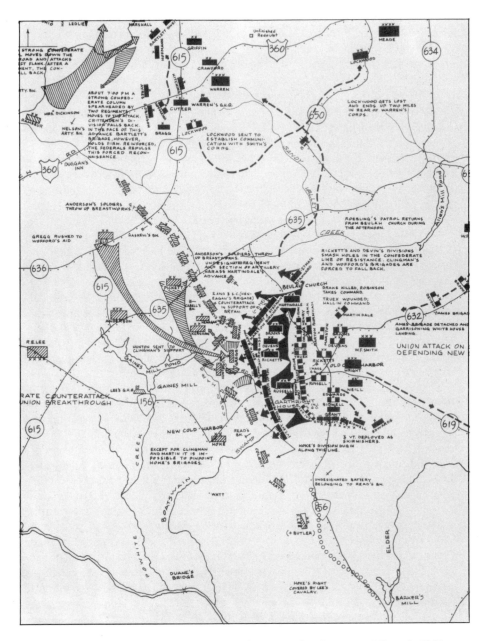

Position of Clingman's Brigade at Cold Harbor on the afternoon of June 1, 1864

Cold Harbor, Map 4

a piece of shell after seeing him first in an ambulance and started off and having met General Clingman who had come to see how Captain White was we then returned to the brigade formed in line of battle directly across the road.

We passed the night very quietly and I was very much refreshed by my sleep which was very uninterrupted considering my state of health. Weather fair and warm.

Wednesday June 1st 1864

About daybreak our brigade moved back about seventy yards to a better position and with their hands and bayonets in a short time threw up quite a good line of breastworks. Some skirmishing during the day and about 5:00 p.m. as the skirmishers commenced a more brisk fire every one strengthened the entrenchments and it was not before long till the Yankees charged us and as our left was entirely unprotected by the moving of Hagood's Brigade (which had been till a short time previous in front of us and on our left) to the right the enemy got completely round our left flank and in overwhelming numbers. The 8th North Carolina Regiment on our left was almost surrounded but managed to get off, losing its Lieutenant Colonel ([John R.] Murchison) commanding killed. Our line had then to be completely changed but as the enemy had entirely flanked us and were not more than fifty yards from our next left regiment to the 8th the men fell back in some disorder. The 31st [North Carolina] Regiment being behind the hill had not suffered as yet and had not seen the enemy owing to the hill and the very thick woods. I, by permission of the general, ordered the 31st [North Carolina] to file to the left out of the breastworks, front and charge the enemy while the 51st [North Carolina] Regiment swept the enemy, would lie down flat in the ditch and await till the 31st should charge and then the 51st would cooperate with the 31st and also charge the Yankees. But as the 31st was somewhat long in forming, the enemy pressed up to the 51st and made them give way first as the 31st were coming to their assistance; and the 31st being unprotected had also to fall back. I rallied the men somewhat about a one hundred yards in rear and about the center of the 61st [North Carolina] which regiment still kept in the trenches, though I had ordered its Colonel James D. Radcliffe by permission of General Clingman to file also to the left front and stop the advancing enemy and act as a nucleus for our men to form on but which order as it was not obeyed I imagine he did not understand. A regiment from General Colquitt's Brigade (27th Georgia) having come to my assistance and we having formed on a line with it, simultaneously charged the enemy. We had not charged but about fifty yards (and I in front of the 51st [North Carolina] Regiment and near the colors) when I received a tremendous blow which struck me I thought about the knee making me fall like an ox and suffering intense pain; I knew I [was] very painfully wounded and I thought my knee joint was shattered. Colonel McKethan grasped my hand and asked me how I was wounded and I told him I thought it might be mortally. He expressed great concern at my being wounded and ordered four of his men to carry me off. I was put in a blanket and carried off some distance where we met Lieutenant [Harvey C.] McCallister, 8th North Carolina Regiment, and some half dozen men who relieved the four that we[re] carrying me. After a while they obtained a stretcher and carried me to our Brigade Hospital about two and a half miles. About 11:00 p.m. Dr. Tamill, Division Surgeon, and Dr. [Samuel B.] Morrisey, Brigade Surgeon, put me under the influence of chloroform and probed and dressed my wound which they told me had struck about one-half inch below the right knee planing the bone and passed out making a painful but not dangerous wound. Weather fair and warm. Was struck about 7:00 p.m. while charging and driving the enemy. Captain Blake, A. A. G., was seriously wounded below the left knee while going for reinforcements and on his way back.

Wednesday June 2nd 1864

About 12:00 noon an ambulance having been obtained Captain Blake and myself started for Richmond, Pompey accompanying me. About mile from Richmond met a man (sent into the city by Major Erwin to deliver a note to a Dr. [Charles G.] Barney (particular friend of my Father's) to notify him I was wounded) who said my Father was at Dr. Barney's waiting for me and that I was to come directly to Dr. Barney's and not go to a hospital. Was assisted into his house by some gentleman of the Ambulance Corps and comfortably fixed and after drinking a cup of tea fell asleep and passed a moderately comfortable night. Weather fair but about 4:00 p.m. commenced to blow and rained some.

Friday June 3rd 1864

Dr. [Alexander Y.P.] Garnett, Chief Surgeon, called to see me in the morning and prescribed for me and Dr. Spence in the afternoon. Passed as quiet a day and night as I could expect. Weather cloudy.

Saturday June 4th 1864

Father having then the kind assistance of Dr. Garnett got me sixty days furlough. We started on the 4:30 p.m. train for Petersburg. Rode on an open car and as it rained some got a little wet. Mr. Archer [Archibald Graham] McIlwaine, Sr.,[38] met us at the depot and insisted on my going to his house for which I was much obliged. Passed a moderate night. Weather rained some during the afternoon and night. Wrote a note to Mrs. Robinson on arriving at Petersburg for my trunk. Before starting from Richmond sent Pompey to camp and got ready to start with my [illegible].

— END OF BOOK THREE —

* * * *

Headquarters of Clingman's Brigade near Petersburg
June 25th 1864

My dear Colonel [Henry K. Burgwyn, Sr.],

After long delay your letter reached me in the trenches where I have been for more than fifty days. I have delayed answering it for a week or two in the hope that I might get to some place when I could write with ink but believe it altogether uncertain when I can do that.

You wish me to state particularly what has been the conduct of your son Captain Burgwyn while on my staff. This it gives me great pleasure to do; he had always shown himself intelligent energetic and efficient.

While at New Berne I had an opportunity of seeing that he carried out orders with the same alacrity in danger that he did out of it. In the campaigns in this state

---

[38] Prominent Petersburg wholesale merchant and public benefactor.

he was equally courageous and prompt. In the charge on the enemy at Drewry's Bluff which decided the contest and defeated the entire army of the enemy though made with only two of my regiments he was in the front rank of the attack. Both then and at Bermuda Hundred he rendered good service.

At the latter place he became so unwell that I ordered him to the rear. Nevertheless I was surprised that he insisted on following the brigade when it went through Richmond. Just after we had gotten through a severe fight on the evening of the 31st of May in which with only three regiments of my brigade and some cavalry two corps of the enemy were held in check and that position saved he came to me in the night though so feeble that I endeavored to induce him to go to the rear. He insisted on lying with me on the ground that night and next day was in the hard struggle of June 1st in which my brigade defeated the enemy in front and though attacked in flank and rear because [General William T.] Wofford's Georgia Brigade ran away from our left still held its ground and saved to General Lee's Army that most important position. Captain Burgwyn was very active in assisting to form the new line of battle and while advancing with it to the attack I learned afterwards was wounded. I must have been within a few yards of him at the time on the right of the line but owing to the confusion and noise of the occasion and the many duties that devolved on me I was not aware of the accident to him at the time. It was not until we had retaken our position that I learned from Colonel McKethan that he had been wounded near him and sent to the rear.

While I deeply regret the injury to him yet I trust he will soon be able to return to the field. I learn that the new staff bill gives me two adjutant generals and I shall be pleased to give him one of them if he cannot do better. As I have formerly told him I will give him preference over any one else if he should prefer to return to me which I hope he will be able soon to do.

As to your other son [George] I know not what temporary employment I could give him that would suit him and hence as he is so soon to return to school [V.M.I.] again had he not better remain at home.

I have written this note finally amid the hissing of bullets and the roar of artillery. I have not been out of the trenches for any length of time for more than fifty days. If you think proper you can have this copied with ink. I do not know when it will reach as the mails [illegible] interrupted. I shall always be pleased to hear from you and to serve you if I can. In haste,

Yours truly & c,
T.L. Clingman[39]
Brigadier General

---

[39] Clingman would be wounded on August 19, 1864, defending the Wilmington-Weldon Railroad during the Federal offensive. He was replaced by Colonel McKethan. Clingman's Brigade would remain with Hoke's Division, along with those of Colquitt, Hagood, and Kirkland.

Clingman convalesced with W.H.S.B.'s parents (September 9, 1864-December 6, 1864). (Ann Greenough Burgwyn Diary)

CHAPTER 5

BOOK FOUR: SEPTEMBER 29, 1864 - MARCH 11, 1865[1]

Thursday September 29th 1864[2]

Visited and inspected our lines this morning; found things in good conditions. Inspected the brigade infirmary and I in returning [to the] wagon yard about dinner time heard from Captain White, A. A. G., that the division had been ordered off for Chaffin's farm. About 6:00 p.m. took the train for Drewry's Bluff from Dunlop's house.[3] On arriving at Drewry's Bluff marched immediately on to Chaffin's farm where we arrived about 10:00 p.m. Stayed all night in the road about one half mile from the farm. Weather very much like rain and sultry. Received a letter from Mother.

Friday September 30th 1864

About 6:00 a.m. moved up to our entrenchments one mile distant and waited till about 12:00 noon when we moved to take position in line of battle preparatory to charging the enemy out of the works he had captured from us yesterday [Fort Harrison]. About 2:00 p.m. everything having been arranged and our artillery having opened on the enemy we started on the charge. General [Charles W.] Field's Division to charge at an obtuse angle to us and on our left and General [Willliam W.] Kirkland's and Hagood's Brigades and I think General [Alfred M.] Scales' Brigade also to charge on a line with us and on our right. General Colquitt's Brigade was immediately in our rear and to act as our support all the line to charge simultaneously. As soon as we saw General Field's men charging we were to start. At 2:30 or 3:00 p.m. General Field having [once] commenced to charge and been driven back started again and word came for our brigade to go forward. I had been ordered by Major [James M.] Adams, Division Inspector, to take charge of a line of skirmishers in the rear to keep the men forward but at my solicitation he permitted me to charge with the brigade. We started slowly up the hill till we came on top then with a yell we started on the charge. I with the 31st [North Carolina] Regiment having been sent towards the right by Colonel McKethan as he did not know how it would do as it was under new regimental commander [Lieutenant Colonel Caleb B. Hobson]. As we started the whole Yankee line opened on us in plain view and about four

---

[1] W.H.S.B. wrote in the front of the book used for this part of the diary: "Bought while a prisoner of war at City Point. October 3rd, 1864. Price 50 cts in greenbacks."
   W.H.S.B. had returned to active duty on July 21, 1864. (C.P.E. Burgwyn, M.D.)

[2] "Will left for Gen. Clingman's Headquarters at Petersburg July 21, 1864." (Anna Greenough Burgwyn Diary)

[3] This house, a retreat of David Dunlop, a wealthy Petersburg tobacconist, was located on the railroad near Swift Creek, north of Petersburg.

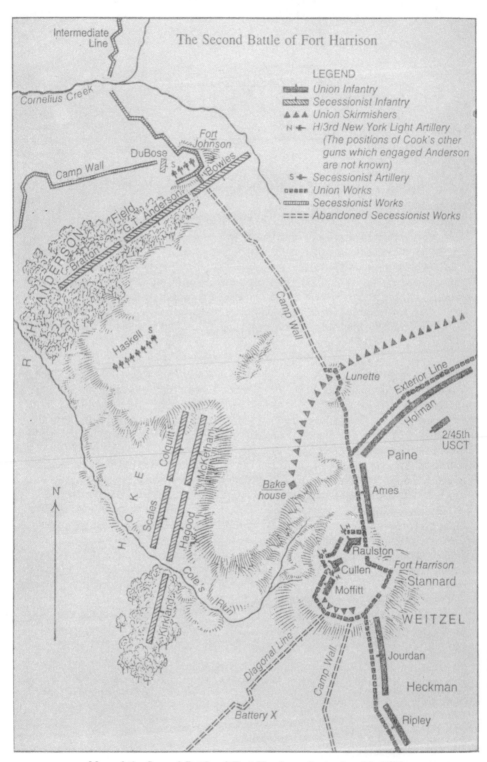

Map of the Second Battle of Fort Harrison, September 30, 1864
Sommers, *Richmond Redeemed*, p. 138

hundred yards and as I afterwards found the Yankees had massed their troops in the works right in our front having virtually vacated the works to their left and I suppose they were three lines deep behind their works and as they were all armed with seven shooters the fire was awful. By the time we got [with]in about seventy yards of their works our line was entirely broken not from any falling back but literally from the men being cut down by piles [*sic*] by the brigade's fire and our support, Colquitt's Brigade, having returned behind the hill being appalled at the sight of the mortality and fire. What remained of our brigade lay down on the ground somewhat protected by an undulation between the hill from where we started and the hill [where] the enemy were. I, though falling down twice from my spurs catching in the grass, kept up with the men though I would not go ahead as I generally do as I promised my Father I would not. From the time we lay down about 3:00 p.m. till dusk there we lay about seventy yards from the enemy line, some entirely exposed and some shielded from view by some weeds and grass, but all entirely at the mercy of the enemy but they did not fire at us knowing we could not get away (though some did) except we faced almost certain death to do so. About dark as I was getting ready to run the gauntlet, favored by increasing darkness, when the enemy sent forward a line of skirmishers who captured almost without a single exception all who had not surrendered. As I got up to see if I would have to surrender or not I saw a Yankee about ten yards with his gun pointed towards me calling out to surrender or he would shoot. I then took out my handkerchief and waved it and gave up my sword to a Yankee captain and was hastened to their lines and sent from there to General [Godfrey] Weitzel's headquarters and from his to General [Benjamin F.] Butler's about four miles off. At General Weitzel's headquarters we were treated very gentlemanly and also at General Butler's. As I began to examine about me I found my clothes pierced through in several places and my haversack was shot off me. We stayed all night at General Butler's headquarters. Weather cloudy and rained at intervals but about 3:15 p.m. when it commenced to rain and rained off and on all night. I think our failure to take the works was owing to Field's Division failing to drive the enemy or turn their right flank and to General Kirkland's and Hagood's Brigades not charging on the right and to Colquitt's Brigade not supporting us. I do not know how much we lost but I think our brigade lost at least two-thirds in killed, wounded, and prisoners and I fear three-fourths. I think the other troops lost but inconsiderably few.

Saturday October 1st 1864

About 6:00 a.m. we started on the march from General Butler's headquarters to Deep Bottom about four miles. At 4:00 p.m. we started in a steamer for Bermuda Hundred. Took something to eat there and as no boat arrived to carry us to City Point we remained at Bermuda Hundred all night and slept out in the open air and on the soaked ground and it raining. Wrote Father a short note and the Provost Marshal promised to send it. Weather rained very hard during the day and about all day.

Sunday October 2nd 1864

Took the boat for City Point about 6:00 a.m. after eating some breakfast. After we had remained some time under guard at City Point and had eaten dinner we were separated from the enlisted men and put in a confined place which was guarded by Negro troops from the 10th Pennsylvania Negro Regiment. The space was about fifty yards long and thirty wide with a large house to sleep in. The Yankees report that they have possession of the Southside Railroad. Weather cloudy and fair by turns and towards night clouded up and misty rain. Heard we were ordered to be kept here till further notice.

Monday October 3rd 1864

Passed a dull unmeaning day. Went to the Sanitary Commission under guard by a Negro who are exclusively our guards and got some paper and envelopes by which I wrote Mother. We are allowed to buy anything we want and if we have greenbacks can live quite well. Weather cloudy and misty. Seventeen deserters from Pickett's Division arrived today and were put in the same enclosure which we are in which is extremely repugnant to us. Got coffee and meat and crackers in the morning about 9:00 which were to last all day with a cup of bean soup in the afternoon about 5:00 p.m.

Tuesday October 4th 1864

In the morning heard we would possibly go north today but certainly tomorrow. Had two meals a day; one about 9:00 a.m. and second about 6:00 p.m.; had coffee, crackers, and meat in the morning and bean soup in the evening. We are guarded entirely by Negroes and when you wish to go anywhere had to be escorted by one of them by permission of a Negro sergeant. Weather fair and warm.

Wednesday October 5th 1864

At 10:00 a.m. we started for Washington City in the steam ship *Manhattan*. Enjoyed the scenery very much. Passed a good number of recruits in transports going to join Grant's army. Slept in the extreme bow end of the boat and slept pretty comfortably. Weather fair and warm. Reached Fort Monroe on the way about 1:00 p.m.; saw a very pretty young lady on the Baltimore boat. Was very glad to go farther north.

Thursday October 6th 1864

Arrived at Washington City at 9:00 a.m. and were marched immediately to the Provost Marshal's about two and a half miles and again back to the Old Capitol Prison about two and a half miles. Fourteen of us officers were put in a room twenty by fifteen feet with no windows and the door kept constantly shut making the air very close and suffocating. Had two meals one at 9:00 a.m. and another at 3:00 p.m. having at breakfast cold bread, meat, and vinegar eaten with a knife only and afternoon bean soup and cold bread eaten by a knife. After each meal fifteen to twenty minutes exercise and then we have to go to our rooms and spend the remainder of the day. Wrote Father and Uncle David [Stoddard] Greenough[4] at Boston, Massachusetts. We can buy any edibles from the sutler at the prison who charges enormous profits. They gave us two blankets apiece. Could get your clothes washed by paying ten cents a piece to a private soldier staying at the prison. Weather fair and warm.

Friday October 7th 1864

Sent my two letters off at roll call at 8:00 a.m. One officer from a room is allowed to go down stairs at a time but he has to carry a wooden peg in his hand as an

---

[4] Brother of W.H.S.B.'s mother, married to Anna Parkman.

indication he has permission. Lieutenant Colonel [John M.] Maury C.S.A. who was captured on the 29th ultimo [at Fort Harrison] had a lunch sent him by some friends in the city and the lunch, except four apples, was considered contraband and confiscated for the use of our jailers. I am afraid our health will suffer from want of exercise. Weather fair and warm. Borrowed ten dollars Yankee money from Major [Andrew J.] Rogers 8th North Carolina Regiment who sold his gold watch for $120.00.

Saturday October 8th 1864

I was detailed as orderly for the room and brought water, coal, swept up the room, etc. Sent out by a sentinel and bought me a shirt for $4.00 which if I had bought from the sutler would have cost $5.50. Weather turned very much colder and fire was necessary. We are allowed plenty of fire.

Sunday October 9th 1864

Had the divine service today. Read the Testament and religious books and no novels. A fire in the room all day was pleasant. We are allowed plenty of coal. Wrote Mother. Weather fair and cool. A gentlemen brought us some tracts in the afternoon which were acceptable.

Monday October 10th 1864

Wrote Sister yesterday but as we are not allowed to write but one letter a day I sent mine to Mother and wrote Sister a new letter today. Had coffee and bread at 4:00 p.m. instead of bean soup. Heard we had captured from the enemy in front of Richmond 1,300 prisoners and fifteen pieces of artillery. Also that [General Philip H.] Sheridan was falling back from Harrisonburg [Virginia] and saw in a Yankee paper a dispatch from him glorying in having destroyed 2,000 barns full of grain and two hundred mills full of flour in the valley and burnt every house for five miles to square for the death of Lieutenant [John R.] Meigs, Engineers Corps. Weather warmer than the day before and also fair.

Tuesday October 11th 1864

Amused myself principally in reading a book called "Harry Lorrequer."[5] Asked the sutler to get me a small pocket edition of Shakespeare's works which he promised to do. Weather fair and warm.

Wednesday October 12th 1864

Occupied myself principally in reading. Bought a pair of slippers for $2.25. Weather cloudy and rained some and turned cool towards night.

Thursday October 13th 1864

Received a very kind and affectionate letter from Uncle David Greenough enclosing $100.00 Wrote him a letter in reply. Bought a towel from the sutler at $1.00. Heard there had been a large fight at Petersburg but no particulars. Weather cloudy and cool also fair part of the time.

---

[5] Charles James Lever's *The Confessions of Harry Lorrequer.*

Friday October 14th 1864

Wrote a letter to Uncle David in reply to the one received from him yesterday but it was returned to me as I had written him to get Mr. [William] Dehon[6] to send me a uniform of of [sic] grey cloth which was not allowed unless I got especial permission from Colonel Wood, Superintendent. Weather cloudy and warm. Colonel Maury changed from our room to room Number 5 as ours was very much crowded.

* * * *

Old Capitol Prison Washington City, D.C.
October 14th 1864

My Dear Father,

I received a very kind and affectionate letter from Uncle David yesterday enclosing me $100.00 from him and offering more as Mr. Dehon was not in the city. He also wrote desiring me to come and stay with him as a prisoner if possible; he said he had received a letter from Mother which was "as a star in a cloudy night" and the only letter received from any of the family in over three years. He himself is in very feeble health and walks with difficulty with the help of a stick but all of his family are well. Mr. Dehon is also in very bad health and consequently spends but little of his time in Boston but is expected there every day. Uncle David's address is Number 40 State Street, Boston, Massachusetts. Mr. Sumner,[7] he writes, has been dead about three years. With the help of the $100.00 I will get along very well. I wrote asking Mr. Dehon to get me a pair of pants, jacket, and vest of grey cloth which will make me quite comfortable. The only drawback or want experienced is books but I think I may buy some. I have sent for Shakespeare's works pocket edition.

I am in hopes of hearing at any day from home. Never forget to write particularly how is the health of those at home and the Devereux family.

I am in very good health and only very anxious to get exchanged. Write frequently and address your letter to Captain William H. Hatch, Assistant Adjutant of Exchange, War Department, Richmond, Virginia or to Colonel [Robert] Ould and they will be sent here. Write if my horses trunk and Pompey got home safely. My best love to all, dear Father.

Your most affectionate son,
W.H.S. Burgwyn, Captain and
Acting Assistant Inspector General
Clingman's Brigade

* * * *

Saturday October 15th 1864

Wrote another letter to Uncle David and one to Mother both of which I imagine went as they were not returned. Bought yesterday two pairs drawers $4.00 each,

---

[6] William Dehon and his family were Boston friends of the Burgwyn family. W.H.S.B.'s grandfather, John Fanning Burgwyn, had visited with them before the war and they, in turn, had visited at Thornbury plantation. Mr. Dehon managed property for the Greenough's and especially Anna Greenough's inheritance.

[7] Colonel William Hyslop Sumner, married Maria Foster Doane Greenough, widow of Colonel David Stoddard Greenough. Sumner and Doane had no children. Among Maria Doane Greenough's eight children was Anne Greenough, W.H.S.B.'s mother. Colonel Sumner had died in 1861.

tooth brush 60 cents, haversack $4.50. The prices most exorbitant. Weather fair and warm. Had coffee and bread for breakfast instead of meat and meat for dinner instead of bean soup.

Sunday October 16th 1864

Heard preaching in the morning held in the yard of the prison in the morning by a Presbyterian clergyman. I liked it on account of its entire freedom from sectional matters. Read some religious papers and books. Weather fair and warm. Bought a pair of very inferior thin socks at 75 cents and one hat $5.00 and steel collars $2.00.

Monday October 17 1864

Passed a day without anything occurring of interest. Weather fair and warm. Read a book of Thackeray called *Lovel the Widower.*

Tuesday October 18th 1864

Lent Major Rogers, Captain [?]Mims, and Lieutenant Butler five dollars apiece. Lieutenant Jones' brother came to see him from Kentucky who had been here since Sunday endeavoring to see him; though he brought Lieutenant Jones a uniform suit of gray and shorts, etc., they would not let him have but an undershirt two linen shorts and pair of drawers. Also Captain Jackson was treated in the same manner. Weather fair and warm. Wrote Uncle David Greenough a letter to have me a uniform suit made having obtained from Mr. Clarke, Assistant Superintendent, as my uniform coat was torn and of very thin summer cloth.

Wednesday October 19th 1864

Heard it rumored we were to be sent to Fort Warren, Boston harbor, but hardly believed it. Wrote Father a letter; am getting very impatient for a letter from loved ones in Dixie but think the authorities are conscientious in sending off our letters and in delivering those written to us. Weather fair and warm.

Thursday October 20th 1864

Was very much disappointed in not receiving a letter from home as several arrived from Dixie. Was officer of the day. Weather cloudy and disagreeable.

Friday October 21st 1864

About 2:00 p.m. Mr. Clarke, Assistant Superintendent, informed us we would leave at 6:00 p.m. for Baltimore to get ready. He turned over my knife and money he had belonging to me. About 6:00 p.m. left our prison but did not start from Washington till about 8:20 p.m. Rode in passenger cars nicely made and clean and we went very fast for a Southern man accustomed to the speed of our railroads. A short distance a [*sic*] from Baltimore a Captain Curry, quartermaster, General [John H.] Morgan's command, who had been in prison over fifteen months made his escape from the window in the privy attached to the coach. He was discovered but they did not apprehend him. Did not change cars at Baltimore but kept right through to Philadelphia where we arrived at 4:00 a.m. next morning. They made us keep our windows and blinds down when passing through Baltimore. Weather cloudy and disagreeable.

Saturday October 22nd 1864

Marched from the depot to the wharf about one mile from there to Provost Marshal's Office about two miles. Received breakfast of bread and coffee and at 12:00 noon marched back to the wharf but found the boat gone. Remained at the wharf in a house till about 5:00 p.m. when we marched back to the Provost Marshal's and they then gave us coffee and bread again. Several schemes for escape were started by different officers but none were carried out. Weather rained a little very early in the morning and all day cloudy and cool wind blowing. At 7:00 p.m. wrote a note to Hon. George M. Dallas[8] to let him know my Aunt and all were well when I last heard from them.

Sunday October 23rd 1864

Started from Philadelphia for Fort Delaware about 10:00 a.m. in two small tug boats. Reached Fort Delaware about 2:00 p.m. Before being put in the bull pen we were thoroughly searched; all but about one dollar of our money taken away, oil cloth, canteen, but left us our clothes. Those who had watches were also deprived of them. They allow us to draw our money in sutler's tickets they exacting one percent for their trouble in doing so though. We were compelled to give up the money a real Yankee trick. Saw several officers of our brigade here. We not being as yet furnished with blankets I slept with a friend Captain Sturdivant, Confederate States Artillery. Weather fair and moderately warm.

Monday October 24th 1864

Called our division (No. 35) to order and appointed Lieutenant Colonel Maury President. One post master, two mess sergeants, and an adjutant. Had two meals one at 9:00 a.m. and the other at 2:00 p.m. Bread and meat in the morning at [sic] bread meat and soup in the afternoon. Am told a perfect system of bribery is going on between the prison officials and the prisoners, numbers of whom have bribed the officials to get them exchanged before their times by from fifty to a hundred dollars but a prisoner reporting the fact to General [Albion F.] Schoepf (Commandant) it has been stopped or rather it is feared it will be. Wrote Mother a letter. Weather fair and moderate.

* * * *

Fort Delaware. Delaware
October 24th 1864

My Dear Mother,

You will perceive that since my last letter to you my prison has been changed consequently when you write direct here. Fort Delaware. It is much colder here than at Washington and our quarters more airy but withal as comfortable as could be expected. As I passed through Philadelphia I wrote Mr. George M. Dallas telling him that Aunt Emmie and Uncle Tom and all were well, etc. I saw his address in

---

[8] Dallas served as vice-president under President James K. Polk and as the United States ambassador to Great Britain (1856-1861) under President James Buchanan. He was ill in October, 1864, and died two months later. Aunt Emily had been presented to Queen Victoria during a visit to Great Britain in 1858-1859 and Burgwyn family members surmise that Ambassador Dallas made the arrangements. W.H.S.B.'s aunt (Sarah Emily Pierpont Burgwyn) and uncle (Thomas Pollok Burgwyn) had lived in Philadelphia, as had also W.H.S.B.'s cousin Mary Katherine MacRae (Cousin Kate). Emily and Kate returned to North Carolina in 1860 or 1861.

a directory and thought Aunt Emmie would like for the ladies of his family to know that she was well when I last heard from her. I heard Mr. Frederick Brown, Sr., had been dead about five months.

I continue in very good health and at this prison we have abundance of room for exercise though of the two prisons I would much prefer Washington City. I am getting very anxious to hear from you and think it must be time for me to receive a letter.

I saw this morning Captain Leayton Gales who was captured at Fishers Hill; he is very well but very anxious to hear from his home which he has not heard from since his capture. Up to which time Tom Devereux[9] he said was well. I imagine by this time George must be at Lexington [Virginia at the Virginia Military Institute]; give him my best love.

Longing to hear and see you all at home and my but dearest love, I remain,

> Your most affectionate son,
> William H.S. Burgwyn, Captain and
> Acting Assistant Inspector General
> Clingman's Brigade and Division,
> Army of Northern Virginia

* * * *

Tuesday October 25th 1864

Wrote Uncle David asking him to send me the clothes enclosing the permit for them to pass. Had beef and potatoes and soup for dinner. Bought a coffee pot and paid $1.25 for it. Borrowed yesterday a copy of Shakespeare from Division 26 through Captain Sturdivant. There are regular gambling establishments in operation in the prison of faro [illegible] etc. which attracts large crowds and is openly carried on the yard without molestation. Weather fair and pleasant and but cold at night.

Wednesday October 26th 1864

Entered into a mess with a Captain [William] Clarke and bought $11.05 worth of mess furniture, etc. Bought for myself one overshirt, $3.50; looking glass and comb, fifty cents; and pair of socks, eighty cents. Wrote Cousin Minnie Anderson[10] to Louisville, Kentucky. Took a wash about 1:30 p.m. in the yard which was very cold. Had an examination of sick and wounded soldiers to be exchanged and I presented my old wound for examination but could not pass as I did not pretend to be injured by it. Some fifty prisoners captured in the valley on the 19th arrived during the night. Weather fair and pleasant.

Thursday October 27th 1864

We were very unceremoniously evicted of Division 35 and ordered to procure other berths and I after a little research got quite a good one in Division 24. Had a very good breakfast and dinner which we cooked with our coffee pot arrangements. Read twenty-five pages in Shakespeare. Weather cloudy and about dusk it commenced to rain and also blew quite hard; did not rain all night.

---

[9] Thomas Pollok Devereux, son of John Devereux and Margaret Mordecai Devereux, was brother of Anne Devereux. He served as a courier throughout the war, first on the staff of General Junius Daniel, then on the staff of General Bryan Grimes.

[10] Mildred Ewing Anderson, widow of General George Burgwyn Anderson, W.H.S.B.'s second cousin.

Friday October 28th 1864

This island is built on a marsh which at high tide floods it about four to five feet. It is diked around and dirt put on the forward marsh for a foundation which as at high tide is below the surrounding water about six feet cannot be drained but once a day and together with the former marshy soil in rainy weather is nothing but a bog and couldn't be walked on. There are several large ditches running across the island which are filled daily by the bay water and which furnish the water for washing. Our drinking water is brought from Brandywine Creek about ten miles and which water (the ditch water) is sometimes almost filthy and generally looks so. Read twenty-five pages in Shakespeare. Managed to get a plank and put up a shelf which we needed very much. Weather rainy and cloudy.

Saturday October 29th 1864

Had a general whitewashing of all the Divisions which though very necessary puts the prisoners to a good deal of trouble moving about their baggage. Received a letter from Uncle David dated 27th instant. Was very much annoyed by being kept waiting after getting our meals till the whole "Bull Pen" had eaten which arrangements was made by the authorities to enable them to put the proper number of rations on the tables and also to prevent a man's taking more than one ration which, as they are very small, tempts many to do. Weather fair and pleasant.

Sunday October 30th 1864

Not knowing at what time service took place I was very late for which I was sorry since was held in Division 33 by Reverend Mr. [Charles] Kinsolving, Episcopal clergyman. Wrote Uncle David Greenough and Mr. William Dehon. Weather cool and somewhat cloudy. The sick and wounded soldiers who passed the examining board last Wednesday [remainder blank]

Monday October 31st 1864

The book (Shakespeare's works) that I had been reading was sent for by the overseer and I was deprived of the pleasure of reading. Borrowed a blanket from Captain [Charles U.] Williams, aide de camp to General Corse and sewed the four blankets up and made a bag of them which was much warmer than to leave them open. Weather fair and cool.

Tuesday November 1st 1864

Quite a cool day and very cold night; had a fire in the stove in the Division for the first time which made the Division quite comfortable. Find almost as much trouble now to get the sutler to buy things we want which he has not on hand as at Old Capitol Prison. Borrowed another book of Shakespeare's works. Weather cloudy and cold.

Wednesday November 2nd 1864

The whole prison was turned out and ordered to take all their covering (bed clothes etc.) with them and there three or four sergeants examined each officer as he passed through into the enclosure again taking away blankets from those who had more than one and a half apiece and gave one blanket of those taken to those who had none. Wrote Father a letter. Spent today the last cent of money I possess for eatables. Weather cloudy and cold.

Thursday November 3rd 1864

Played several games of chess with my messmate Captain Clarke which was very interesting as we were both very equally matched. Weather cloudy and cold and rained during the night.

Friday November 4th 1864

Cleared up today. A Yankee lieutenant of the guard said it was in the Washington papers that all prisoners would be exchanged before cold weather but I do not believe the report. Had a meeting of the Confederate States Christian Association in our Division tonight. Reverend Mr. Harris, Baptist preacher, was president. Determined to join the association. Was one of forty who have five dollars Confederate money to elect President Davis a life director that being the constitution of the association to give two hundred dollars in Confederate money to elect any person life director. Weather cleared up very fair.

Saturday November 5th 1864

Felt the want of money to buy us some things and more so as I have over sixty-five dollars in greenbacks owing me. Took a nice wash before going to bed in a tub I borrowed. Weather cold and windy and sleeted a little about 1:00 p.m.

Sunday November 6th 1864

Attended divine service by the Reverend Mr. Kinsolving, Episcopal Minister but had no sermon. Was also introduced to Mr. Kinsolving today and had quite a long conversation with him. Weather fair and very pleasant but rained in the night.

Monday November 7th 1864

Rained all day but not hard. Received a letter from Uncle David dated November 4th and one from Cousin Minnie Anderson dated November 3rd which gave me considerable pleasure. I occupied myself in reading and playing chess. Weather moderate and rainy.

Tuesday November 8th 1864

Received a letter from Uncle David dated 5th instant saying my clothes had been sent. Though this is a great day of election for President of the United States nothing unusual occurred till night when the sentinels were doubled and one shot a hole through the privy for some cause or other and they say there is a great riot going on in New York City and Chicago. The island went about 300 majority for Lincoln. Weather cloudy and moderate.

Wednesday November 9th 1864

Lieutenant Butler having paid Captain Clarke and myself some money he owed us, we started our cooking establishment which had suspended operations a few days ago on account of want of money. Election returns I am afraid indicate Lincoln will be elected though nothing is definite can as yet be determined. Weather rained some and the yard perfectly covered with water and mud.

Thursday November 10th 1864

They would not allow any papers to come in today which as is done when they contain good news for as we have construed that something good has turned up for our side. Some (New Fish) prisoners arrived today who report that McClellan has been elected. I do not believe it. Was disappointed in not getting my new clothes today. Weather cloudy but very moderate though cold at night.

Friday November 11th 1864

Election returns show that Lincoln was elected and I don't know but that it is better for us. Was surprised I did not get my valise or a letter today. Weather cloudy but warm.

Saturday November 12th 1864

Was again disappointed in not getting a valise. Received a letter from Mr. Dehon Boston dated November 9th containing one hundred dollars what I wrote for. Weather cold and cloudy and very cold at night.

Sunday November 13th 1864

Mr. Kinsolving, Minister, being sick Episcopal service was read by Adjutant [Lieutenant Francis A.] Boyle 33rd North Carolina Regiment. Wrote Uncle David Greenough, Cousin Minnie Anderson, and Cousin [Nathaniel] Hill Burgwin.[11] Weather cold but moderately fair.

Monday November 14th 1864

Had roll call of each Division. Weather very cold and the Division very uncomfortably cold it being the largest Division in the barracks and the supply of coal for the stove is deficient. Weather cold and cloudy.

Tuesday November 15th 1864

Wrote General Clingman a letter. Did not receive my valise which delay I couldn't account for. Weather cloudy and sleeted a little and suffered at night. Now cold very much.

Wednesday November 16th 1864

This day being appointed by President Davis as a day of thanksgiving and praise it was kept by us all. Had Episcopal service in the morning and afternoon. Wrote Father. Weather cloudy and cold.

Thursday November 17th 1864

The Divisions were whitewashed again and we all were very much inconvenienced having to move everything out and then clean up the Division. Weather cloudy and about dark began to rain a little. About twenty officers of [General John] McCausland's Brigade Cavalry captured in the [Shenandoah] Valley arrived tonight.

Friday November 18th 1864

Wrote Mrs. General James G. Martin asking her to inform my mother where I was on her return south. Weather rained slowly during the day but cleared up at night.

---

[11] W.H.S.B.'s first cousin and youngest son of George William Bush Burgwin was a lawyer in Pittsburgh, Pennsylvania.

Saturday November 19th 1864

Good news came in today's papers that General [John C.] Breckenridge had defeated the enemy in Tennessee. Cannot imagine why my valise does not arrive. Three surgeons arrive today captured somewhere in the west. Weather fair and moderate.

Sunday November 20th 1864

Reverend Mr. Kinsolving administered the Holy Communion and I was glad to partake of it. Weather rainy and moderate.

Monday November 21st 1864

A Dr. Smith in the barracks said General Schoepf informed him that a general exchange was going and we all would be exchanged in two or three weeks. Weather rainy. Suffered a good deal at night from cold. The sutler was closed till afternoon and then had nothing much to sell his contraband goods being hid away on account of the visit of the inspector.

Tuesday November 22nd 1864

Found accidentally this morning that my valise had arrived two weeks ago and they had neglected to inform me of it. Everything arrived safely and of excellent material but I was not allowed to receive the sack coat by Sergeant Fink in charge and I then wrote to General Schoepf asking for it. Wrote Uncle David. Weather fair but very cold and night very cold and we all suffer from it.

Wednesday November 23rd 1864

So cold last night the water in the tanks froze up and it was some time in the day before we could get water. Put newspapers between our blankets we lay upon to make them warmer which I think was of some good. Weather fair but cold.

Thursday November 24th 1864

Sergeant Fink said Captain [George W.] Ahl, A.A.A.G., said in reply to my note to General Schoepf that Sergeant Fink did wrong in giving me the overcoat that he should have kept it and given me the undercoat. Had double rations of bread for breakfast some said because it was Thanksgiving Day; others that the bread was given out to prevent it from spoiling. It was very old bread. Weather fair and cold. The tanks froze.

Friday November 25th 1864

Nothing happened worth recording. Weather fair and not very cold.

Saturday November 26th 1864

Had many reports about a general exchange but not reliable. Was very much disappointed in not getting a letter. Weather fair and moderate.

Sunday November 27th 1864

Mr. Kinsolving being in the hospital Adjutant Boyle from Plymouth, North Carolina, read the services and also an excellent sermon on the "Prodigal Son." Weather very fair and moderate. Wrote Cousin Hill Burgwin again.

164

Monday November 28th 1864

Received a letter from Uncle David dated 25th and one from Cousin Hill Burgwin dated 23rd. Wrote Cousin Hill and a Judge [Asa Owen] Aldis[12] at St. Albans, Vermont. Weather fair and moderate. Got no newspapers today.

Tuesday November 29th 1864

Wrote Uncle David. We infer from the news the papers contain today that General [William T.] Sherman is in rather a tight place and will most probably be destroyed. Weather fair and moderate.

Wednesday November 30th 1864

No important news from Sherman. Weather very fair and moderate.

Thursday December 1st 1864

No important news from Sherman in today's paper. Weather fair and very pleasant. Had not meat for dinner today. I don't know why.

Friday December 2nd 1864

Had no meat for dinner again but a double ration of bread. Weather cloudy and rained during the night a good deal. Papers report a fight between two corps of [General John B.] Hood's Army and [General George H.] Thomas' whole army and Hood was repulsed but the enemy fell back fifteen miles nevertheless from Franklin to three miles of Nashville.

Saturday December 3rd 1864

No very important news about Sherman today. General Grant telegraphed to Secretary [of War] Stanton a Richmond papers [sic] thinks Sherman will get to the coast. Weather cloudy and about 4:30 p.m. a heavy cloud appeared but no rain.

Sunday December 4th 1864

Had Episcopal service; Mr. Kinsolving read it. Weather very raw and cool. Many reports of a general exchange are floating about with some show of probability as General Schoepf says there will be one very soon.

Monday December 5th 1864

Several surgeons left for Dixie among them a Dr. Chas I. A. Smith of General [Patrick R.] Cleburne's command, Army of Tennessee, who I gave forty dollars in Sutler's checks to give to a surgeon here to put my name down on the list of sick and wounded to be exchanged. Dr. Smith told me he had made all the arrangements with the surgeon and only needed the money to consummate it. Weather fair but cold.

Tuesday December 6th 1864

The Federal surgeon above mentioned said to me today that Dr. Smith had never spoken to him about getting me off nor had he given him any money. I conclude the said Dr. Smith is a consummate rascal and has cheated me of the forty dollars. Received a very affect [sic] letter from Judge Aldis in reply to mine. Encouraging news came about Sherman today. Weather cloudy a little sprinkle of rain. Wrote Judge Aldis tonight.

---

[12] A friend of H.K.B., Sr.s', who became acquainted with the Burgwyn family on a trip to North Carolina in early April, 1861. He served on the Vermont Supreme Court from 1857-1865.

Wednesday December 7th 1864

Weather cloudy and rainy during the day. Encouraging news still about Sherman and his chances diminishing daily.

Thursday December 8th 1864

Nothing important from Sherman. Richmond papers consider the fight at Franklin as a Confederate victory. Weather fair and windy and cold night extremely cold and suffered from cold very much.

Friday December 9th 1864

Weather cold but night not quite so cold; snowed some during the night. No news of importance.

Saturday December 10th 1864

Snowed a little during the day. Weather cold and very disagreeable. No important news from General Sherman.

Sunday December 11th 1864

Found when changing my clothes that the heretofore Dr. Smith had taken off with him a pair of my new woolen drawers and handkerchief. Had Episcopal services by Reverend Mr. Kinsolving in Division Number 27. Weather cold and intensely cold night. Suffered very much from cold at night.

Monday December 12th 1864

Sergeant Fink being ordered by General Schoepf to give me my coat and he having given it away to an officer in the barracks as he said gave me a very poor substitute in its place of poor material of thin but to make up for its thinness he also gave me a sack of woolen material. News today gives me great concern as I see a large force under General [Gouverneur K.] Warren have left the front of Petersburg and started for near my home Weldon, North Carolina. General [Robert B.] Vance received Beales Circular[13] today about furnishing Confederate officers with clothing, blankets, etc., etc., and he had the chiefs of divisions in his room to make arrangements about it. Weather very cold but as they gave us plenty of coal to burn we did not suffer so much at night. Received a letter from Uncle David dated 10th instant was called out in the afternoon to get my coat they had detained from me my Uncle having written to General Schoepf about it but though the Sergeant Fink had promised to keep it for me he had given it away the day after he made the promise and I only got what I have previously described.

Tuesday December 13th 1864

Wrote Cousin Minnie Anderson yesterday. No news from General Warren and the Yankees are anxious about him. May God let his column be destroyed before it reaches Weldon. No news from Sherman. Weather cold but moderated towards night and rained during the night. Many officers enjoyed themselves sliding on the ice formed in the pen. Put up a notice about my coat but could not hear anything of it.

---

[13] Under those arrangements the United States and Confederate States governments would supply their respective prisoners of war with necessary supplies. The Circular authorized the formation of Confederate States prisoner committees to (1) determine the necessary supplies, (2) prepare lists of officers, privates, and citizen prisoners, and (3) appoint officers to issue supplies when received. [*O.R.*, Series II, vol. 7, p. 1207.]

Wednesday December 14th 1864

Papers report General Sherman in line of battle five miles from Savannah a battle hourly expected. General Warren has returned after going as far as Hicksford [Virginia] and I am very grateful for it. Weather moderate but turned cold during the night.

Thursday December 15th 1864

Wrote yesterday Captain Ahl, A.A.A.G., a letter informing him that Dr. Smith went off owing me forty-two dollars, etc. Received a letter from a Mr. William Samuel Johnson[14] dated 11th ultimo from Stratford, Connecticut, a relation offering me money, etc. I replied. No important news from Sherman but papers state he has invested Savannah and intends to attack it. Weather moderate and about dark it snowed some.

Friday December 16th 1864

No news from Sherman but papers state General Thomas attacked Hood yesterday driving his left about five miles but right stood firm. Weather moderate and rained during the night.

Saturday December 17th 1864

No definite news from Sherman. General Thomas telegraphs that he drove Hood the first day's fight but says nothing about the second day's battle and we do not know the result. Weather moderate and misty. Wrote Uncle David.

Sunday December 18th 1864

Attended Episcopal service in Division 34. Wrote Father. Weather cloudy and misty and rained during the night.

Monday December 19th 1864

Yankee papers confirm Hood's defeat and I am afraid he was somewhat worsted. I heard today that I was reported killed in the papers when I was captured. The report gives me great concern and I can only hope some of my letters have reached home. Weather cloudy, misty, and moderate.

Tuesday December 20th 1864

News not quite so bad about Hood. No news from Sherman. Weather cloudy and moderate.

Wednesday December 21st 1864

Very bad news if true from Hood. Papers report nine thousand prisoners reported taken from him and about all of his artillery. Weather commenced to snow at daybreak but did not snow much and moderate. Received a letter from Cousin Susan E. J. Hudson[15] saying she had got a letter from Father concerning me which relieves me very much as they know I am not killed. Replied to her letter and wrote Cousin Hill Burgwin.

---

[14] William Samuel Johnson was the father of Susan Edwards Johnson Hudson. He was a second cousin, once removed, through the Edwards family, to W.H.S.B. These New England Johnsons were related to the North Carolina Johnsons.

[15] Susan Edwards Johnson Hudson, of Stratford, Connecticut, daughter of William Samuel Johnson, was a third cousin of W.H.S.B. She had been married to William Henry Hudson, a prominent New York importer and merchant, who was killed on May 7, 1864. Her aunt, Sarah Elizabeth Johnson, was married to George Pollok Devereux, and her great-great-aunt Eunice Edwards, sister of William Samuel Johnson, had been married to Thomas Pollok of North Carolina.

Thursday December 22nd 1864

No news from Hood and none of importance from Sherman. Weather windy and cold and very cold night. Received a letter from Dr. Smith from a Camp Hamilton, Virginia, dated 8th instant, saying he had left an order with Captain Ahl for all of his money that should arrive for him to be paid to me and Captain Clarke my messmate.

Friday December 23rd, 1864

No important news from anywhere. Weather cloudy and cold.

Saturday December 24th 1864

Heard from some officers lately arrived that I had been published in the papers as dead and my obituary written. Weather sort of fair and moderate. The Butler-Porter expedition has appeared off Wilmington and General Bragg telegraphs he can hold the place.

Sunday December 25th 1864

Can not but contrast my situation on this Christmas and that of last and while I am depressed at being in prison and in the complete power of my ruthless and bloody enemies I can not but be thankful and return thanks to Almighty God that he has preserved me to be even here though the numberless dangers I have passed through between this and last Christmas. Had divine service by Reverend Mr. Kinsolving in Division 25. Never was more impressed with our beautiful prayers in the prayer book than I was today. Had double rations of bread. Weather beautiful and God seems to smile on us though man seems to frown.

Monday December 26th 1864

Bad news for us today; Savannah fell on the 21st instant, General [William J.] Hardee evacuating the city but 25,000 bales of cotton fell into the enemy's hands. No mail today. Weather rained about all day.

Tuesday December 27th 1864

Received a letter from Cousin William Samuel Johnson dated on the 22nd enclosing $50.00. No papers today. Weather misty and cloudy and rained hard during the night.

Wednesday December 28th 1864

Good news from Wilmington. General Bragg has repulsed a land attack on Fort Fisher. Felt very badly today and had a chill about 8:30 p.m. Weather rainy and moderate.

Thursday December 29th 1864

Felt better today and had no chill. Better news still from Wilmington. General Bragg telegraphs to President Davis the enemy have reembarked on their transports. Weather snowed a little and turned cold fast but during the night it moderated.

Friday December 30th 1864

Confirmatory reports of our great success at Wilmington. General Butler's command has reembarked for Fort Monroe. Felt much better today. Received a letter from Cousin Hill Burgwin dated Christmas day. Wrote Mother. Weather very beautiful and moderate.

* * * *

Fort Delaware Prison
December 30th, 1864

My dear Mother,

I have at last heard indirectly from the South. Cousin Susan Johnson has received Father's letter of the 8th of November and wrote to me in Washington which letter I received a few days ago here. You may imagine how glad I was to hear even indirectly from you as I heard a few days previous to the reception of Cousin Sue's letter from some officers recently captured that I had been reported killed in the papers and my obituary even written and I did not know how long you might have been under that impression. Was I so reported? I can't conceive how I could have been.

I have just received a letter from Cousin Hill Burgwin; his family are all well and he wished you to let Cousin Hassel [Burgwyn] know it.

I have been uniformly well since my capture and am getting along pretty well if there is any possible chance for a special exchange, I hope Father will effect one. I could not but contrast my present Christmas and last years' and though my captivity is very irksome to me I feel very thankful to God for his preservation of me and that my lot is not worse than it is.

I am pretty confident I will hear from you soon as I understand a flag of truce boat went to Aikens Landing last Tuesday. We are confined here to a half page. I don't know if you are so or not. Write all you can and frequently. With best love to all dear Mother,

Your affectionate son,
William H.S. Burgwyn, Captain
and Acting Assistant Inspector General,
Clingman's Brigade

* * * *

Saturday December 31st 1864

Commenced snowing a little before daybreak and continued slowly all day. Felt better today. No papers today. Received a letter from Cousin Sue Johnson dated 29th instant. Weather not very cold. Wrote [remainder is blank]

Sunday January 1st 1865

Had a very severe chill and for some time was afraid it was worse than a chill. Weather very cold. Was too sick to attend divine service.

Monday January 2nd 1865

No important news today. Felt very much better and missed my chill. Weather fair and cool.

Tuesday January 3rd 1865

No important news. Had all night a severe pain in the bowels. Weather commenced snowing about dark and snowed nearly all night.

Wednesday January 4th 1865

Received a letter from Judge Aldis containing $25.00 dated Christmas day. No papers today. Wrote Cousin Hill Burgwin. Weather fair but cold and very cold night.

Thursday January 5th 1865

No papers today owing I believe to the ice. Weather cold and fair.

Friday January 6th 1865

Notwithstanding the snow was on the ground we tried to move out everything out of doors and let the Division be whitewashed. Weather moderate and about 5:00 p.m. commenced raining and rained [remainder blank]. Received a letter from Cousin Minnie Anderson dated January 1st 1865.

Saturday January 7th 1865

Wrote yesterday Cousin Minnie Anderson and Mrs. Judge Aldis. No news of importance. Weather commenced to turn cold about 9:00 a.m. and very cold night.

Sunday January 8th 1865

Had divine service in Division 23. Mr. Kinsolving is to be librarian for the island as an especial favor and I am afraid we will lose him as a Pastor. Weather very fair and moderate.

Monday January 9th 1865

Papers today report the exchange has been resumed. No other news today. Weather fair and moderate.

Tuesday January 10th 1865

A letter to an officer in the barracks informed him arrangements for a general exchange had been completed. No news in the papers. Weather rainy and moderate but turned cold during the night. Wrote Mother today.

Wednesday January 11th 1865

No important news except that General B.F. Butler has been removed from command for his failure at Wilmington. Weather fair and moderate.

Thursday January 12th 1865

No important news. I see by papers that Colonel Munford has returned from Richmond or Varina Landing and there will soon be a Dixie mail. Weather fair and moderate. The Yankee sergeants came around counting the blankets today.

Friday January 13th 1865

No news of importance. Weather fair and moderate.

Saturday January 14th 1865

Weather turned cold towards evening and very windy. Received a letter from Cousin Susan E. J. [Hudson] dated January 12th.

Sunday January 15th 1865

Had Episcopal service in Division 22. Adjutant Boyle reading the services. Three political prisoners came in today. One man with one leg and one very old man, victims of Yankee despotism came from vicinity of Savannah, Georgia. Weather fair and cold. Wrote Cousin Sue Hudson.

Monday January 16th 1865

I forgot to state that on last Friday the Yankees made a requisition on the chiefs of Divisions for all the blankets in their Divisions over one and a sixth each man in the pen. Our Division sent fifteen blankets in accordance with requisition. Today about 4:00 p.m. without any notice the Yankees made us turn out with everything and confiscated all boxes and blankets that any officer might have obtained for his comfort. Weather cold and cloudy and windy.

Tuesday January 17th 1865

Commenced to snow about 10:00 a.m. and continued till about 3:00 p.m. No important news.

Wednesday January 18th 1865

Was much depressed by the news that Fort Fisher had fallen under the combined attack of [Admiral David D.] Porter and [General Alfred H.] Terry.[16] Weather cold and cloudy and very cold night and suffered from cold.

Thursday January 19th 1865

Was much depressed and disappointed today in not getting a letter from home as a "Dixie" was received. Confirmatory news of the fall of Fort Fisher arrived today. Weather cold but fair.

Friday January 20th 1865

Was again disappointed that I did not get a Southern letter as the mail is still being distributed. Received a letter from Cousin Sue Hudson dated 17th January. Weather fair and cold.

Saturday January 21st 1865

Received two letters from Father dated October 21 and November 15 and one from Mother dated November 9. The first letters from home since my capture and they gave me intense pleasure to receive them. Weather commenced to snow about 4:00 p.m. and continued till 10:00 p.m. Wrote Cousin Hill Burgwin and sent for some underclothes also wrote Cousin Sue Hudson and Father.

Sunday January 22nd 1865

Had Episcopal service in Division 30, a Captain Dwight officiating. Weather fair but cold.

Monday January 23rd 1865

Did not get any mail today as was customary. Weather rainy and moderate.

Tuesday January 24th 1865

My spirits were enlivened by receiving two more letters from home, one from Mother dated October 22 and one from Sister dated November 16. They both write very cheerfully. Weather fair and very cold night.

---

[16] Fort Fisher fell on January 15, 1865.

Wednesday January 25th 1865

The Dixie mail still continues to be issued; did not get a letter. Our cotton for blankets for our prisoners has arrived at New York. Weather fair and cold.

Thursday January 26th 1865

No letter again today was a little disappointed as I am afraid they have given all the Dixie letters that remained today. Weather very cold and cloudy.

Friday January 27th 1865

Papers report Mr. [Francis P.] Blair, Sr. has returned from Richmond. Our little fleet from Drewry's Bluff made an attempt a day or two ago to destroy City Point buildings but did not succeed. Weather cloudy and very cold.

Saturday January 28th 1865

No news of importance. Was happy in getting two Southern letters, one from Mother dated Raleigh, November 16th, and one from Father dated December 30th. Weather very cold and fair.

Sunday January 29th 1865

Had divine service in Division 27. Weather fair and more moderate. Wrote Father, Uncle David and Misses Read and Dehon.

Monday January 30th 1865

The papers report the Blair visit a humbug and say Mr. Lincoln authorized the report. Weather cloudy and moderate.

Tuesday January 31st 1865

Received a letter from Cousin Sue Hudson dated 27th instant saying she would do all she could for my parole. Weather beautiful and moderate.

February 1st 1865

Papers report that Judge [John A.] Campbell, Vice-President [Alexander] Stephens, and a Mr. [Robert M.T.] Hunter from Virginia have passed their lines on the way to Washington City as Peace Commissioners from President Davis to Mr. Lincoln. Weather cloudy and moderate.

Thursday February 2nd 1865

The peace commissioners have certainly passed the enemy's lines and Secretary [William H.] Seward has gone to Fort Monroe to meet them. Weather fair and moderate. Received a letter dated January 26th from Mrs. C.H. Jenkins, No. 146 East 31st Street, New York.

Friday February 3rd 1865

The papers report that Mr. Seward returned to Washington and Mr. Lincoln and he returned to Fort Monroe to meet our commissioners. Weather fair and moderate but snowed about dusk. Received a letter from Cousin John Greenough[17] dated January 31st 1865.

---

[17] Son of W.H.S.B.'s uncle David Greenough.

Saturday February 4th 1865

Wrote yesterday Judge Aldis and Mrs. Jenkins. More prospects for peace the papers state. A number of privates have been paroled previous to an exchange. Received a letter from Cousin Hill Burgwin dated January 23rd and a speech by Honorable James Brooks from New York sent by Cousin Sue Hudson and a pocket chess board from Cousin John Greenough. Weather cloudy but moderate.

Sunday February 5th 1865

Attended Episcopal service in Division 24. Weather very windy and cold. Wrote Sister and Cousins Sue Hudson, Hill Burgwin, and John Greenough.

Monday February 6th 1865

The newspapers report the peace conference a rupture, each side determined to fight it out. The papers report a general exchange agreed upon. Weather very windy and cold.

Tuesday February 7th 1865

Exchange report currently reported today. No mail or papers today on account of the weather which commenced to snow about 10:00 a.m. and snow heavily till dark.

Wednesday February 8th 1865

General Grant has moved on Petersburg on our right flank; no definite results known. Exchange news current. Weather cloudy and cold.

Thursday February 9th 1865

Papers report General Grant repulsed and I conclude badly. About seventy-five officers were paroled preparatory to their exchange and a general exchange was reported in the papers. Weather fair and cold.

Friday February 10th 1865

Confirmatory reports of General Grant's repulse. General exchange again reported in the papers. Weather fair and moderate. Received a letter from Mr. Dehon dated February 7th in reply to mine.

Saturday February 11th 1865

Had a chill about 11:00 a.m. Remained in bed all day. Weather fair but cool and clouded up about 11:30 p.m. and snowed till 11:00 a.m. next day. Received a letter from Father dated November 2nd 1864 and one from Cousin Sue Hudson dated 7th instant.

Sunday February 12th 1865

Remained in bed all day felt somewhat better. Today was the coldest day we have experienced during the winter and many officers had to go to bed to keep warm. Yesterday and today there was no water in the tanks and the only water we could get was by melting snow. The night was excessively cold and very windy as was all the day.

Monday February 13th 1865

About 7:30 p.m. was taken with a chill and had a pretty severe one. Weather more moderate than yesterday. Received a letter from Cousin Hill Burgwin dated 10th instant.

Tuesday February 14th 1865

Remained in bed all day and had a severe pain in the left breast. Weather fair and moderate. Received a letter from Sister dated 22nd January and one from Mother dated 4th and one from Father dated 24th January.

* * * *

Fort Delaware Prison
Tuesday February 14th 1865

My Dear Father,

I was prevented from writing you my accustomed Sunday letter last Sunday on account of being confined to my bed by an attack of chills and though I wrote today am far from feeling well but think I will be in a few days.

Today yours of 24th January and Mother's of 4th and Sister's of 2nd January came to hand and on last Saturday yours of November 2nd. It was very gratifying to get the letters as I had not received any for three weeks and also to know all were well at home. I am glad you have started one-half of two [*sic*] force for Franklin County. I have been directing my letters lately to Thornbury but as I see by your last letter Mother and the family have gone to Raleigh shall address them there. I wrote Sister last Sunday since when I have received a reply to my letter from Mr. Dehon written as you suggested and he says his government prohibits his paying the means of Mother's estate to either her or your order and as the United States send prisoners of exchange free a coat he don't see that I will need any money but if I will make it clear to him that I do need it he will advance me $100.00 and signs the letter for himself and Mr. James Read.[18] I don't think I shall trouble Mr. Dehon to advance me any.

We are searched preparatory to going on exchange and all surplus clothing over a change is confiscated. Uncle David has received a reply to his request for a parole for me to visit him that it was entirely inadmissable. Cousin Sue Hudson is trying for the same thing but I have not heard the result.

I am very glad you have got that letter from General Clingman. What has become of him? You don't say a word about him. The Northern papers say a general exchange has been agreed upon; I pray God it may be so. I don't think I ever will be captured again. I feel confident you must have lately received many letters from me. With dearest love to all and hoping to see you soon,

Your affectionate son,
William H.S. Burgwyn, Captain
Prisoner of War

* * * *

Wednesday February 15th 1865

Felt somewhat worse till about 5:00 p.m. when I put on my left side a mustard plaster; found I had a slight attack of bronchitis. Received a letter from Judge Aldis dated February 9th.

Thursday February 16th 1865

Felt somewhat better today and sat up most of the day. Weather fair and moderate. Wrote Judge Aldis.

---

[18] A longtime friend, confidant, and business advisor of the Greenough family.

Friday February 17th 1865

Felt some better today. It is generally believed a general exchange has been agreed upon. Weather fair and moderate. Wrote Cousin Sue Hudson.

Saturday February 18th 1865

Am steadily improving. Weather fair and moderate. See in the papers Confederate prisoners passing through Baltimore on exchange in large numbers.

Sunday February 19th 1865

Heard Mr. Harris, Baptist preacher, preach in Division 33. Weather fair and moderate. Wrote Mother and Cousin Minnie Anderson.

* * * *

Fort Delaware Prison
February 19th 1865

My dear Mother,

I trust as I write this in the expectation it will be the last letter I will write you from Fort Delaware and soon after it reaches you if God permits I may according to present appearances follow it in person. I wrote Father last Wednesday since which time I have not heard from you. I acknowledged in that letter Father's of 24th January and yours of 4th January and Sister's of 2nd January.

It pains me very much you do not receive my letters. I cannot account for it.

I have been improving slowly for the last four or five days and hope I may not have another attack of chills though I did not have a severe attack at all.

I have received a letter from Judge Aldis in reply to my letter and also in reply to one he received from Father. He wrote me he had written to Judge Coleman to get me a parole either to visit my relations in the North or to go to Richmond to get me a special exchange. I will hear I think in about a week and by that time will hear from Cousin Sue on the same subject.

Tell Mr. Lightbourne that I knew the intercourse I had with him last summer and the fall of 1863 would work wonders in him and regenerate him entirely which I think is conclusively displayed in his playing the "Beau Chavalier" at Mr. Randolph's and that I have no doubt but that he did himself in that trying occasion entire honor. Raleigh must be much more gay than last winter with marriages and the sitting of the legislature and I hope you and all are similarly affected.

With my best and dearest love to all and hoping to see you all soon I remain,

Your affectionate son,
William H.S. Burgwyn, Captain
Prisoner of War

* * * *

Monday February 20th 1865

All officers who had Confederate money or watches at the fort were ordered to go out and get them. The best sign of an exchange yet. Papers report Columbia, South Carolina, evacuated. Weather fair and moderate.

Tuesday February 21st 1865

No papers today. Weather fair and moderate. Received a letter from Cousin Sue Hill dated February 17th.

Wednesday February 22nd 1865

Wrote Mr. William Dehon yesterday. Was very unexpectedly taken out and paroled to go on exchange tomorrow through Cousin Hill Burgwin's influence.[19] My gratitude knows no bounds. Papers report Charleston evacuated and thirty-seven guns were fired today for Washington's birthday. Weather fair and moderate. Received a letter from Aunt Anna Greenough[20] dated February 19th. Wrote Aunt Anderson, Cousin Hill Burgwin, Cousin Sue Hudson, Minnie Anderson, Judge Aldis, and Mr. Dehon.

Thursday February 23rd 1865

Did not leave today as was expected but expect to leave tomorrow. Papers report Fort Anderson below Wilmington [had fallen]. Weather rainy till afternoon.

Friday February 24th 1865

Was disappointed again in not leaving. Papers report Wilmington evacuated. Weather fair and beautiful.

Saturday February 25th 1865

Was again disappointed in not leaving the island. Weather misty and cloudy. Received a letter from Cousin Minnie Anderson dated February 22nd.

Sunday February 26th 1865

Did not leave today; don't know why as we were twice ordered to get ready. Weather fair and warm.

Monday February 27th 1865

At last we started this morning about 12:00 noon in the steam transport *Cressandra* and my feelings were beyond expression as I left and I hope for ever all the privations of Fort Delaware. We were all put 400 privates and 200 officers in the between decks in bunks so close together you could not sit up and sentinels put on the hatchways and we were compelled to stay in there. Weather fair and moderate.

Tuesday February 28th 1865

Reached Fort Monroe about 12:00 noon and about four miles of City Point about dark. Weather rainy but not stormy.

Wednesday March 1st 1865

Reached Varina about 12:00 noon and laid off of it all day and night. Found another transport with prisoners of war on board waiting exchange. Weather cloudy and mild.

---

[19] And the intercession of Colonel William Norris, of Baltimore, Confederate States Commissioner of Exchange.

[20] Wife of David Greenough, Anna Augusta Parkman Greenough.

Thursday March 2nd 1865

About 9:00 a.m. left the *Cressandra* and we all marched about three miles to where our commissioners were waiting for us and my feelings as we passed the last Negro picket were undescribable. Had to march to Richmond but I went to General Custis Lee's headquarters [?]Capnis house and got an ambulance and rode to Richmond which I reached about dark. Weather rained all day.

Friday March 3rd 1865

Got a furlough from General [Richard S.] Ewell till exchanged and transportation to Weldon, North Carolina. Called on Dr. Charles Barney. Met Miss Margaret Stuart on the streets and called to see her at General Lee's headquarters and was introduced to Miss Mildred Lee and took charge of a package for her to Raleigh. Went to see my brother George at the cadet's barracks but found him on furlough. Started for Raleigh at 6:30 p.m. Telegraphed Mother. Weather cloudy and rained some.

Saturday March 4th 1865

Reached Danville [Virginia] at 1:30 p.m. three and a half hours late and missed connection; remained all night in Danville and slept at the hospital. Weather fair and mild.

Sunday March 5th 1865

Left Danville 10:00 a.m. and reached Greensboro at 7:00 p.m. about four hours late on account of another train ahead being off track and some other causes. Found General Joe Johnston's army passing on its way to Fayetteville. Passed the night at Greensboro till 3:00 a.m. next day. Telegraphed Mother again. Weather fair and mild.

Monday March 6th 1865

Left Greensboro at 3:00 a.m. and at 11:00 a.m. reached Raleigh where I met Sister and Cousin Annie Devereux and Reverend Mr. Lightbourne who came to meet me. Rode up home in Uncle Tom's carriage. Found my dear Mother wonderfully improved and was much rejoiced. Called in the afternoon on Mrs. Lucy Byrum to inform her of her son's death but she was not at home. Called to see Aunt Emmie and Uncle Tom who I saw on my way from depot home. Weather fair and mild.

Tuesday March 7th 1865

Called to see Miss Maggie H. and delivered her Miss [Mildred] Lee's package. Called with Uncle Tom in the carriage at the Devereux's[21] but found them about but see the little darlings Mary [Livingston Devereux] and Laura [Margaret Devereux] for whom I had some presents. In the afternoon at home not feeling very well. Weather fair and pleasant.

---

[21] Major John Devereux II, Chief Quartermaster of the North Carolina Troops during the Civil War, also managed the details of the state's blockade running efforts. He was married to Margaret Mordecai of Raleigh; their oldest daughter was Anne. See March 26, 1863. The Devereux's had eight children.

Wednesday March 8th 1865

Was prevented from going and spending the evening at Major [John] Devereux's on account of the rain. I did not but spent the evening at Dr. [Charles Earle] Johnson's. Weather cloudy and rained all day. Wrote a number of letters to prisoners' friends that I had been requested to write.

Thursday March 9th 1865

Called upon Miss Maggie MacRae and a Mrs. Broughton for her son, a prisoner of war and Miss Mary H. and Sue Branch. Took dinner at Uncle [?] Lorris and took tea and spent the evening at Major Devereux's. Weather cloudy and rained the afternoon but cleared up at night.

Friday March 10th 1865

Being a fast day appointed by President Davis went to church in the morning and afternoon. My brother George unexpectedly arrived from plantation on his way to Richmond to rejoin the cadets. Weather fair but cool.

Saturday March 11th 1865

To spend the evening had Cousin Annie [Ann Devereux] and Kate [Katherine Johnson] Deveraux, Miss Sue Branch and Cousin Katie MacRae and Dr. Philips, Captain DuHaume, and Lieutenant Collins. Had a most delightful time. Wrote Father I would start for Weldon Monday.

Sunday March 12th 1865

[no entry]

— END OF BOOK FOUR —

ABBREVIATIONS

Cold Harbor	*Troop Movements at the Battle of Cold Harbor*
H.K.B., Jr.	Henry K. Burgwyn, Jr.
H.K.B., Sr.	Henry K. Burgwyn, Sr.
N.C. Troops	*North Carolina Troops*
N.C.D.A.H.	North Carolina Department of Archives and History
O.R.	*The War of the Rebellion: A Compilation of the Official Records of Union and Confederate Armies*
O.R.A.	*Atlas to Accompany the Official Records of the Union and Confederate Armies*
S.H.C.	Southern Historical Collection, University of North Carolina
W.H.S.B.	William H.S. Burgwyn

BIBLIOGRAPHY

Manuscripts

William H.S. Burgwyn Letters November 12, 30, December 3, 1862; June 3, July 18, August 12, 1863; M.W. Ransom's letter December 20, 1863: Collection of Margaret Burgwyn Cooley.

William H.S. Burgwyn Papers: North Carolina Department of Archives and History.

Papers of Henry K. Burgwyn, Jr.: Southern Historical Collection, University of North Carolina.

Typescript of Anna Greenough Burgwyn Diary: Collection of Collinson P.E. Burgwyn, M.D.

Books and Pamphlets

Ashe, Samuel A., Weeks, Stephen B., and Van Noppen, Charles L. *Biographical History of North Carolina*. 8 Vols. Greensboro: Charles L. Van Noppen, 1911.

Atlas to Accompany the Official Records of the Union and Confederate Armies. Washington: Government Printing Office, 1891-1895.

Battles and Leaders of the Civil War. 4 Vols. ed. Robert Underwood Johnson and Clarence Clough Buel. New York: The Century Co., 1888.

Burgwyn, Henry King, Sr. *Considerations Relative to a Southern Confederacy* with *Letters to the North on the Preservation of the Union, and a Note from the Secret History of the Emancipation in the English West Indies.* Raleigh: "Standard Office" Print, 1860.

Clark, Walter. *Histories of the Several Regiments and Battalions from North Carolina in the Great War 1861-1865.* 5 Vols. Goldsboro, Nash Brothers, 1901.

Davis, Archie K. *Boy Colonel of the Confederacy: The Life and Times of Henry King Burgwyn, Jr.* Chapel Hill: University of North Carolina Press, 1985.

Jones, Walter Burgwyn, *John Burgwyn, Carolinian [;] John Jones, Virginian.* Privately printed, 1913.

Manarin, Louis H. and Jordan, Weymouth T. *North Carolina Troops, 1861-1865.* Vols. 3-12. Raleigh: North Carolina Department of Archives and History, 1971-1990.

Richmond Civil War Centennial Committee: *Troop Movements at the Battle of Cold Harbor.* Richmond: Richmond Civil War Centennial Committee, 1964.

Sommers, Richard J. *Richmond Redeemed.* Garden City: Doubleday & Company, Inc., 1981.

The War of the Rebellion: A Compilation of the Official Records of the Union and Confederate Armies. Washington, D.C.: U.S. Government Printing Office, 1880-1901.

Peace, Samuel Thomas. *"Zeb's Black Baby" Vance County, North Carolina, A Short History.* Henderson: n.p., 1955.

Scott, James G., and Wyatt, Edward A., IV. *Petersburg's Story: A History.* Petersburg: Titmus Optical Co., 1960.

INDEX

In some cases, first names could not be found.